HOME [illegible]
from HOME

Arms of Sir Everard Home, 1st Baronet, as recorded in the Lyon Register on 19 July 1813. These incorporate the 'red hand of Ulster' of his recent baronetcy, as well as the augmentation of honour bestowed upon him for his treatment of the Duke of Cumberland's head wound three years earlier. (Reproduced with the permission of the Lord Lyon King of Arms.)

HOME *away* *from* HOME

A. W. BEASLEY

Central Institute of Technology
Te Whare Wananga O Whirinaki
Wellington

in association with

Grantham House
New Zealand

First published 2000

Central Institute of Technology
Te Whare Wananga O Whirinaki
Wellington

in association with

Grantham House Publishing
6/9 Wilkinson Street
Oriental Bay
Wellington
New Zealand

ISBN 1 86934 076 0

Edited by Lorraine Olphert

Typeset and designed by Bookprint Consultants Limited, Wellington.

Printed by Bookprint International Limited, Hong Kong.

CONTENTS

Office of the President
Mr Barry Jackson MS PRCS

THE ROYAL COLLEGE
OF SURGEONS OF ENGLAND

35-43 Lincoln's Inn Fields London WC2A 3PN
Telephone 0171-405 3474
Fax 0171-973 2135
E-mail president@rcseng.ac.uk

I have long had an interest in the life and times of Everard Home senior. Owing to his being the brother-in-law of John Hunter (about whom library shelves almost sag with the weight of accumulated biography) Home's story is fairly well known. Mainly remembered for destroying the major part of Hunter's writings he was, nevertheless, one of the leading surgeons of his day, being both Master and President of the Royal College of Surgeons, Serjeant-Surgeon to the King and, in 1813, the co-founder of the Hunterian Oration, a prestigious lecture which continues to be given on or near Hunter's birthday to this day. Indeed, the following year Home senior was the first to deliver what was then called *the Hunterian Oration in Honour of Surgery and in memory of those practitioners by whose labours it has advanced.* One of my prize possessions is a copy of this Oration in its original wrappers and printed in an elegant Baskerville type. Of Everard Home junior, however, my knowledge has been but scanty.

Scanty, that is, until reading the fascinating account of his career which is recounted so ably and readably by Wyn Beasley in the text which follows. A midshipman aged 11 years, a captain before he was 40, he served in Chinese and Australasian waters doing battle in the opium wars and keeping the peace with the indigenous population of New Zealand. When not engaged in matters military, he spent time contributing to the greater knowledge of natural history by collecting botanical specimens, some 1200 for the British Museum with more for Kew. Being a Fellow of the Royal Society and a Companion of the Order of the Bath, he straddled science and service to his country in a way that would be nigh impossible today.

An ancient proverb says 'Like Father, like Son'. The story herein casts doubt on the veracity of this adage for a more dissimilar pair it is difficult to imagine. Different again, was the progenitor of the duo, Robert Boyne Home, compatriot of John Hunter in the Belleisle Campaign. But I digress: read on and be captivated by a story of three generations told by a master medical historian.

Barry Jackson

INTRODUCTION

In some ways this story might be regarded as a sequel to my earlier book *Fellowship of Three,* which dealt with the association between James Cook the navigator and John Hunter the surgeon, and the link between them that was provided by Joseph Banks - who sailed with Cook and collected for Hunter, but in the final reckoning did much more than that to bridge the careers of his older colleagues.

On the other hand, this may be seen as the story of three generations of a family: of Robert Boyne Home who worried about his allowances as he moved round Portugal; of the older Everard who achieved on a grandiose scale and yet finished his career poorly regarded; and of his son who made amends for some of his father's transgressions and died enjoying great respect, but who is today one of the neglected men of the early days of European settlement in Australia and New Zealand.

In this story John Hunter becomes a link, rather than a principal character, yet his influence is pervasive (and, with John Hunter, how could it be otherwise?). Cook appears very little, Banks rather more, but many of the same people drift in and out of the tale, for the London of the late eighteenth and early nineteenth centuries was a small place and its society very close-knit. You could throw a blanket over the Home residence in Suffolk Street and the houses in Jermyn Street and later Leicester Square where John and Anne Hunter lived (and Everard stayed with them before his marriage) – and Everard's own home in Sackville Street afterwards. The same blanket would almost have covered Joseph Banks's house in New Burlington Street, before he removed to the relative remoteness of Soho Square. No wonder the gentlemen of the Royal Society thought it necessary to add that apologetic insert – 'of Mile End' – after Cook's name when proposing this Eastender for Fellowship.

I had known of the younger Everard Home as naval commander on the Australian station because of Stokes's renaming of Cook's Point Hicks, and mentioned this when talking of the Hunterian influence in the Antipodes at a conference on early modern history, *Freedom and Modernity,* in Wellington in 1994. Another speaker at the conference was Donald Kerr, the curator of rare books in the Auckland public library, and from him I learned that this same naval officer had given books to Sir George Grey, who in turn gave them as part of the basis of a library for Auckland on completing his first term as governor here in New Zealand. From Donald Kerr and his colleague Peter Hughes, then librarian at the Auckland Museum, I gained some insight into, and detail of, the role played by the younger Everard in this country. And from there it was simply a matter of following up leads – and, in the process, of discovering several more.

The title I have chosen may be interpreted as the reader chooses; certainly the younger Everard seems to have differed from his father in character, just about as widely as their last resting places are separated. For that matter, the student of heraldry might note that the lions which form the supporters of Everard's arms look not at each other as supporters commonly do, but away from one another, and might speculate that this fact inspired the title. As it happens, it did not – but only perhaps because the title came to mind before I had studied the arms themselves.

As to pronunciation of the Home family name, I have obeyed the terse injunction 'Home (not Hume)' contained in Sir Thomas Holmes Sellors' Hunterian Oration of 1973. I received encouragement in this decision – at least so far as the two Everards are concerned – from the rendering of the name by a succession of clerks recording land tax returns for the parish of Long Sutton. There the name is never spelled with complete accuracy, but it is always in a form (Holms, Holmes, even Holmnes) that demands the anglicised pronunciation. Robert Boyne Home, though, would probably have reverted to the Scottish 'Hume' in his retirement. And in one place at least (Hudson's *Nelson and Emma*) the younger Everard's mentor appears as 'Sir Hume Popham' so that he, too, seems to have favoured the Scottish form.

While I was still reading round the subject, the Central Institute of Technology awarded me a professorial research fellowship, and subsequent work has been done under the auspices of, and with support from, the institute. Being charged with promoting and coordinating research within my faculty, I have felt a compulsion to set an example of diligence. I am sure the discipline of this compulsion has done me good - whatever effect it may have had within the institution.

Another stimulus was the Cowlishaw symposium, which I devised as a way of making more widely known and appreciated the historical collection in the library of the Royal Australasian College of Surgeons. The first such symposium was held at the college in Melbourne in October 1996 and it is now a regular part of the college calendar of events. The speakers at this symposium take as their starting point one of the books in the collection, and for my book I chose the final volume in the older Everard's *Lectures in comparative anatomy.* The resulting paper was published (under the same title as this present publication) in the Proceedings of the symposium in the *Australian and New Zealand Journal of Surgery.*

The final element, in a process of agreeable serendipity, came when I was in the library of the Royal College of Surgeons of England, examining documents relating to Clift and Home. There I received an invitation from Professor Bertram Cohen, chairman of the Hunterian Trustees of the College, to participate in a symposium in October 1999 to celebrate the bicentenary of the trustees. Just as his invitation was despatched to New Zealand, he learned that I was 'on the premises' and we were able to discuss the matter before I left London. Publication of this book in time for release about the time of the symposium then became a matter of some importance.

I must acknowledge the help I received – help that was cheerfully given in so many places and is greatly appreciated. In some sort of north-south order, I should mention Sir Malcolm Innes of Edingight, the Lord Lyon King of Arms in Edinburgh; Mrs Carol Trotter of Greenlaw, who introduced me to Gibson's history of the town – and the hospitable folk at the Blackadder Hotel who introduced me to Mrs Trotter. I am much indebted to Tina Craig and her staff in the library of the Royal College of Surgeons of England; to the Royal Society; to Mr R. Vickery at the Natural History Museum in Kensington; the library staff at the National Maritime Museum, Greenwich; the Public Record Office and the Royal Botanic Gardens, both in Kew; the Hampshire Record Office in Winchester. Mr Ronald Brown of Bentley guided me on my way to Well, where Mr and Mrs R.M. Matheson, the present owners of the Manor, extended much consideration and friendship to a total stranger who appeared on their doorstep one Saturday morning. Mr and Mrs E.R.A. de Unger, the present owners of the Manor House in Ham, have been equally hospitable. At the Royal Hospital, Chelsea, the curator, Major R.A.G. Courage, and his assistant, A/CSM M. Ford, were able to locate the older Everard's tombstone for me; and in Australia, Mr Derek Leon took me on a return visit to the Camperdown cemetery, on a Sydney day so brilliant as to facilitate the fuller reading of young Everard's inscription. There, too, the State Libraries of Victoria and of New South Wales were most helpful, especially in guiding me through the intricacies of their newspaper rooms; and the Alexander Turnbull Library here in Wellington has helped me document the younger Everard's service in New Zealand waters. My debt to Donald Kerr and Peter Hughes is already apparent from what I have described above.

I am most grateful to Mr Barry Jackson, MS PRCS, who has been kind enough to provide the foreword for this book. I have attempted to give form to my appreciation by choosing Baskerville (the type face of his prize possession, Everard Home senior's Hunterian oration of 1814) on this occasion.

Lorraine Olphert has again been gently meticulous in her editing, and Graham Stewart has further demonstrated his ability to realise an author's aspirations. I remain indebted to them both.

A.W. BEASLEY
Wellington, New Zealand

The Royal College of Surgeons of England became established in Lincoln's Inn Fields at a critical stage of the events described in this book. Its first building (top left) was designed by George Dance the younger, its next (top right) by Charles (later Sir Charles) Barry. Barry's building has been added to, but its general form is still clearly recognisable today (lower).

FOR

SALLY HUME

John Hunter's army service in Portugal brought him a surgical reputation, the basis of his collection, and friendship with the Home family, into which he would later marry. The Royal College of Surgeons of England's portrait of him, entitled 'The Anatomist', used to be attributed to Gainsborough, but recent evidence would indicate that it is by John Zoffany (1733-1810) and is in fact painted over a Zoffany self-portrait. Zoffany came to England in 1758; the painting was probably done about a decade later, and certainly before Hunter's first heart attack in 1772. (RCS)

1

ENTRANCES INTO PORTUGAL

> There are so many entrances into Portugal, the whole country being frontier, that it would be very difficult to prevent the enemy from penetrating.
>
> Arthur Wellesley, 1st Duke of Wellington (1809)

For Britain the eighteenth century opened with war imminent and ended with the country locked in conflict on a scale hitherto unknown. During that century, indeed, Britain spent over 40 years at war, all but three of them against France. Her preoccupations – apart, that is, from the loss of the important part of one Empire, and steps towards its almost casual replacement with another and greater Empire – were three in number: to cobble together coalitions to allow her to fight the French, to accommodate to the swings and roundabouts of Spanish policy, and to take up the challenges and opportunities provided by the traditional alliance with Portugal. The Seven Years' War afforded a good example of these preoccupations.

Britain was then allied with Prussia against the French. For a start the French in North America raided into British territory, capturing Fort William Henry at the head of the Hudson Valley while the British commander-in-chief, Lord Loudon, concentrated on preparing to attack Louisburg, which is situated on Cape Breton Island, guarding the southern approach to the St Lawrence. Loudon was therefore replaced as commander-in-chief by Abercromby, under whom Amherst did capture Louisburg before being shifted to the Hudson Valley, so leaving Wolfe to achieve the capture of Quebec – at the cost of his own life.

The later stages of the war saw Loudon restored to a command, this time of a British expeditionary force into Portugal,[1] after Spain aligned herself with France and sent troops pouring down the Douro valley towards Oporto, effectively slicing Portugal into two. Britain's response was to assemble four regiments from the garrison of Belleisle and two from Ireland.[2] When the medical services for Loudon's force (which was to operate under the overall command of the Prussian Count von Lippe) were assembled, they included two men who are central to this story. One, John Hunter, is recognised as the founder of scientific surgery and is, moreover, a significant if under-rated figure in natural history; the other, Robert Boyne Home, is an inconsiderable figure in surgery but was the head of a notable family. He would become Hunter's father-

The farmhouse at Long Calderwood, where John Hunter grew up, is now a museum to him and his older brother William.

in-law as a consequence of the friendship the two formed in Portugal.

To deal first with John Hunter's background: he was the tenth and youngest child of a Scots farmer, of Long Calderwood near East Kilbride out of Glasgow. A wilful child, he was thought stupid because he ignored formal education and spent his days studying nature. 'When I was a boy,' he wrote in later life, 'I wanted to know all about the clouds and the grasses and why the leaves changed colour in the autumn, I watched the ants, the bees, the tadpoles, and caddis worms; I pestered people with questions about which nobody knew or cared anything.'

At the age of 17 he was put to work for one Buchanan, husband of one of his older sisters and a cabinetmaker in Glasgow, but three years later he took himself to London where his older brother William had established a reputation as an anatomist. He began as a technician in William's anatomy school, realised that he had found his calling, secured an attachment as pupil to two of London's leading surgeons – Cheselden and Pott – and after five years entered St George's Hospital as a pupil, advancing to become house surgeon in 1756.

In 1759 his health cracked up as a result of the long hours he was devoting to work and research, for already the scientific curiosity that was to drive his career had become evident. According to Ottley, one of his early biographers,[3] 'he was attacked with inflammation of the lungs, which left behind symptoms that threatened to end in consumption'. There was in the Hunter family a strong history of tuberculosis – indeed, six of the ten children had fallen victim to the disease even before John left home, and as a teenager he had watched three of these family members die.

The attack on Belleisle, 1761. Here Hunter had his first taste of service as an army surgeon. (NMM)

Ottley goes on, 'he was strongly advised to leave London, therefore, and seek a more southerly climate'. Hunter's response to this advice was to join the army. It took him out of London, certainly, and to a more southerly climate as well, though we would have to wonder just how military service in the eighteenth century rated as a rest cure! On 30 October 1760 he was commissioned by Robert Adair, surgeon-general of the army (the ardent Robin Adair of the old ballad). On 29 March 1761 he sailed with the force sent to capture the island of Belleisle at the mouth of the Loire and embarrass traffic using the river.

For a 'side-show' it was a substantial combined operation. with 10,000 men under General Hodgson (a force larger than the 9000 with which Wolfe had captured Quebec a couple of years before). The naval commander was the Hon. Augustus Keppel,[4] whose reputation would later be tarnished in an unseemly dispute with his second-in-command, Sir Hugh Palliser, over their respective performances at the battle off Ushant in 1778. But at Belleisle things went well enough and the operation achieved its objective, though unlike Quebec its effects were meagre.

During the waiting period on shore after the occupation, Hunter amused himself studying natural history, and one of his specimens is still to be found in his museum. This shows the ability of a lizard to regenerate its tail, not once but twice – but on each occasion the replacement becomes more primitive. When the Allies responded to the Spanish invasion of Portugal, the Belleisle troops, now otherwise unemployed, formed the basis of Loudon's expeditionary force. In February 1762 Sir William Fordyce, surgeon to the 3rd Foot Guards, today's Scots Guards, was tasked to draw up a medical scheme for the force.[5] His paper begins:

Hunter's specimen of a lizard, obtained at Belleisle, showing its ability to regenerate its tail – not once but twice. (RCS)

'For 5000 men or eight regiments and supposing each regiment to have 100 sick...' and makes the point that the number of sick per regiment tends to stabilise at this figure except after a long period spent encamped in one place. It makes no mention of figures for wounded. The assumption that one man in six would be incapacitated by sickness provides an interesting commentary on warfare of this period.

At this time there were two fairly distinct groups of army medical officers: those posted 'to the hospital appointed to attend our Forces' or some similar formula, and those serving, with surgeons' mates to assist them, with specific regiments. In this latter category was Robert Home, surgeon to General Burgoyne's 16th Light Dragoons, which were joined up with the four infantry regiments from Belleisle.

Robert Boyne Home (1713-86) came of a junior branch of the notable Scottish Home family. From Sir Christopher Home of that Ilk was descended Sir Alexander, ambassador to England in 1459, who became Lord Home in 1473; and the sixth Lord Home was advanced in the peerage to become the first Earl of Home in 1605. A descendent of Sir Christopher's brother Sir David of Wedderburn became Baron of Polwarth, and from him descended the Earls of Marchmont. Patrick, a younger brother of the second Baron, was the ancestor of our Robert Boyne Home, who practised as a surgeon in Hull before joining the army. He served first as surgeon to the Royal Welsh Volunteers, then joined Burgoyne's regiment of Dragoons.

John Burgoyne himself was a dashing if controversial figure: educated at Westminster, he eloped at the age of 21 with Lady Charlotte Stanley, daughter of the Earl of Derby. Commissioned two years later, he spent five years up to the outbreak of war in France as a fugitive from his creditors, but in 1759 he raised his regiment of light cavalry and in 1761 (just before the foray into Portugal) gained election to the Commons as member for Midhurst. He became brigadier-general in 1762. His later career was equally colourful: as a parliamentarian he led attacks on Clive and Hastings; as a soldier he censured his brother officers in New England in 1775 and his superior in Canada the following year; and after being made commander-in-chief in Canada he surrendered at Saratoga in October 1777. In among these activities, he found time to be a dramatist of some repute.

'Gentleman Johnny' Burgoyne was a colourful character. Robert Boyne Home served as medical officer to Burgoyne's regiment of dragoons. (NPG)

His regiment became the 16th Lancers in 1816 and was amalgamated with the 5th Lancers (formerly the Royal Irish Dragoons) in 1922 to form the 16th/5th Lancers. It seems that Home, though serving with the regiment throughout the Portuguese campaign, entertained hopes of transferring to the strength of the hospital:

> Mr Home Surgeon to the 16th Regiment of Dragoons begs the favour of Brigadier Fraser to make his most humble comp^ts to the Earl of Loudoun. He received a letter about the time of the Regiment embarking for Portugal informing him that Mr James Pringle had been so good to recommend him to his Lordship's favour and Protection in case a Vacancy should happen in the Hospital; but it has been his great misfortune that it has never been in his power to pay his respects to his Lordship.

The transfer did not eventuate. But Home had another pressing concern, and the letter goes on:

> Mr Home was informed in England that he would have an Allowance of Baggage for carrying his Medicine Chest, but he has not received any, tho' the Surgeons to the Regiments of Foot have long ago, if his Lordship has any doubts concerning his right to it, Coll^e Chancey (he is told) is the properest person to inform his Lordship what is the establishment in Germany.

The letter reached Loudon and was endorsed by him but without comment. Even after returning to Lisbon following the cessation of hostilities, Home was seeking his due.

> Lisbon March 29th 1763.
>
> Sir,
> You will oblige me in applying to his Excellency the Earl of Loudoun to beg the favour of his Lordship to give an order to Mr Bembridge, deputy Paymaster General for paying me an allowance of Baggage money for carrying the Medicine Chests of Brigadier General Burgoyne's Regiment of Light Horse which as yet I have never received, neither in England nor here.
>
> I am not informed what allowance was in Germany but in England it is Ten pounds for a Horse and Forrage money to the amount of seven or eight pounds more, which Mr Tomkins, surgeon, can inform his Lordship of.
>
> I am with Respect
> Your most obedient and most humble servant
> ROBT HOME *Surgeon.*

As any one with a background of army service can testify, the obtaining of allowances can be a tedious process.

Hunter, unlike Home, was on the strength of the hospital attached to Loudon's expeditionary force; such an attachment was familiar to Loudon from his North American days. The Director of Hospitals in the United Kingdom, one Cathcart, reported to Loudon on 4 May 1762 that the hospital stores were on board *Neptune*, and five days later Adair as surgeon-general gave him a nominal roll for the hospital – the Director, William Young, two physicians, three surgeons including Hunter, two apothecaries and 16 mates. These appointments were backdated to 10 February 1762.

There were also, classified as servants, a Matron, Mrs Sullivan, on 2s 6d a day, two head nurses, three cooks and five washerwomen at a shilling – and 18 women nurses at sixpence. The pay relativity, as between cooks and washerwomen on the one hand and women nurses on the other, is interesting. So is the fact that, a century before Florence Nightingale, women were employed as army nurses – but perhaps 6d-a-day nurses were not quite what Florence demanded!

Hunter sailed from Belleisle to Lisbon in the first half of July 1762, probably in the hospital ship *Betty*, to find a general

The houses which were built after the 1755 Lisbon earthquake are now considered of sufficient architectural interest to merit preservation of their facades. It was in houses such as these that the expeditionary force's hospital was established.

hospital being set up there. Lisbon at that time was recovering from the earthquake of 1755, which destroyed virtually all the mediaeval city apart from such massive structures as the castle. The city was being rebuilt up the steep hillsides from the harbour, and in four separate buildings (one at some distance from the rest) the hospital was established. .The houses of Lobo and Panteas were calculated to receive 100 and 196 patients respectively; they may well have resembled the houses that are still to be found today – and, given the seismic history of Lisbon, these are now of an age that justifies retention of their facades when rebuilding is undertaken. The Casa de Almirante (Admiralty House) accommodated one surgeon, five mates and 50 patients; the Fort, with three mates and 150 patients, was described in the adjutant-general's report as 'much the worst hospital, the rooms small and is removed at least a quarter of a mile from the others'. The bed state stood at 202 on 6 July. The hospital standing orders laid down, *inter alia*, that

> The guard will also send frequent patrols to the Tipling houses in the neighbourhood to prevent any men drinking and quarrelling with the inhabitants.

In the three weeks after Hunter's arrival 373 men, probably all sick cases, passed through the hospital. In spite of the patrols, the

John Hunter set up a forward hospital in the monastery which commands the square in Santarem.

The castle at Abrantes dominates the town and overlooks the Tagus plain.

'Tipling houses' doubtless contributed to this number.

He hoped to become deputy director of the hospital, an appointment he was more or less promised from England; but so too (and with certain documentary evidence to support him) did his colleague Maddox. Hunter made an issue of it, even though Maddox withdrew gracefully and provided the medical escort for his own patron Lord Trelawley's return to England. Possibly because of Hunter's outburst no deputy was appointed.

Meanwhile the troops were being moved by boat up the Tagus as far as Muge, before undertaking a march to Santarem (in which 11 men died of heat stroke), and in Santarem a forward hospital was established with Hunter as surgeon. This soon had to move to larger quarters in the Jesuit monastery which dominates the city square.

The 'grain' of the country runs roughly east and west. It will be recalled that the original Spanish thrust had been on the line of the Douro, but all the passes further south were at risk. Von Lippe had his headquarters at Abrantes, which sits on a crag overlooking a bend in the Tagus, dominated by its castle in a manner reminiscent of some of the Rhine castles. He set General Townshend, the British field commander, to cover the valleys of the Mondego and Zezere, to keep open the links with Oporto and to defend Coimbra, the old capital and still then the cultural centre of Portugal. Coimbra lies near the mouth of the Mondego, close

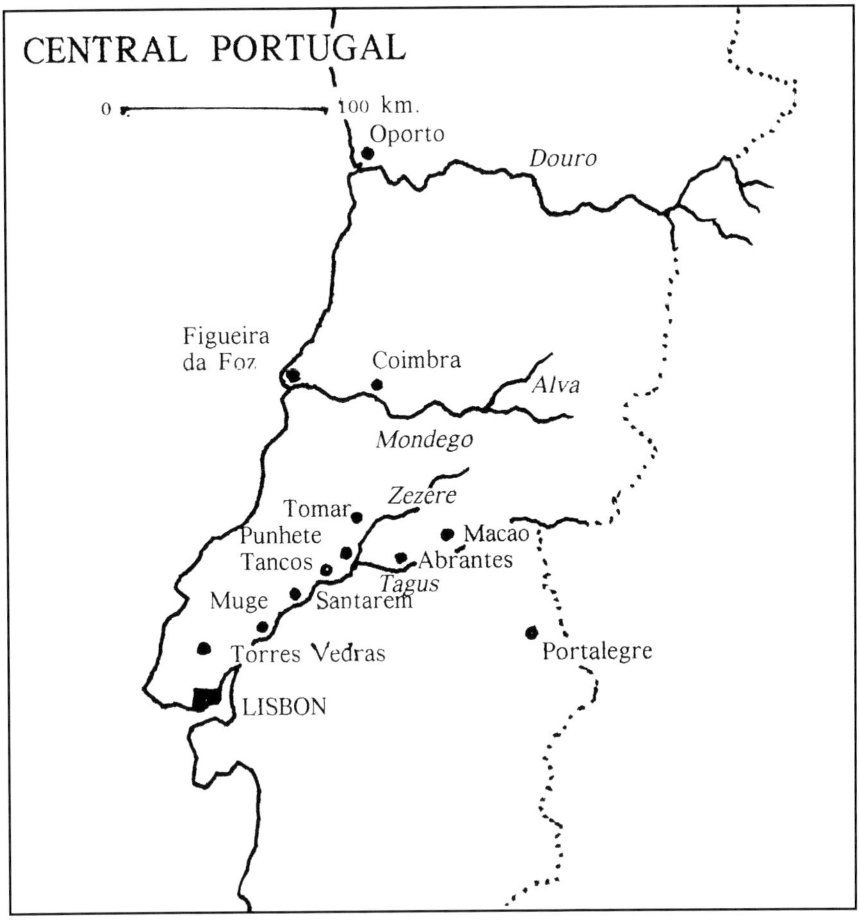

to the site of the Roman city of Conimbriga. The resulting deployment had the British forces operating in a wedge of country extending from north to north-east of Santarem.

To give medical cover to these dispositions Hunter took himself to Punhete (present-day Constancia, at the junction of the Zezere and the Tagus) where he later drew up plans for a 'Temporary', a sort of casualty clearing station, from which further evacuation by river would be possible. Then at Tancos, a pleasant town a few miles to the west, he established one of several forward hospitals, comparable to the advanced dressing stations of more recent wars, and here he worked himself almost into the ground during August. On 8 September Young, the director, reported to Lord Loudon:

> I have a letter this day from Mr Hunter at Tomar. [Tomar is some distance up the Coimbra road from Tancos.] He does not downright say he is sick but that he is almost knocked up. He has had too much to do. He says he is stopped at Tomar for want of a carriage, but hopes to set out soon.

Hunter's 'setting out' took him north to Coimbra. Beyond the city Townshend's men were blocking the Alva, a southern tributary of the Mondego, and here, transport for the sick being at a premium (one hears little of wounded from this campaign) he proposed evacuation by sea from Figueira da Foz, at the river mouth about 20 miles below Coimbra, down the coast to Lisbon. His proposal came up against red tape, and he wrote to Lord Loudon:

> MY LORD
> When I returned from Venda Nova [about ten miles east of Coimbra] I immediately waited upon Mr Nash to get his assistance in procuring what was necessary for the removal of the sick. When I told him your Lordship's pleasure he found the following difficultys, viz., that it was very uncertain, the getting a vessel fit for the purpose at Figuera. When got, that it would cost above fifty Moidores: that it might wait some time for a [tide to carry it over the] Barr: and on entering the river Tagus might be embarrassed by the Health Office.
> If these are not sufficient objections I shall pursue the first plan... it will be necessary to have an order from your Lordship to press a ship, if she is to be found there. If your Lordship did not think it tedious, a ship might be ordered from the river Tagus to Figuera, viz. the Hospital ship from Bellisle... The ship's name is the Betty Transport, Captn Pescore Master... Or if your Lordship was not desirous of having them at Lisbon immediately I dare say that they might all be removed by land in a fortnight's time; for above one half will be able to walk to Santarem, if their accoutrements are carried and slow marches; and the others will be able to do it with a little assistance from carriages. They are all so well that one Mate is sufficient to take care of them...

This lucid presentation of the options made Loudon's response easy, and he replied forthwith:

> SIR
> You are hereby directed upon the receipt of this Order to hire Vessels proper and sufficient to transport the Hospital and Baggage now under your care and direction at Coimbra to Lisbon, for which purpose I shall make immediate application for Convoy.
> *To Dr Hunter.*

Because Townshend's force had von Lippe's base at Abrantes well covered from the north, the Spanish now attempted a 'left hook' across the Alentejo plain to the south of the Tagus. Von Lippe adopted a 'scorched earth' policy, denying them supplies as they advanced, so that the thrust soon petered out and with the approach of winter the Spanish withdrew to the frontier. (Wellington, having read diligently the accounts of the 1762 campaign, frustrated the French in the same way before Torres Vedras 48 years later.)

As the Spanish retreated, von Lippe moved his headquarters forward from Abrantes, where he had been able to overlook their discomfiture from his crag, to Macao; and Hunter accompanied

From his crag at Abrantes, von Lippe was able to watch the discomfiture of the Spanish invaders.

him on this move. He had put in for an appointment as physician back in Lisbon when Cadogan went off sick (physicians attracted pay of one pound a day, surgeons 10s only) but was unsuccessful.

At the end of October, as the Spanish withdrawal continued, he moved even further forward to Portalegre on the Alentejo uplands, where he became busy following the armistice in mid-November, determining which of the sick were fit to be moved, pleading for better transport for their evacuation – each of the wagons used for this purpose contained six 'beds' made of

Tancos, basking in the sunshine, looks a pleasant site for a forward hospital.

Although it is now close to the bustle of Trafalgar Square, Suffolk Street remains a quiet cul-de-sac. Here John Hunter got to know the Home family, and especially the older daughter Anne.

slabs of cork! – but still finding time to study the geology of the plateau.

By 8 January 1763 he was back at Santarem; on 10 February the Peace of Paris was signed. Two days later he wrote 'an account of the sick in the hospital in Lisbon', and here he was able to renew his acquaintance with Robert Home when the latter returned from the field and pursued his quest for baggage money. The expeditionary force left Lisbon about 13 April, and the staff of the hospital were taken off the pay roll as from 14 May.

Hunter and Home had established a friendship sufficient to see the younger man welcomed into the Home household in Suffolk Street, Pall Mall,[6] after their return to London. It was a household of some military tradition, for Mrs Home was herself the daughter of Colonel Alexander Hutchinson. Here Hunter met and courted Anne, the older of the Home daughters, to whom he was married eight years later – on 22 July 1771, at St James's Church in Piccadilly, a Wren church of which its builder was rather proud.

The length of their courtship has attracted speculation: it was probably dictated by Hunter's need to establish himself in civilian practice before inviting a well-provided young woman to share his life. As his brother-in-law Everard described it, 'the expence of his pursuits had been so great, that it was not till several years after his first engagement with this lady, that his affairs could be sufficiently arranged to admit of his marrying'. Anne was, after all, fourteen years younger than her husband, and entitled to expect a 'comfortable' marriage. She achieved even more: theirs was a happy marriage between two people of strong personality, and they managed to pursue their respective careers without becoming strangers to one another for, as will emerge, Anne was a distinguished figure in her own right.

John put the years of their engagement to good use: in 1767

John and Anne were married in 1771, in St James's church, Piccadilly.

he was made FRS, and the following year he became a member of the Incorporation of Surgeons (equivalent to achieving the Fellowship of a College of Surgeons these days) and was appointed to the surgical staff of St George's. In the year of his marriage to Anne, he published his first book, *The natural history of the human teeth.*

They were an interesting family, these Homes. There were seven children, including William who reverted to using the spelling 'Hume' and was in the East India Company's service. Apart from Anne three are of particular interest. Anne's sister Mary, named after her mother, married Robert Mylne the architect in 1770 – and perhaps this younger sister's marriage served as a stimulus to John Hunter and Anne.

Robert Mylne was descended from a long line of Scottish builders, many of whose works survive. (NPG)

Mylne was descended from an extraordinary line of Scottish master-masons: John, who died in 1621, repaired the Dundee harbour works and built a bridge over the Tay; his son, also John, built the steeple of the Aberdeen Tolbooth and worked on fortifying Dundee 1643-51, dying in 1657. The next John (1611-1667) designed the Tron Church in Edinburgh, built Heriot's Hospital and Edinburgh College, was master-gunner of Scotland in 1646, on the Town Council 1655-64 and member of parliament for Edinburgh 1662-63. His brother Alexander (1613-1643) was a sculptor who assisted John in his work, and Alexander's son Robert (1633-1710) reclaimed the foreshore and built the sea-wall at Leith, superintended the rebuilding of Holyrood Palace after the fire of

Mylne's Mount – the name has been blurred to 'Mills Mount' – clings to the rock overlooking West Princes Street Gardens where, in the time of its construction by an earlier Robert Mylne, the North Loch provided an additional defence for Edinburgh Castle. A cafe and restaurant now occupies the building that surmounts it.

1650 and built 'Mylne's Mount',[7] one of the bastions of Edinburgh Castle.

Robert's son William (1662-1728) was another master-mason, and William's son Thomas, who died in 1763, was city surveyor of Edinburgh. It was Thomas's son Robert – our Robert – who, after studying in Rome and travelling through Switzerland and Holland, gained the commission to build Blackfriars Bridge in London. Here he became embroiled in controversy with Dr Johnson over the relative merits of semicircular versus elliptical arches, the combative doctor being quite undeterred by the Mylne lineage.[8] The bridge occupied Mylne's energies for the decade 1760-69, but its proceeds enabled him to marry Mary Home the following year. His other projects included the Gloucester and Berkeley canal and the drainage of a portion of the Fens, as well as works throughout

England and Scotland, and in 1766 he was appointed surveyor of St Paul's Cathedral. The following year he became a Fellow of the Royal Society and he was an original member of the Architects' Club in 1791. His younger brother William, who died in 1790, was architect to the city of Edinburgh and there built the North Bridge in 1765-72. Robert and Mary's son William Chadwell Mylne (1781-1863) inherited from his father the post of engineer to the New River Company in 1811 and was much involved in projects in connexion with water supply and drainage. He too became FRS, in 1826, and FRIBA in 1834.

Robert Home junior (1752-1834) studied under (and, according to Gibson, later married) Angelica Kauffman,[9] who was one of the 36 original members of the Royal Academy and painted the ceiling of the council chamber in Burlington House. He in turn became an artist of some note, who painted John Hunter on at least two occasions – one portrait is in the possession of the Royal Society, another at the Royal College of Surgeons – and exhibited at the Academy and in Dublin. He subsequently moved out to India, where he became chief painter to the King of Oudh, and where his subjects included Sir Arthur Wellesley (the future Duke of Wellington) some six years before Torres Vedras. Guedalla records that the commission was undertaken 'at the modest price of 500 rupees'.[10]

Robert Home junior (this is his self-portrait) prospered as a painter in India. (NPG)

And the baby of the family was Everard. Born in Hull on 6 May 1756, while his father was in practice there, he was a king's scholar at Westminster[11] – the school of his father's old commander, 'Gentleman Johnny' Burgoyne – when his sisters were married. He won a scholarship to Trinity College, Cambridge, but resigned this and became a pupil of John Hunter in 1772.

On the way to an illustrious career in India, the younger Robert Home painted his brother-in-law on two occasions. (RCS)

NOTES

1 The alliance between England and Portugal, because of which Spain invaded and in terms of which the British expeditionary force came to the aid of Portugal, dates from 1373, when a treaty was signed between Edward III of England and Ferdinand and Eleanor of Portugal. Their agreement ran: 'In the first place we settle and covenant that there shall be from this day forward true, faithful, constant, mutual and perpetual friendships, unions, alliances, and needs of sincere affection and that as true and faithful friends we shall henceforth, reciprocally, be friends to friends and enemies to enemies and shall assist, maintain and uphold each other mutually by sea and by land against all men that may live or die.' It has been a very durable pledge.

2 From Belleisle came the 3rd Regiment of Foot (The Buffs), the 67th (Boscawen's), the 75th (Crawford's) and the 85th; from Ireland, Armstrong's and Blayney's. The Buffs became part of the Queen's Regiment in 1966.

3 Drewry Ottley, a young St George's man, wrote a biographical sketch as introduction to J.F. Palmer's 1837 edition of Hunter's works.

4 Keppel and Adair were brothers-in-law (in 1758 Adair married Lady Caroline Keppel, who wrote the verses).

5 The medical aspects of the Portugal campaign are described in Gask, G (1950) *Essays in the History of Medicine.* London, Butterworth. pp. 116-144.

6 Robert Boyne Home later retired to the ancestral home, Greenlaw Castle just north of the border. It is uncertain whether he died there or in Hull, where he had earlier practised. Greenlaw, formerly the county town of Berwickshire, nestles in the valley of the Blackadder; but the castle was demolished in the nineteenth century and its stones used for other building. Only an area of flat ground marks its site.

7 Scots usage has blurred the name to 'Mills Mount'. It is now surmounted by a cafe.

Robert Boyne Home retired to Greenlaw, the seat of his branch of the family. Greenlaw Castle, on the outskirts of the village, was later demolished, and only a few trees and a patch of flat ground remain to mark its former site. The churchyard is full of Home (and Hume) tombstones, but there is no indication whether these include Robert Boyne's. The windows in the kirk tower are a reminder that the building also served as the town gaol.

8 Boswell, in his *Life*, seeks to justify Johnson's incursion into architecture. 'Johnson's regard for his friend Mr Gwyn induced him to engage in this controversy against Mr Mylne... If it should be remarked that this was a controversy which lay quite out of Johnson's way, let it be remembered, that after all, his employing his powers of reasoning and eloquence on a subject which he had studied on the moment, is not more strange than that we often observe in lawyers, who... are sometimes obliged to pick up a temporary knowledge of an art or science, of which they understood nothing till their brief was delivered, and appear to be much masters of it. In like manner, members of the legislature frequently introduce and expatiate upon subjects of which they have informed themselves for the occasion.'

A footnote carries the apologia further: 'It is ungraciously suggested, that Johnson's motive for opposing Mr Mylne's scheme may have been his prejudice against him as a native of North Britain... So far was he from having any illiberal antipathy to Mr Mylne, that he afterwards lived with that gentleman on very agreeable terms of acquaintance, and dined with him at his house.' (This is the final item for 1759 in Boswell's *Life*.)

9 Gibson, R (1905) *An old Berwickshire town*. London, Oliver & Boyd. According to Gibson, Robert Home first married Angelica, and later Anne Paterson. The DNB, however, has Angelica Kauffmann marrying 'the imposter count de Horn' (and after his death, Antonio Zucchi), and it may well be that Gibson's informants misled him in the matter of this first marriage.

10 Guedalla, P. (1931) *The Duke*. London, Hodder & Stoughton. p.113.

11 The School Register records his admission on 17 January 1770 at the age of 13.

In *The Pickwick Papers* Dickens refers to the White Hart hotel in Bath 'where the waiters, from their costume, might be mistaken for Westminster boys, only they destroy the illusion by behaving themselves much better'.

On his return from Jamaica, Everard Home became Hunter's assistant, and he was admitted to Fellowship of the Royal Society in 1787. (RCS)

2

A DIFFERENT MAN

He is quite a different man from Mr Hunter.

William Clift, letter to his sister(1793)

Everard Home spent six years as Hunter's pupil – a comprehensive medical education, especially if we bear in mind that a six-year course was introduced into New Zealand as recently as 1923, and certain Australian universities have reverted to a five-year course. During that time, and later when he was back in London as a single man, he was a member of John and Anne's household, first in Jermyn Street (where John took over his brother William's house in 1769) and after 1783 at the establishment created in Leicester Square by the purchase of two properties, one fronting on to Castle Street,[1] the other to the square itself.[2] Hunter joined the two already sizeable houses with a building that provided a reception area and lecture theatre on the ground floor and museum space above.

He had already accumulated widely, specimens documenting the broad range of his curiosity – but also illustrating his conviction of the essential importance of the links between structure and function in living creatures. The Belleisle lizard had been joined by geological specimens from the Alentejo uplands in Portugal, and in 1771 – the year before Everard Home's arrival as a resident pupil – the collection was augmented by specimens brought back by James Cook and Joseph Banks from the *Endeavour* voyage. These specimens were given for sorting and cataloguing to a young man who was already a pupil, Edward Jenner, who accomplished his task with such ability as to be proposed as naturalist for Cook's next voyage, which was being planned by Cook even before *Endeavour* reached home. Jenner chose, however, to complete his time with Hunter, then return to work as a country general practitioner in Berkeley in Gloucestershire. His observations of the healthy complexions of milkmaids led him to propose cowpox inoculation as a protection against smallpox, and the outcome guaranteed his place in history. But his time with Hunter was significant, in the refining of his abilities, in the friendship which grew up between the two men and – for that matter – in the opportunity he considered but rejected, of becoming a part of the Cook legend.

Everard Home, for his part, made the acquaintance of Cook's 'partner' from the *Endeavour* voyage, Joseph Banks. Half a generation younger than Hunter and Cook, who were strict contemporaries, Banks was in turn half a generation older than

Edward Jenner completed his time with Hunter, then returned to his native Gloucestershire, to a practice in the old vicarage in Berkeley. The house is now a museum.

John Hunter was a pupil of William Cheselden, who was then recognised, with Pott, as London's leading surgeon. Cheselden's portrait by Jonathan Richardson is in the possession of the Royal College of Surgeons of England; a copy was given to the Australasian College by Professor Wood Jones, who 'bought it for "a song" at the Caledonian market'. Richardson's preliminary sketch is in the National Portrait Gallery. (RACS)

Everard; but Banks's friendship with Hunter (whom he had met in 1766 at the introduction of a Scottish physician at St George's Hospital, George Fordyce) and their shared interest in natural history made him a frequent visitor, often bearing gifts of specimens but – even more – bringing a 'starter dose' of dilettantism into a household ruled by zeal and professionalism. It was a dose that would come to affect Everard Home.

Hunter's first heart attack occurred in 1772, and for the last twenty years of his life he was subject to angina, his life (as he once described it) 'at the mercy of any rogue' who cared to anger him.[3] He did not allow his symptoms to affect the tempo of his work: his consulting, his research and collecting and writing (but it is his museum that has been called his 'great unwritten book'), his teaching.

His willingness to take pupils was in accordance with eighteenth-century practice. He himself had, it will be recalled, been a pupil first of William Cheselden and then of Percivall Pott, and these two men were the leaders of surgical thought and practice in the beginning and middle part of the century. William Cheselden (1688-1752) was, like Hunter, of farming stock and like him carried his boyhood recollections into his surgical career. As a boy he suffered a fracture of the forearm which was treated by a bonesetter with a bandage stiffened with eggwhite and wheaten flour. Remembering the technique, Cheselden used it successfully over many years in the treatment of club foot, with success enough to bring him a substantial referred practice. He was even more celebrated as a lithotomist in a period when cutting for the stone was one of the few relatively safe operative procedures, albeit a major ordeal. (Samuel Pepys, at the end of his diary some 11 years after the event, still celebrated the anniversary of his own

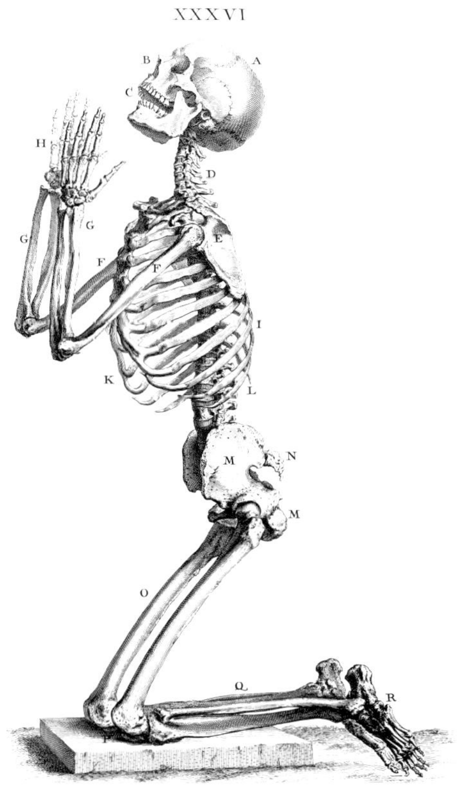

Cheselden's *Osteographia* is distinguished as a work of art, quite apart from its significance as an anatomy text.

operation.) Cheselden's career as an anatomist culminated in the publication of his *Osteographia*, which is notable as a work of art, as a reference work on anatomy and, for that matter, as an advance in the understanding of infection in bone. His career in surgical politics saw him closely involved in the schism between the barbers and the surgeons, and master of the newly formed Surgeons' Company. His skills as an architect were applied to the design of the old wooden Putney bridge of 1729, but they could not secure him the commission when Surgeons' Hall was built in the Old Bailey! He was surgeon to St Thomas's Hospital for two decades, moving to St George's at its foundation in 1733 and to Chelsea four years later, and it was here that Hunter was his pupil a couple of years before his master's death.

Percivall Pott (1714-88) was surgeon at St Bartholomew's and received Hunter as a pupil when the latter ended his time with Cheselden. His large practice included such notables as Samuel Johnson and David Garrick; he became FRS in 1764 and one of Cheselden's successors as Master of the Company of Surgeons the following year. He described the fracture at the ankle that bears his name, and the paralysis that can be associated with tuberculous disease of the spine.

Hunter's experience of the teaching of these men, coming on top of his exposure to the influence of his brother's teaching, established his conviction that the sharing of surgical knowledge is a prime responsibility of the surgeon and that teaching is a prime concern of a hospital. (It was a dispute over moves to restrict teaching at St George's that precipitated his final heart attack.) But his zeal for teaching was magnified by his own scientific curiosity and the urge to bounce ideas off his pupils. His friendship with Jenner led to a prolonged exchange of letters between London and Gloucestershire – often on matters of natural history: it was in the context of hedgehogs and their hibernation that Hunter offered the celebrated injunction to Jenner: 'I think your solution is just; but why think, why not trie the Exp^{t}...'

Hunter's teaching was freely offered (not until 1775 did he make public advertisement of his lectures) and warmly received. Young Everard was not alone in being a resident in Jermyn Street during his student years – in the years between 1770 and 1774 Hunter taught his pupils in his own house and without fee apart from a weekly charge of 2 guineas for board and lodging; and this was a house which, unlike the Leicester Square 'centre' later on, was not designed for such extra activities.

Even more spectacular extra activities were, however, possible at the Earl's Court house which Hunter built after his return from Portugal. He bought two acres in what was then a mere hamlet, a couple of miles outside London close to the Great West Road, and there built what Paget, his biographer, described as 'a most complex and heterogeneous structure; a farm, a menagerie, an institute of anatomy and physiology, and a villa decorated in the fashion of the period'.[4] The institute afforded Hunter a degree of relaxation and the opportunity to pursue his interest in and observation of natural history. At times the relaxation aspect was illusory: Hunter used to wrestle with a small bull which had been presented to him by Queen Charlotte (wife of King George III). On one occasion the bull won and Hunter had to be rescued by the servants. On another a pair of leopards, normally kept chained, escaped and got in among the dogs. Hunter appeared as one of them tried to get over the wall, grabbed them both and returned them to their den, before they could respond or he, for his part, had time to appreciate his own hazard.

Everard Home's student days, therefore, were punctuated by excursions out to Earl's Court and there, observing his brother-in-law engaged about the place, he was able to appreciate the man he would later describe as a short stocky Scot, 'uncommonly strong and active, very compactly made, and capable of great bodily exertion'.[5] But he was also concerned to note that John's heart condition continued to affect him. In 1776 (as Home later observed, in his introduction to the book he published as Hunter's executor) Hunter was 'extremely ill' and took himself to Bath to convalesce. His illness rather took the gloss off his appointment that year as surgeon-extraordinary to King George III.

The following year there was another attack severe enough to prompt a return visit to Bath, with giddiness that persisted for ten days. Hunter wrote to Jenner describing this episode, and

At Earl's Court Hunter established 'a most complex and heterogeneous structure'. (RCS)

Jenner travelled over from Berkeley to see his old chief. He identified the condition as that which William Heberden had described, ten years earlier, as pectoris dolor or (the name that has stuck) angina pectoris. Heberden wrote:

> They who are afflicted with it, are seized while they are walking (more especially if it be uphill, and soon after eating) with a painful and most disagreeable sensation in the breast, which seems as if it would extinguish life, if it were to increase or to continue; but the moment they stand still, all this uneasiness vanishes... The pain... very frequently extends from the breast to the middle of the left arm.

Heberden had recognised the disorder as progressive, writing

> After it has continued a year or more, it will not cease so instantaneously upon standing still; and it will come on not only when the persons are walking, but when they are lying down, especially if they lie on the left side... The termination of the angina pectoris is remarkable. For if no accident intervenc, but the disease go on to its height, the patients all suddenly fall down, and perish almost immediately.[6]

But he did not appreciate that the condition arose from impairment of the coronary blood flow. Jenner, on the other hand, recognised the cardiac basis of the pain. Out of consideration for Hunter he did not mention his belief when they met in Bath, but he confided his opinion privately to Heberden, writing

> How much the heart must suffer from the coronary arteries not being able to perform their functions I need not enlarge upon.

He also communicated with his Bath colleague Caleb Parry, whose 1799 text on angina advanced views soundly documented and with appropriate acknowledgment to Jenner, but views that would not be generally accepted for a century or more.

On completing his six years of training – in effect, of apprenticeship – Home was admitted in 1778 to membership of the Company of Surgeons and entered the naval medical service. He was posted to the naval hospital at Plymouth and here was involved forthwith in the care of sailors wounded in the engagement off Ushant on 27 July 1778 – one of the opening moves in the war of American Independence. The French admiral, d'Orvilliers, had been given conflicting orders and settled for prudence, electing to fight only on his own terms. The Honourable Augustus Keppel (naval commander at Belleisle in the previous war) tried to force the French to fight but fell victim to a combination of wind shifts and poor communications between him and his second-in-command, Hugh Palliser. The immediate result was an inconclusive skirmish – and because the two British commanders were of opposing political beliefs (Keppel was a Whig, Palliser a Tory), there ensued an unseemly political uproar which affected the naval careers of both men, even if the next Whig administration did choose Keppel as First Lord of the Admiralty! It was heady stuff, and the young naval surgeon could feel himself almost a part of it.

The Hon. Augustus Keppel was the naval commander at Belleisle in 1761, and again in an indecisive battle off Ushant in 1778. Everard Home was a young surgeon at the naval hospital at Plymouth at the time. (NMM)

When the focus of the war shifted across the Atlantic, Home went with it. Between 1779 and 1784 he served as a staff surgeon with the army in Jamaica, a position analogous with that held by Hunter in Portugal.[7] Here he survived the hurricane of October 1780, and was a close observer of Rodney's campaigns from the time, early in 1780, when that colourful officer arrived.

Mahan wrote of Rodney: 'Of distinguished courage and professional skill, but with extravagant if not irregular habits, money embarrassments had detained him in exile in France at the time the war began.'[8] But Rodney was no stranger to the West Indies: he had first become commander-in-chief on the Leeward Islands station in 1761 and the following year, while John Hunter and Robert Home were moving into Portugal, he was reducing Martinique and taking possession of St Lucia, Grenada and St Vincent. (Under the Peace of Paris in 1763, Martinique and St Lucia were returned to France; but then, as John Wilkes remarked, the Peace of Paris resembled the peace of God, in that it passed all understanding.) Between 1771 and 1774 Rodney was back commanding at Jamaica, until his financial difficulties drove him to take refuge in France.

His first encounter with the French admiral de Guichen came

on 17 April 1780 but was inconclusive; so were two further engagements the following month. De Guichen then sailed back to France after a Spanish squadron sent to reinforce him had succumbed to sickness, but Rodney, unaware of this, split his force and sailed with half his ships to New York, thus himself escaping the hurricane. On his return to the Indies he learned of Holland's entry into the war and promptly seized a couple of small Dutch islands, St Eustatius and St Martin. While he was thus engaged, the Comte de Grasse succeeded in doubling round Hood's force left to guard the approaches to Fort Royal in Martinique. Linking up with the four French ships blockaded there gave him a four-to-three superiority which he did not exploit – so attracting Mahan's acid comment: 'can a policy or a tradition which justifies such a line of conduct be good?'

Rodney's victory over de Grasse in the battle of The Saints in 1782 foreshadowed the end of 'a disastrous war'. (NMM)

Rodney took sick leave later in 1781, handing over the Indies command to Hood. Further north, de Grasse had more success when, after landing reinforcements in Chesapeake Bay, he saw off Admiral Thomas Graves's ineffectual attempt to take him as he emerged. Graves trickled back to New York, leaving Cornwallis and his army to their fate. Hood, second-in-command to Graves in this encounter, had been so deployed as to be unable to get into action against the French at all; but off St Kitts in January 1782, he had a more respectable skirmish with de Grasse as the latter returned to the Caribbean to threaten Jamaica.

A month later Rodney returned to resume the command, and off Dominica the British fleet cornered de Grasse, encumbered as he was with a flock of transports. On 12 April off the tiny islets named Les Saintes the two fleets, on opposing courses, began a traditional and punishing action with each fleet in line; but a fortunate wind shift allowed Rodney to abandon tradition and

break the French line (so setting a precedent that Nelson would refine into a new naval strategy). De Grasse's flagship *Ville de Paris*, at 130 guns the largest in the world, was obliged to surrender with 300 dead and not a single round of shot left. A contemporary cartoon depicted Rodney receiving de Grasse's sword. It was captioned:

Rodney: You have fought me handsomely.

De Grasse: I was glad of the opportunity.

By the battle of the Saints, the threat to Jamaica was lifted and the garrison, for whose medical services Home and his colleagues were responsible, was relieved. This 'great victory', Sir Arthur Bryant wrote, 'and the stubborn three years' defence of Gibraltar by General Eliott, turned the scale. A disastrous war dwindled into stalemate. The British faced the facts and in 1783 made peace. Their former colonies became the United States of America.'[9]

In the year after the Treaty of Versailles Everard Home returned to London and to residence with the Hunters,[10] now established in Leicester Square. That environment was in sharp contrast with conditions in Jamaica, for in the West Indies yellow fever, the *vomito negro*, could reduce the ten companies of an infantry battalion of the time to just one company's strength in less than a year and, as Haswell relates, 'British units garrisoning Jamaica, the Bahamas, the Leeward Islands and Barbados wasted away, and battalions had to be replaced after only a year's service because of the diseases afflicting the men.'[11] It was, indeed, an achievement that Home himself came through his four-year posting in good health. Moreover, from Barbados he had been able to send back to Hunter specimens of marine animals, the sea anemone *Actinia* and the polychaete worm *Serpula*, made accessible by the effect of the hurricane on the seabed.

No longer a pupil, he was now effectively Hunter's assistant, lecturing for him when he was unwell or obliged to be away. In 1785, for a start, Hunter suffered another attack which drove him once again to Bath. 'He declares,' wrote John Lettsom the physician, 'he was the other day dead for four minutes, not having pulsation in the heart or arteries.'[12] A recurrence in 1786 brought episodes of pain with the least exertion and 'never afterwards', according to Home himself, 'was he entirely free from complaint, or capable of his usual bodily exertions'.

Home was, as Holmes Sellors describes him, 'a good practical surgeon, if a little rough'.[13] (Hunter had been moved to comment on his clumsiness: 'those fingers of yours are all thumbs', and again 'he will never have sense enough to tie down a bottle'.) By ballot on 15 February 1787 Home became a Fellow of the Royal Society – with Hunter as one of his sponsors (despite his reservations about Home's genius). Others included William Pitcairn, then president of the Royal College of Physicians, and his nephew David, and Charles Blagden, a physician from

Edinburgh who became Banks's friend and later the Society's secretary. Home's nomination form noted that 'his account of a new sea animal is published in the Philosophical Transactions' – a slender recommendation, perhaps, but the criteria for admission were somewhat generous in those days.

The Royal Society's more serious resolution in 1787 was its award of its Copley medal to John Hunter. This medal, in gold, was awarded for the most important scientific achievement of the year; in its way, it was a precursor of the Nobel prize. Hunter's friend Cook had received it back in 1776, immediatcly upon his election to Fellowship, and it was at the hands of their mutual friend, now Sir Joseph Banks (his baronetcy came in 1781, three years after he succeeded Sir John Pringle in the presidency), that Hunter received his award.

Things were not, at this stage, going quite so well for Home. He had become assistant surgeon to Hunter at St George's in 1787, and in 1788 a vacancy for a senior surgeon occurred. Hunter lobbied for his brother-in-law, but the post went to the older Gunning's protégé, Thomas Keate.[14] More to his liking, Everard Home obtained a grant of arms in 1788. Whether this was in anticipation of the hospital appointment that did not eventuate is unclear, but in the Lyon Register is recorded:

> 183.
>
> EVERARD HOME Esquire Surgeon in London fourth son of Robert Home of Sharplaw in the County of Roxburgh Esquire by Mary eldest daughter of Colonel Alexander Hutcheson which Robert was only son and heir of William Home of Sharplaw Esquire by Anne second daughter of Sir Alexander Purves second Baronet of Purveshall in the County of Berwick Sollicitor for Scotland to King James the 7th which William was son and heir of William Home of Greenlaw Castle in the County of Berwick Esquire descended from Patrick Home the first of Coldinghamlaw a younger son of Sir Patrick Home second Baron of Polwarth Ancestor of the Earls of Marchmont BEARS Vert a Lyon rampant between two Piles ingrailed issuing from the chief Argent all within a Bordure ingrailed of the last charged with six Pepingos of the first beaked and membered Gules CREST a Lyons head erazed proper collared Sable charged with a Flower de lys Or. Motto TRUE. Matriculated the 9th of May 1788.[15]

In 1788 Everard Home received a grant of arms.

Finally in 1792 Home was able to secure an appointment at St George's as lecturer in anatomy, and on 4 November of that year he was married to Jane, daughter of the Rev. James Tunstall DD and widow of Stephen Thomson. She is a shadowy figure, and the obituary of her son, though recording her family connexions, does not even specify her first name.

Upon his marriage Home moved out of the Leicester Square house into one nearby; but earlier that year Hunter had gained a new staff member. On his 17th birthday, which also happened to be Hunter's 64th, William Clift became amanuensis and laboratory

Anne Hunter's old school friend Mrs Gilbert was instrumental in gaining William Clift his appointment as Hunter's amanuensis and laboratory assistant.

assistant. He had grown up in impoverished conditions in Bodmin, in Cornwall, but his abilities had prompted a Mrs Nancy Gilbert to take an interest in his welfare. She and Anne Hunter were old school friends who had kept in touch, and when Anne described the difficulties her husband was experiencing in replacing his assistant and draughtsman William Bell (Bell went, in 1790, to a lucrative surgical post in Bencoolen in Sumatra, where he died only a couple of months after taking up his duties) Nancy replied that 'she knew a very clever boy who was accustomed to come into her kitchen in Cornwall and make drawings with chalk on the floor, who would with proper instruction become an excellent draughtsman, and so, from the ability which he displayed, would probably answer his purpose very well in other matters'.[16] Told of this, Hunter invited Mrs Gilbert to go ahead, and she and her husband took the lad off to be indentured to Hunter for six years, his work to be in return for his keep, clothing and instruction.

It was an inspired arrangement. In the twenty months that he was employed prior to Hunter's death, he gained an appreciation of the significance and purpose of his master's collection, such that he was to devote his entire life to its demands.

Soon after taking up his post, Clift drew a plan of the Leicester Square establishment, in which Hunter had joined two houses with a lecture theatre. (RCS)

He was also, in a sense, to become Everard Home's nemesis.

His first acquaintance with Hunter he recorded in a letter home: 'I had the pleasure to see Mr Hunter... and I go to write almost every night from eight to eleven... he is a very curious man, and plain as well for he has hair as white as snow and has never got it drest. I believe there is not a bit of Pride in him and all his clothes so plain (but very rich) that I am sure you wou'd not think he was such a grand gentleman.' A grand gentleman – well, Hunter had become acknowledged, with the death of Pott in 1788, as the first surgeon in England. In 1789 he was elected to the Court of Assistants of the Company of Surgeons (equivalent to the Council of today's Royal College of Surgeons) and in 1790 he became surgeon-general of the army – the post held by Robert Adair all those years ago, when he commissioned a young man into the service.

For a start, young Clift enjoyed his acquaintance with Home, and the older man took a jovial interest in the boy. At their first meeting Home (thinking perhaps of the bodies in the dimly-lit dissecting room) asked Clift if he believed in ghosts. 'I don't know, sir,' replied Clift, 'I never saw one. But I was never afraid of my school-fellows, though bigger boys than me.' Home laughed heartily.

He took an interest in the boy's artistic ability. 'I have last week,' Clift wrote home, 'been drawing a bird from nature for Mr Hunter has a great collection of stuffed birds and Mr Home, Mr Hunter's brother-in-law, Mrs H.'s brother, came into the room where I was drawing and said he thought it was done very well and went through to the other house and told Mr Hunter and in the evening when I went to write he told me he was in hopes I should do very well in a little time.'

Not long after Clift began work, Sir Joseph Banks dispensed with his own museum, giving half his specimens to the British Museum and the rest to Hunter. Clift was given the task of sorting these and remounting the ones that were to be incorporated in Hunter's own collection, which came to number over 13,000 specimens, arranged so as to demonstrate the interdependence of structure and function in nature, and the application of this principle to human anatomy, physiology and pathology.

On 16 October 1793 Hunter set out, in apparent good health and spirits, to attend a board meeting at Sir George's. The discussion, on the hospital's policy in respect of students, became heated; Gunning – some accounts say Keate, but they were cronies – angered him and he suffered what this time was a fatal heart attack. His body was brought home that afternoon in a sedan chair. The family was down at Brighthelmstone (present-day Brighton, a village of little account until the Prince Regent made it fashionable) and Matthew Baillie – the physician son of Hunter's sister Dorothea, and five years younger than his fellow-executor Everard Home – went in haste to fetch them. Home had to go off to Deal, before

Anne and her children returned, to see some wounded men returned from the continent,[17] where Britain was once again at war with France, and the Duke of York's 'ten thousand men' were floundering through the Flanders mud.

Clift was devastated, not only by the loss of his beloved master, but by apprehension over his own prospects. 'I am afraid our house will be turned quite upside down now the wall and support is gone... I hope God will provide for me. I should like to live in London very much but I don't think I should ever like any Master as well as Mr Hunter. Perhaps Mr Home might take me to serve out my time with him to look after the dissecting rooms but then all my future hopes of learning to draw would be quite put a stop to, and I suppose I should never learn anatomy under him for he is quite a different man from Mr Hunter as Mrs Gilbert well knows.'

He pondered on the character of the master he had lost. 'From the very beginning I fancied, without being able to account for it, that nobody about Mr Hunter seemed capable of appreciating him. He seemed to me to have lived before his time and to have died before he was properly understood... the more I have seen, the more I have known, the more I have learned and the more I have thought, the stronger the conviction grows that I shall never look upon his like again.' And Holmes Sellors, in a Hunterian Oration 180 years later, reflected on 'a very contrasting pair – the brother-in-law, Everard Home, who probably never really understood what John was aiming at, and the poor lad, William Clift who, though he only knew Hunter for a period of months became his most valuable disciple'.

It fell to Home to conduct Hunter's autopsy. He discovered widespread calcification in the dead man's coronary vessels, a finding that confirmed Jenner's views, and one which he duly communicated to Jenner. 'The coronary arteries,' he recorded, 'had their branches... in the state of bony tubes, which were with difficulty divided with the knife, and their transverse sections did not collapse, but remained open. The valvulae mitrales... were in many places ossified... the aorta, immediately beyond the semilunar valves, had its cavity larger than usual, putting on the appearance of an incipient aneurism... and the internal membrane of this part had lost entirely the natural polish, and was studded over with opaque white spots, raised higher than the general surface... The internal structure of the brain was very carefully examined, and the different parts... were found in the most natural and healthy state; but the internal carotid arteries... were ossified... The vertebral arteries ... had also become bony.'[18]

As Hunter's executor Home was confronted with two immediate tasks. The first was relatively straightforward: he saw through to publication the book *On the Blood, Inflammation and Gun Shot Wounds* which represented the fruits of Hunter's experience during the Seven Years' War and in his career

Everard Home saw Hunter's final book through to publication in 1794.

thereafter. The book came out in 1794 in a quarto edition for George Nicol. It embodies views on wound management which have been derided in more recent years, principally because due allowance has not been made for the septic conditions in which wounds were treated in the eighteenth century (where any interference with tissues carried a substantial risk of introducing or spreading life-threatening infection) or for the low velocity of missiles of the period (which produced minimal tissue death alongside their track, as compared with the devastating effect of the shock wave that accompanies a high-velocity projectile). Two papers, presented at a meeting of the Royal Australasian College of Surgeons in Hobart, Tasmania, in 1994 (one subsequently published in the *Australian and New Zealand Journal of Surgery*)[19] help to show how much better acquainted with wound ballistics was John Hunter than many of his later detractors.

Another item in this posthumous work may be remarked: Hunter documented for the first time the rise in the erythrocyte sedimentation rate that occurs in infective conditions. The viscosity of the serum diminishes so as to allow the red cells in blood to settle more rapidly, producing a clear zone at the top of a thin tube of blood stood upright for a time. The test, though not specific for infection (rheumatic conditions and certain malignancies can also produce a rise) is of great value because the presence – and commonly the level – of an increased ESR provides a simple warning of the existence of a problem, and its fall in response to treatment offers reassurance that the treatment is proving effective.

Home's second task proved more difficult, and a great deal more tedious. During Hunter's married life he had been able to

George Stubbs was noted as an animal painter; but his anatomical knowledge gave him a good deal of common ground with his friend John Hunter. His painting of a rhinoceros is in the possession of the Royal College of Surgeons. (RCS)

provide for his wife so that her talents made her salon one of the more sought-after centres of culture and good conversation, attracting the likes of Sir Joshua Reynolds, who lived nearby and died a year before John; Stubbs the animal painter who did work for John and painted the kangaroo whose skin and skull came back with the *Endeavour* voyagers (the skull went into the museum);[20] Benjamin West, the American who succeeded Reynolds as president of the Royal Academy and shocked the Establishment by painting the dying Wolfe in uniform rather than the classical robes which had previously been the required dress;[21] and Fanny Burney (Mme d'Arblay) the diarist, whose father was the encyclopaedist of music in his time, and whose brother James went with Cook and sought to render Polynesian chants in musical notation.

Anne herself was a poetess of some distinction, a Romantic before the Romantics, and described as 'singularly dignified and lady-like, possessed of a cultivated mind with special gifts for poetry and music'. When the composer Joseph Haydn came to London at the beginning of 1791 he was referred to John Hunter who proposed operating on his nasal polyps. He escaped from John and was gathered into Anne's circle; and on his next visit, a year after John's death, he set to music a number of her verses (the best known is *My mother bids me bind my hair*) which he dedicated to her. She in turn wrote a libretto for his oratorio *The Creation*, one which flows much better than the usual English libretto which has barely survived its translation into German and back. This text of Anne's, however, languished at the College of Surgeons for almost two hundred years before receiving its premiere (very

Anne Hunter was as talented in her own fields – as poetess, musician and society hostess – as her husband John had been in his. (RCS)

largely because of the initiative of Dr Aileen Adams) in a performance at the Royal Festival Hall in London during the bicentenary commemoration of Hunter's death, on 15 September 1993.

After John Hunter died, it was apparent that the proceeds of a lucrative practice had gone into supporting an establishment of about three dozen persons – in London and at Earl's Court – and developing the museum. With practice income no longer coming in, Anne was left penniless. It was thus Everard's concern (with his fellow-executor, Matthew Baillie) to dispose of the collection, and that not simply because Hunter's will stated 'I... give to the said Matthew Baillie and Everard Home all my collection of natural history, and the cases, and other things belonging thereto, or used therewith, upon trust that they offer the same to sale in one entire lot to the Government of Great Britain' but in order that his sister Anne might have something to survive on. Hunter's books and paintings were able to be auctioned off promptly at Christie's, the paintings on 29 January 1794. These included works by Titian, Rubens, van Dyck, Canaletti, Ruysdael, Loutherbourg (who subsequently painted the battle of the Glorious First of June, fought later that year) and, of course, Reynolds – who certainly painted Hunter – and Zoffany who probably did.[22]

Hunter's nephew William Baillie was Home's fellow executor. (RCS)

On the following Saturday, 1 February, the books were sold: a wide selection of reading – anatomy and physiology, medicine and surgery; the arts, Virgil and Bacon, Adam Smith; Blackstone on the law and Hartley on the mind; Newton and Priestley, Bougainville and Cook. But nothing by way of Romantic literature.

The sale of the paintings, it appears from Clift's records, yielded £1000; of the books, £634.4.6. With the proceeds of the two sales, Anne's immediate needs could be met. The disposal of Earl's Court was not so straightforward. Of Booth, the attorney who negotiated the sale, Clift recorded that it 'was a long time before he could be brought to book, under various pretences for delay'; and he added a wry couplet:

> Full many a time did I after him trot
> And naught but an unsatisfactory answer I got.
> W.C.

It was an even harder matter, however, to persuade the Government to purchase the museum collection. The country was at war and the younger Pitt was desperate for money to fund the war effort; buying 'curiosities' in cases did not stand high in his priorities.[23] It did not help when, in 1796, Sir Joseph Banks responded to a suggestion that the Royal Society might take over the collection by remarking that 'he did not consider Hunter's museum an object of importance to the general study of natural history'. Since half of Banks's own collection had gone to Hunter in 1792, so dismissive an opinion is surprising.

Ultimately the determination of William Eden, Lord Auckland,[24] bore fruit and on 13 June 1799 Parliament voted £15,000 for the purchase of the collection. Its custody was offered to the Company of Surgeons and on 23 December the Court of Assistants (of which Hunter had been a member at the time of his death) voted unanimously to accept the responsibility. As early as 26 April, though, the Court had agreed to accept the collection in the event Parliament 'shall think proper to purchase this valuable Collection for the benefit of the Public and Honour this Corporation by Entrusting it to their Care'.. The acquisition was a significant factor in the evolution of the Company into a Royal College.

During these long years of uncertainty William Clift had remained quietly, loyally, unobstrusively but very methodically at work in Leicester Square, preparing and arranging specimens and copying out what he regarded as the more significant of his master's papers. His initial uncertainty gradually subsided. Writing to his sister of events immediately after Hunter's death he had reported: 'I believe that Mr Home is not going to carry on the lectures and dissecting after this winter and then I suppose when that is over I shall have a place got for me.' When the Leicester Square house was let (and Anne Hunter moved to a cottage at Blackheath) only the housekeeper and the dissecting room steward remained with Clift in the Castle Street portion of the complex; and when Haynes the steward was sacked for taking and selling some of Hunter's clothing, Clift found himself very much in charge.

Everard Home would drop in on him from time to time. He took an interest in the youth, giving him half a guinea on one occasion upon learning that he had no regular income, and advising him to wear away at his best suit – before he grew out of it (which is not bad advice for a smallish eighteen-year-old). But it took a sorrowful letter to Mrs Gilbert, who in turn confided young Clift's difficulties to Baillie, before Home was brought to pay him the £5 he had earlier been promised. However, he was also given permission to learn anatomical drawing, and this was to prove a useful talent in financial as in other respects.

Being obliged to be almost constantly on the premises, so that he could show visitors – even potential purchasers - round the collection, Clift soon reached the point where it would have been difficult for him to contemplate any other calling beyond the one into which circumstances had driven him. With some relief he received Home's proposal, that he should remain in charge of the museum. To his sister he wrote, 'I must trust to providence which hath favoured me greatly beyond what I could ever expect.' His salary was set at £20 per year, but now he had to provide himself with clothing; his anatomical drawings provided a source of additional income, not lavish but welcome. For Matthew Baillie's *Morbid Anatomy* he did 72 plates at a guinea per

Hunter's bust now stands in Leicester Square. Next to the cinema, the site of his old home is occupied by a pub in which historical photographs are generously displayed.

drawing;[25] he observed that Heath, Skelton and Basire (Basire was responsible for an engraving from one of James Cook's portraits, not a particularly distinguished rendering at that) had quoted five guineas.

But of most importance, he read and copied out Hunter's manuscripts. These had been moved over to the Castle Street section of the 'centre' when the Leicester Square house was sold off. Home suggested they should go to his own house at 30 Sackville Street, but they were left in Castle Street until 1800. In one of his own manuscripts Clift owns 'a kind of presentiment that if they were removed to his [Home's] house some accident might befall them, and even then feeling their value, I copied for my own use and information a considerable proportion of them'.

After his marriage in 1792, Everard Home moved out of Leicester Square to a house at 30 Sackville Street. He took Hunter's papers there in 1800, somewhat to Clift's dismay.

When the custody of the collection was settled in December 1799, Clift received the best possible Christmas present – he was appointed to be the first Conservator of the Hunterian Museum. The collection was judged to have been improved by his ministrations since his master's death, and under a Board of Curators he was to have the responsibility for it. The Company of Surgeons itself was reconstituted as a Royal College, but the collection was to be under a Board of Trustees. Thirty in number, the trustees included sixteen public figures serving *ex officio* (including Sir Joseph Banks as president of the Royal Society), the remainder being appointed in the first instance by the Lords of the Treasury, the trustees themselves then having the right of filling vacancies.[26] Baillie was one of the original fourteen, as was Lord Auckland himself, but not Home. The Board of Curators fixed Clift's salary at £80 a year; Home had led him to expect £100 and was supportive enough to give him an additional 20 guineas in each of the next five years.

The Curators (William Long, George Chandler, John Heaviside, William Blizard and Henry Cline) imposed fairly strict conditions on Clift, requiring him

> - to examine into the security of the Museum in every part as to fire and other causes of danger every night before going to rest. In case of danger from fire or any other cause to give immediate notice to the Curators and to the Secretary of the College.
> - not to be absent from the Museum any night without a written leave from two Curators who will give directions for the care of the Museum in his absence.
> - the Museum never to be left unlocked upon any occasion nor during any period.
> - to communicate in writing to the Board every matter respecting the care and improvement of the Museum.
> - to enter in a book every article wanted from time to time in the Museum.
> - no article to be procured except of the most trifling nature or upon a pressing occasion without permission of the Board of Curators.
> - an account to be regularly kept in a book of all expenses.

All this, it may be reflected, was imposed upon the young man who had guarded the collection almost single-handed for seven years with a maturity far beyond his own years – and at a time when the museum's new home was yet to be constructed. The board chose to limit the admission of visitors, whose names were to be entered in a book, to forbid the borrowing (or drawing without their leave) of specimens, to admit visitors on two afternoons a week and to bring in Baillie and Home as well-qualified to advise on 'supplying any deficiencies in the Collection'.

Home had, by this time, become as friendly with Joseph Banks as Hunter had been, and upon him devolved the privilege of receiving specimens sent back by Pacific explorers. The celebrity which Banks (and his public relations machine, two centuries before such devices became general) had achieved after the *Endeavour* voyage with Cook had produced two interesting results. In the first place, it prompted him to claim the role of selector-manager when Cook's second voyage was in the planning stage. He 'chose' James Lind (the 'other' one, not the author of the classic work on scurvy) and, as artist, Johann Zoffany, the society portrait painter. He approached Joseph Priestley, the discoverer of oxygen, then dropped him when he recognised that – as a nonconformist minister – Priestley would not be acceptable to the heavily-Anglican Board of Longitude. Then in a final act of unwisdom he demanded the building of an extra deck on *Resolution*, the larger of the two expedition vessels, to accommodate him and his suite, of fourteen this time, including two horn players to entertain him after dinner. It is possible to understand his reasoning, for anyone who has crawled through the cramped accommodation in today's *Endeavour* replica; what his landsman's instinct failed to impress on him was the effect of extra tophamper on such a shallow-draft vessel. When *Resolution* proved dangerously unseaworthy and the offending structure was removed, Banks withdrew in a huff from any further involvement with the voyage.

But his place as a 'sponsor' of scientific expeditions had been secured. He conceived and promoted Bligh's breadfruit voyages and, when Cook's other former midshipman George Vancouver went in 1791 to explore the north-west of North America, Banks designated Alexander Menzies as Vancouver's naturalist - or, more strictly, as 'his' naturalist aboard Vancouver's ship, for he instructed Menzies to be answerable to him (and warned him to expect little co-operation from Vancouver). The outcome was a flood of botanical specimens for Banks for Kew Gardens, a generally

Banks was influenced, by the cramped conditions he had experienced in *Endeavour*, to demand the building of an additional deck on *Resolution*. Aboard the *Endeavour* replica it is possible to understand Banks's landsman's instinct.

friendly association between Vancouver and Menzies (to the extent that when *Discovery's* surgeon had to be repatriated, Vancouver invited Menzies, who was medically qualified, to take his place, and Menzies agreed) and a shared interest in the sea otter, with which Vancouver had become acquainted on the final Cook voyage. They brought back two adults and two cubs to London, where Menzies and Home dissected the male adult and cub, publishing their findings in the *Philosophical Transactions* of the Royal Society in 1796.

Bligh, for his part, studied and drew the spiny anteater when he was in Tasmanian waters in *Providence* in 1792 during the second breadfruit voyage. He passed his drawing to Banks after his return, and Banks in turn gave this to Home, who published it with an annotation in the *Philosophical Transactions* in 1802. Home was, in fact, becoming a regular contributor to the *Transactions*: prior to Hunter's death, he had produced just three papers, after it, he would publish no fewer than 92. The underlying reason would emerge in time.

By the time of this latter publication, the Homes had a son, born on 25 October 1798 and named James Everard. William Clift, though still labouring at Castle Street while awaiting the building of the collection's new home in the Royal College of Surgeons, had been promised accommodation in the new college building, and found his prospects secure enough to allow him to marry. On 21 January 1801, in the church of St Martin-in-the-

William Clift and Caroline Pope were married in 1801, in the church of St Martin-in-the-Fields where, eight years earlier, John Hunter's remains had been interred in the crypt.

The new Royal College acquired a second house in Lincoln's Inn Fields (at the right of this print) to enable it to meet its responsibilities in respect of Hunter's collection. (RCS)

Fields – just a few yards from Castle Street and the very church where Hunter's remains had been interred – Clift married Caroline Harriet Pope. He was almost 26, his bride 23. Their daughter, also Caroline, was born in September, and the following year Clift was able to invite his sister Elizabeth to join the household and help his wife with the care of the infant. In 1803 a son was born and named William Home Clift, Everard Home standing godfather to the child.

The new Royal College was meanwhile making good progress with its building programme. The previous Surgeons' Hall in the Old Bailey (the one for which Cheselden's design failed to be chosen) had already, as long ago as 1796, been found in need of major repairs; and the company had secured the freehold of 41 Lincoln's Inn Fields prior to its change of status, so that the additional space needed for Hunter's collection dictated the purchase of the adjacent property. Accordingly, number 42 was acquired in 1803, and George Dance and James Lewis were chosen to design a building to house the new college and its new museum.

The younger George Dance (his father, also George, had designed the Mansion House) was the last of five sons. He combined art and architecture, and was responsible for sketches of Hodges, Bligh and John Hunter himself; he also painted Sir Hugh Palliser, Keppel's deputy and Cook's patron. As an architect he taught John (later Sir John) Soane, who designed the Bank of England, accumulated specimens and curiosities and crammed them into his house – on the opposite side of Lincoln's Inn Fields, where (designated 'Sir John Soane's museum') they have become a rival to Hunter's museum in the guide books of the area.

The College applied, with help from Lord Grenville, for a grant from Parliament and in July 1803 received the promise of £15,000 for the erection of 'a proper and commodious building for the preserving and extending the Collection of the late Mr Hunter'. It was soon evident that the £15,000 was a gross underestimate: the final estimate came to £22,650 and a further £12,500 was voted by Parliament. The plans made provision for Clift (and the College secretary) to live in, and Clift moved over from Castle Street when the collection was shifted in 1806. Home had meanwhile, from 1805, begun to deposit with Coutts' bank, for investment in Consols, his annual 20-guinea payment to Clift, a practice he continued until the interest was sufficient to make up Clift's income to the earlier-anticipated £100. These measures, a gratuity from the college (for making a copy of Hunter's provisional catalogue) which soon rose from £25 to £50, and the proceeds of his artistic commissions, saw Clift through the Castle Street years, while reinforcing his loyalty to Home.

In 1806 the new College building was still unfinished, but the Board of Curators elected to give up the lease at Castle Street and move the collection to 41 Lincoln's Inn Fields in the meantime. It had already been decided that both Clift and the College secretary, Okey Belfour, would need to live on the premises. Their respective calculations of the cost of the move did not tally, and Clift found himself with £35 in place of the £50 gratuity he had been voted for superintending the move. On other matters, however, the new neighbours seem to have experienced no difficulties.

Clift's concern was to achieve an arrangement of the specimens that would reflect the underlying thesis of Hunter's 'great unwritten book' – the interdependence of structure and function. To his satisfaction he found most members of the board ready to accept his judgment. He was, after all, in his thirties by now! By 1809 his scientific reputation was such that he was invited to join the newly formed Chemical Society, which certain Fellows of the Royal Society established to promote the interests of the Society itself by gathering in men interested in chemistry, anatomy and physiology. In this way he found himself mixing with men of the reputation of Sir Joseph Banks – now past 30 years as PRS – and Sir Humphrey Davy, Benjamin Brodie the surgeon, Dr Babington who combined medicine and mineralogy, Henry Cavendish who discovered hydrogen and determined the composition of air and water, and William Brande who occupied the chair of chemistry and materia medica at Apothecaries' Hall. With Banks, in particular, he established a friendship that saw them sampling an assortment of exotic meats 'and many other things... by way of experiment that are not usually eaten'. It was a form of applied research that Banks had entered into during the *Endeavour* voyage, when he and Cook sampled a wide variety of animal species.

George III suffered his first major episode of madness soon after his Sudeley visit in 1788, and was seen by John Hunter. Everard Home later became serjeant surgeon to the King, shortly before that unfortunate man was finally disabled, (probably by porphyria) so that his son became Prince Regent.

In 1809, the year of Clift's accession to the Chemical Society, Home became a member of the Court of Examiners of the College of Surgeons. He had been appointed to the Court of Assistants (later the Council) as far back as 1801. In 1807 he even achieved the Copley medal of the Royal Society 'for his various Papers on Anatomy and Physiology printed in the Philosophical Transactions' – an award the Society may later have regretted, for reasons that will become evident.

In 1808 he became serjeant surgeon to King George III, shortly before the advisers of that unfortunate monarch were obliged to declare a regency in the name of his oldest son, the future George IV – who was detested by his father and derided by many of his father's subjects.[27] During a previous episode of (almost certainly porphyria-induced) kingly dementia twenty years earlier, the Prince of Wales's machinations, and those of his circle of advisers, had come close to securing a regency before the King's condition improved – so vindicating the prognosis given by John Hunter,[28] on no particular evidence, that 'the chances were nine to one in his favour'. There were recurrences in 1801 and 1804, and at the 50th anniversary of his accession, on 25 October 1810, he was seen to have 'a decided return of his former malady'. Home's fellow-executor, Matthew Baillie, was among those in attendance (though not, it seems, Home himself). The Regency Act, passed on 5 February 1811, vested the care of the King's person in the Queen, with the assistance of a Council of seven Privy Councillors and the power of declaring the King well and competent; but this time there was no opportune recovery, and the Prince held the office of Regent until the death of the old King in 1820.

On 31 May 1810 – just a few months before the old King's jubilee became so sad an occasion – Home had endeared himself

Ernest Augustus, Duke of Cumberland, was the victim of an attempted assassination at the hands of his valet in 1810. He was treated by Everard Home. (RColl)

to the royal family in unusual circumstances. The King's fifth son, Ernest Augustus, Duke of Cumberland, had returned to his quarters in St James's Palace from a concert that evening and been attended by one of his valets, Neale, before going to bed. At about 2.30a.m. the Duke was awakened by what he later described as a hissing sound; there followed two violent blows on his head and, as he attempted to ward off further blows, he came close to losing a finger. With his vision, already poor, obscured further by the blood pouring down his face, he blundered out of his room, calling out 'Neale! Neale, I am murdered!'

Neale, running to assist his master, tripped over something which proved to be the Duke's own sabre, thrown aside by his assailant. He applied a dressing of sorts and led the Duke down to the office of the porter, who made the outside doors secure and then went with the rest of the servants in search of Sellis, the other valet. They found him – with his throat cut. It was established that he had hoped to murder his master, then return to his own room and clean himself up. Instead, alarmed by the hue and cry, he had decided to take his own life.

As it happens, Cumberland was less flagrant in liaisons than his brothers, and gossip had therefore invested him with a sinister quality all of his own. The gossips and pamphleteers, aware only of the bloodshed, had a field day, asserting variously that he had been sleeping with Sellis's wife or (by way of contrast) that he had been abusing one or other valet, so as to be open to blackmail.

The uniforms are different, but otherwise St James's Palace is little changed from its appearance at the time of Everard Home's treatment of the Duke of Cumberland's head wound.

The inquest verdict of suicide on Sellis (who was discovered – rather late in the day – to have a history of dishonesty and instability) disappointed but did not utterly deter the gossips, such was the attitude to the royal dukes at the time.

Everard Home was called in, a bulletin announced that His Royal Highness's wounds were 'not immediately dangerous, and he is as well as can be expected under the circumstances of the case'. Home operated on the Duke's head wound the next day, removing a bone fragment that was pressing on the exposed brain. He tidied up the other wounds, and the patient was transferred to the Prince of Wales's residence, Carlton House. He made a slow but satisfactory recovery, though the severe scarring from his head wound added to his sinister reputation!

As an augmentation of honour, Home was granted the use of the 'label of three points' by which the Duke's version of the Royal arms was distinguished.

Royal gratitude for Home's services took an unusual form: he was granted an 'augmentation of honour' to the arms he had previously been awarded in 1788, even as Nelson had been acknowledged after the battle of the Nile and Wellington would be after Salamanca. But even among augmentations (themselves rather rare) his took an uncommon form. In place of the black collar with its gold fleur-de-lis that had adorned the neck of the lion's head of his crest, Home was granted a 'label of three points' - the same emblem by which the Duke of Cumberland's personal arms were differentiated from the royal arms of his father the King. And not only were the points of this label charged with a blue fleur-de-lis between two red St George's crosses exactly as in the Duke's case, but the label so charged was applied also to the necks of the two lions 'reguardant' (that is to say, looking outwards over their shoulders) which served as supporters of the arms. The augmentation was made 'by Special Concession and Licence' dated 23 November 1812 'in the Name and on the behalf of His Majesty' and signed 'George P.R.'.

The formal opening of the Museum took place on 18 May 1813, by which time Home had become Master of the now Royal College of Surgeons; and six weeks later, on 27 June, the Master of the

College became Sir Everard Home, first Baronet. He wasted no time, and on 19 July his updated arms were recorded in the Lyon Register in Edinburgh. They displayed not only the 'red hand of Ulster' that indicates a baronet of Great Britain, but of course the augmentation from the previous year. The Letters Patent detail the circumstances and form of the augmentation:

> ... and in order to convey to his posterity a lasting Memorial of the Sense which His Sacred Majesty King George the third entertains of the Services of the said Sir Everard Home Baronet, and particularly of the skill and Attention successfully manifested by him in the cure of the wounds which his Majesty's most dear son Ernest Augustus Duke of Cumberland received from the hands of an Assassin within the Royal palace of St James's on Thursday the 31st day of May 1810 by Special Concession and Licence dated the 23rd day of November 1812, the augmentation following, that is to say
> "In lieu of the Collar beforesaid a Label of three points, the middle point charged with a fleur de lis Azure, and each of the other points with Saint George's Cross; the same being the difference assigned to the Armorial Bearings assigned by his said Sacred Majesty to his said most dear Son Ernest Augustus Duke of Cumberland. –Motto: True. Supporters Two lions reguardant proper, each Gorged with a Label of three points Argent charged as the Crest."

A little over a week later, on 28 July, the Prince Regent himself inspected the museum, devoting an hour and a half to examining the specimens and declaring 'that he had derived high gratification from the visit'. It is fair to observe that Everard Home and 'Prinny' also derived high gratification as drinking companions and, for that matter, that Prinny seldom achieved the heights of gratification from a study of museums! But, for Everard, 1813 was undoubtedly a 'good year'.

In the course of the year he and Baillie, 'being desirous of showing a lasting mark of respect to the memory of the late John Hunter', arranged for the institution of a Hunterian Oration, to be delivered at the college on the 'official' anniversary of Hunter's birthday – i.e. 14 February[29] – by the Master or a member of the Court of Assistants. The orator was to receive the sum of £10, the rest of the endowment interest going to fund a dinner on the day of the oration. Originally an annual event, it subsequently became a biennial one. The first orator (in 1814, by which time he had been succeeded as Master by Sir William Blizard, one of the original Board of Curators) was Everard Home himself, of whom it was reported that 'the Orator's peroration was peculiarly dignified and impressive'.

Later in 1814 Home achieved the further distinction of becoming vice-president of the Royal Society and hence the right-hand man of his old friend Sir Joseph Banks. The office is in the nature of a 'consolation prize' rather than a stepping-stone to the presidency, but Everard treated it as a qualification on the title page of his writings. It would be reasonable to say that Everard Home had 'arrived'.

NOTES

1 Castle Street is now part of Charing Cross Road.

2 The Leicester Square house, No. 28, was bought by Hunter from the painter John Singleton Copley (1738-1815). Boston-born of Irish descent, Copley came to London in 1775 and was a protégé of his fellow American Benjamin West, who succeeded Sir Joshua Reynolds as President of the Royal Academy in 1792. Reynolds himself lived nearby in St Martin's Lane.

3 Brock, R. (1961) Museum, Research and the inspiration of Hunter. *Ann. Roy. Coll. Surg. Engl.* 29:1.

4 Paget, S. (1897) *Life of John Hunter* London, T. Fisher Unwin.

5 In his biographical introduction to Hunter, J (1794) *On the Blood, Inflammation and Gun-shot wounds.* London, Nicol.

6 Heberden, W. (1768), published in Heberden, W. jnr (ed) (1802) *Commentaries on the History and Cures of Diseases.*

7 The Westminster School register records that on 2 December 1782 Home became surgeon to the 1st Battalion of the 60th Foot (later the King's Royal Rifle Corps and, from 1966, the Royal Green Jackets); on 25 December 1782 he was designated Apothecary and Storekeeper in Jamaica.

8 Mahan, A.T. (1890) *The influence of Sea-Power upon History 1660-1783* (1980 illustrated edition, combined with *The influence of Sea-Power upon the French Revolution and Empire* (1892). Greenwich, CT. Bison).

9 Bryant, A. (1986) *Freedom's Own Island.* London, Collins. p.352.

10 He was placed on half-pay on 6 October 1784.

11 Haswell, J. (1975) *The British Army.* London, Thames & Hudson.

12 Pettigrew, T.J. (1817) *Memoirs of John Coakley Lettsom.* London, Nicholls Son & Bentley.

13 Holmes Sellors, T. (1973) *Ann. Roy. Coll. Surg. Engl.* 53: 139,205

14 The Gunnings and the Keates were entwined in the annals of St George's Hospital, and in what the DNB describes as 'violent controversies with John Hunter'. John Gunning was surgeon at St George's 1765-98, Master of the Company of Surgeons 1789-90 and Hunter's successor as surgeon-general of the army in 1793; the younger Gunning (1774-1863) was surgeon 1800-23, apart from service as surgeon-in-chief to Wellington in the Peninsular War. Thomas Keate (1745-1821) defeated Home for the surgical appointment in 1792, succeeded Gunning senior as surgeon-general on the latter's death in 1798, and at his retirement from St George's in 1813 was succeeded there by his nephew Robert (1777-1857). Thomas was Master of the College (into which the Company had now

evolved) in 1802, 1809 and 1818; Robert held the office - now designated President - in 1830, 1831 and 1839.

15 These arms include elements derived from the Marchmont branch of the Homes: the lion (*Argent*, white or silver) on a green field for Home; the engrailed piles - hanging like ragged stalactites - for Polwarth; the pepingoes or popinjays (heraldic parrots) in the border for Pepdie in what is surely a heraldic pun. The term *engrailed* describes the scalloped edges of the piles and the border; the parrots *beaked and membered gules* have red beaks and legs; the lion's head crest is shown as if torn off its body (*erased*; whereas if cut off cleanly, the head would be *couped*); it has a black collar bearing a gold fleur-de-lis.

16 From the recollections of Sir Benjamin Brodie, quoted in Dobson, J. (1954) *William Clift.* London, Heinemann.

17 After being on half pay from 1784, Home had been appointed Staff Surgeon Great Britain on 14 June 1793; he retired in September 1794.

18 Qvist, G. (1981) *John Hunter 1728-1793.* London, Heinemann.

19 Magee, R. (1995) Muskets, musket balls and the wounds they made. *Aust. N.Z.J. Surg.* 65:890-895.

20 It was destroyed when the College of Surgeons was bombed in 1941, along with much of the museum.

21 But it impressed another of Britain's heroes. 'There is one painting whose power I do feel,' Nelson told West. 'I never pass a print shop where your "Death of Wolfe" is in the window, without being stopped by it.'

22 Taylor, S. (1993) *John Hunter and his painters.* London, Royal College of Surgeons.

Beasley, A.W. (1994) John Hunter and his painters. *Bull. Roy. Coll. Surg. Engl.* 76:1:35.

23 When Banks sounded out the younger Pitt, so Clift recalled to Owen in later years, the suggestion was 'ill received by the War Minister of the day. "What! give £20,000 for bottles - we want the money to buy bullets."'

24 William Eden (1744-1814) already held an Irish peerage when created Baron Auckland of West Auckland, Durham, in 1793. His son George (1784-1849), second Baron, as First Lord of the Admiralty in 1834, appointed two officers to command, each of them after a lengthy period 'on the beach': James Everard Home into *Racehorse* and William Hobson into *Rattlesnake.* The circumstances of Home's appointment will be described later. Hobson became lieutenant-governor of New Zealand in 1840, and gave his patron's name to the site on the Waitemata Harbour which he selected to be the capital of the new colony. The capital was later moved to Wellington, but Auckland is today the largest city in New Zealand. Eden was created first Earl of Auckland in 1839 while governor-general of India.

25 Of the originals, 24 are in the Royal College of Physicians of London, the remainder in the University of Melbourne.

26 The Trustees *ex officio* were the Lord Chancellor, the First Lord of the Treasury (i.e. the Prime Minister), the Chancellor of the Exchequer, the First Lord of the Admiralty, the Speaker of the House of Commons, the Secretary at War, the President of the Royal Society, the President and four Censors of the Royal College of Physicians, the Regius Professor of Medicine and the Reader in Anatomy at Oxford, the Regius Professor of Physic and the Professor of Anatomy at Cambridge. The other appointees were: Lord Auckland, the Earl of Euston, Charles Small Pybus, Matthew Baillie, Lord St Helens, Lord Arden, Sir Charles Blagden, Isaac Hawkins Browne, Sir Archibald Macdonald Bt, the Bishop of Llandaff, Edward Whittaker Gray, MD, Charles Long and Sir George Shuckburgh Evelyn Bt (who was replaced in 1805 by the Earl Spencer).

27 Charles Lamb captured public opinion in his verse:

By his bulk and by his size,
By his oily qualities,
This (or else my eyesight fails)
This should be the Prince of Whales.

28 Hunter, it will be recalled, became Surgeon Extraordinary to the King in 1776.

29 Hunter was born during the night of 13-14 February; his birth certificate gives the date 13 February, and this is the date celebrated by the Hunterian Society, but Hunter himself preferred to observe 14 February, and the College follows suit.

It is easy, observing this bust of Everard Home, to picture his intransigence in his dealings with the Board of Curators. (RCS)

3

LIKE UNTO ASHES

Your remembrances are like unto ashes, your bodies to bodies of clay.

Job, *XIII, 12.*

The Hunterian Museum attracted a glittering array of distinguished visitors, hard on the heels of the Prince Regent – on 11 April 1814 the Grand Duchess of Oldenburg[1] came at his suggestion and echoed his approbation by expressing 'the greatest satisfaction at having seen so valuable and splendid a Collection'. In the course of the year came the physician to the King of Prussia, General Wiebel (already the seeds of Prussian militarism were evident), Dr Hamel of St Petersburg who had accompanied the Russian emperor on his visit to England, and the emperor's surgeon Sir James Wylie, one of a flock of expatriates who became part of the Russian scene.

The Archduke Maximilian of Austria showed his appreciation by presenting a book to the Library, for which at this time Clift was largely responsible in addition to his museum duties. Baillie and Home were among the donors who helped build up a modest collection until the bequest of Sir Charles Blicke in 1816 provided

The Hunterian Museum became an instant attraction for distinguished visitors. William Clift sketched the scene in Dance's building. (RCS)

more generous funding. (Even when Edmund Belfour, son of Okey, was appointed Keeper of the Library in 1821, Clift continued to advise on the acquisition of new books.)

The distinguished visitors were given bound copies of a synopsis of the contents of the museum, which was produced by Home with Clift's assistance. The flow of visitors was such that the need for a full descriptive catalogue of the museum was felt to be pressing. In one year Clift conducted no fewer than 1,842 visitors round the exhibits. He enjoyed doing so, but it meant that he had to work late into the night to keep abreast of his other work – and once a full catalogue could be provided, much less time would need to be spent as a guide. Home was regarded as the appropriate person to undertake the task, since he had possession of Hunter's manuscripts; equally Clift was considered the right person to assist him. As far as Clift was concerned, he did not need help or supervision – but he did need the manuscripts, and Home showed no inclination either to start work himself or to pass the documents to Clift for him to work on. It was an awkward situation, and until it resolved itself Clift could do no more than arrange and catalogue new accessions (which were many and varied) and await developments.

At the time, he had no particular suspicions. Home was a busy man, he had his social life (rather too much of that!) and a large practice, and he was in demand as a lecturer. Indeed it is recorded that he gave the Croonian lectures at the Royal Society – which had been endowed by Dr William Croone at his death in 1684, along with funds to establish algebra lectures at Cambridge! – no fewer than 15 times between 1794 and 1826.[3] But at least by now young Everard Home was off his father's hands. After four years at his father's old school, he had been enlisted in the Royal

Like his father, young James Everard Home attended Westminster School. He left to enter the Royal Navy at the age of 11½, as boys still did in his day.

Navy, as a midshipman, at the tender age of 11½ on 10 April 1810, serving first in the Mediterranean in *Euryalus* (Captain the Hon. George Lawrence Dundas), a 5th-rate of 1803 which had seen action at Trafalgar.[2] Not for a couple of years would the minimum age for enlistment be raised to thirteen.

It is surprising, in view of Home's avuncular interest in Clift during the early days (and the naming of William Home Clift), that he discouraged Clift's efforts to secure young William's entry to Charterhouse, giving as his reason that 'by mixing with those boys who might have better prospects, it might give him a disposition to idleness' – so wrote Clift to his old patroness, Mrs Gilbert. This was in 1814, yet when Home fell ill at Lancing (on the Sussex coast near Worthing) in 1817, he insisted that Clift alone should be in attendance on him. Clift wrote to his wife, 'It is almost impossible that I should leave him till some change for the better takes place... for he can hardly get anything done to satisfy him unless I do it for him.' And a week later, 'I have hardly stirred from the house all the week and am not likely to do so as Sir Everard is so very nervous and weak.'[4] It must appear that Home was perfectly willing to trade on Clift's loyalty.

At the College of Surgeons there is a revealing 'balance sheet' in Clift's handwriting. On one side he lists the payments he had received from Home, including refunds for materials bought by Clift for 'jobs' at Sackville Street; on the other he documents his services over many years, referring to 'sheer work besides funding Paper and Ink, Colours, Pencils & Drawing Paper'. At the foot of the page he comments, rather sourly, 'When a man *expects* and *gets* Sixpennyworth of anything for a halfpenny he has no reason to boast of his Liberality or Generosity.' Other documents make it plain that Clift was expected to act as Home's 'troubleshooter' when, for instance, he became embroiled in a dispute with Geo. Nicol, the publisher, over payments for art work.

The sense of having his good nature exploited was coming to affect Clift's friendship with the man of whom he had hoped for much, and with whom circumstances threw him into such close association. It is unfortunate that the relationship should have cooled in this way, because it had been a rewarding one: in his reminiscences to Richard Owen, for instance, Clift recalled that 'Mr Home occasionally employed him to assist in his operations on private patients, or in the dissection of rare animals'.

It will be recalled that Home and Banks were old friends. Their association had developed against the background of their shared interest in natural history, and in 1804 Home had treated Banks for a severe attack of gout, putting him on a diet of vegetables and milk, with benefit enough to persuade Banks that Home was a doctor of profound ability. Thereafter they were boon companions. Sir Benjamin Brodie (who followed Home in the presidency of the College, just as he followed Banks in the presidency of the

Royal Society) recalled in later life that

> not very long after I had ceased to be house surgeon [which suggests a date about 1805 or shortly after] ... Mr Home introduced me to Sir Joseph Banks. Sir Joseph took much interest in any one who was in any way engaged in the pursuit of science, and as I suppose partly from Home's recommendation and partly from knowing that I was occupied with him in making dissections in comparative anatomy, was led to show me much kindness and attention, such as it was very agreeable for so young a man to receive from so distinguished a person. He invited me to the meetings which were held in his library on the Sunday evenings which intervened between the meetings of the Royal Society.[5]

In announcing the award of the Copley medal to his friend, Banks went so far in adulation as to refer to Home's 'latest paper' on the spleen, and its assertion of

> the probability that the principal use of this hitherto unexplained organ, is to convey from the cardiac part of the stomach to the urinary passages by a short road, all excess of fluid, beyond that which is necessary for the digestion of solids

and speculate that this was a finding

> which gives just reason for believing that he is on the brink of perfecting a discovery in human Anatomy of greater importance to the advancement both of Pharmacy and of Surgery, than anything which the investigations of at least a century past were fortunate enough to discover.[6]

Even had Home's hypothesis been accurate, it could hardly have justified such an accolade.

It was natural, though, that Banks turned to Home when his librarian, Jonas Dryander, needed surgical advice. Dryander, like Daniel Solander before him, was a Swede and a pupil of the great Linnaeus; he helped Banks with the *Flora Kewensis* and took over from Solander when the latter died after a stroke in 1782. He was less sociable than Solander but dedicated to his work. Brodie recalled that

> Dryander was indeed a pattern as a librarian. The library over which he presided was to him *all* in all. Without being a man of science himself, he knew every book, and the contents of every book in it. If anyone enquired of him where he might look for information on any particular subject, he would go first to one shelf, then to another, and return with a bundle of books under his arm containing the information that was desired.[5]

When Dryander complained in 1810 of problems that, Banks surmised, might be more serious than piles, Home proposed to operate and offered his assurance that quite a minor procedure would deal with the condition. Accordingly, Banks went off to his Lincolnshire estate, Revesby Abbey, after arranging for the bachelor Dryander to be looked after at Soho Square during his convalescence. 'My wish,' he told Home, 'is that every kind of accommodation the house can afford be given to my good friend and that the maid and porter should show him every attention.'

But in the first half of the nineteenth century operative surgery was still a hazardous business. Eleven days later, Banks was writing to Home once more:

> I was so stunned by the unlooked for Blow I received from the Perusal of your letter that I was utterly unable to answer by return of Post. I have lost my right hand & can never hope to provide a substitute...

but his confidence in Home was untouched:

> If an unerring hand, guided by Skill, Practice and what is best of all superior Talents and a warm heart could have saved him he would still have been with us.

Home thus continued to be Banks's trusted friend and adviser. He had commissioned Banks's portrait by Phillips – it was presented to the Linnean Society on 24 May 1809, and was perhaps even by way of acknowledgment of the 1807 award of the Copley medal. This is one of two variants of the Royal Society portrait (with Banks's challenging pose unaltered, but his surroundings less formal) that Phillips painted that year.[7]

Everard Home commissioned the portrait of Banks (a variant of the presidential portrait at the Royal Society) which is in the possession of the Linnean Society. (LS)

As Banks's mobility became more impaired, their correspondence became more important to the friendship (and Banks in particular was an avid letter-writer). On 27 August 1818 he reported:

> My dear Sir Everard
> I was overturned two days ago by a drunken coachman, but received no hurt. Lady Banks and my sister and I were driving home from dining with Sir A. McDonald. We are all three rather heavy[8] and I, as you know, quite helpless... we are all now quite recovered from the effects of our accident, except my sister, who has a cut on her head filled with lint and doing very well.

In April 1820 it fell to Home, as vice-president, to convey to the Royal Society a letter of resignation from its president, after an unrivalled term of 42 years. The Council urged him to reconsider and Banks, 'gratified in the extreme' by his Council's attitude, agreed to stay on, so that it was as president that he died three weeks later, on 19 June 1820.

His successor in the chair, Sir Humphrey Davy, has been derided for his assessment of Banks:

Sir Humphry Davy succeeded Banks as PRS; his opinion of his predecessor has been criticised, but is in fact a perceptive analysis. (RSoc)

> He was a good-humoured and liberal man, free and various in conversational power, a tolerable botanist and generally acquainted with natural history. He had not much reading, and no profound information. He was always ready to promote the objects of men of science, but he required to be regarded as a patron and readily swallowed gross flattery. When he gave anecdotes of his voyages he was very entertaining and unaffected. A courtier in character, he was a warm friend to a good King. In his relations to the Royal Society he was too personal and made his circle too like a court.

It is in fact a perceptive analysis; and to discount it on the basis that Davy was 'of humble origin and largely self-taught; all his life he remained socially inept'[9] – however true all that may have been - is to misunderstand Banks himself.

It is possible to feel that he died mourned more by his friend Clift and by young Benjamin Brodie than by his trusted friend and adviser Sir Everard Home, for years later Clift confided to his son-in-law Richard Owen that 'Sir Evd. attended Sir Jos. Banks without fees – in hopes of a legacy but got none. Sent in a bill and recovered £4000.'

Home's grief may well have been more sincere the following year when his sister Anne, John's widow, died on 7 January at the age of 79. An obituary observed, 'with every grace that could make her interesting in society, she had every personal and social virtue that could command respect and attachment'. Baillie and Home had, kindly we may feel, refrained from heroic measures in the management of her final illness.

Her long widowhood had not been a happy one, apart from her friendship with Haydn. Her son, John Banks Hunter, had gone into the army, but he and his mother became estranged, and her daughter Agnes's marriage to Sir James Campbell was not a success. (In a codicil to his will Campbell complained of her 'misconduct, ingratitude and folly' and cut her out of an annuity from his Scottish property; but two years after his death – and only a few months after her mother's – she married Lieutenant-Colonel Charlewood of the Grenadier Guards.)[10]

In other respects, 1821 was another of Everard Home's 'good years'. Once again, he became Master of the Royal College of Surgeons in London (it did not become 'of England' until 1843); and he secured the royal bounty of an appointment as surgeon to Chelsea Hospital. The circumstances of this appointment are uncertain. Clift's version recalled that 'Sir Everard, on receiving intelligence of Mr Keate's death,[11] repaired to Carlton House and when admitted to the King's presence, fell down on his knees, and held up his hands – pleading his age, his poverty, and his large family[12] – and in fine obtain'd the Royal promise of the Surgeoncy to Chelsea Hospital'. (The story gets better: 'he met the D. of Y. on the stairs as he was returning, who was coming on the same errand in favour of Mr McGregor, afterwards Sir P. Bt.' But then, even in

After the death of Thomas Keate, Everard Home was appointed surgeon to the Royal Hospital, Chelsea. Whether this was the result of his own pleadings or a 'consolation prize' is debatable.

Flanders, the Duke of York had been slow off the mark.)

Brodie, on the other hand, ascribed Home's Chelsea appointment to the episode of the King's sebaceous cyst. (The former Prince Regent had succeeded to the throne as King George IV in 1820.) 'His majesty,' wrote Brodie,

> had one of the common encysted tumours which occur on the scalp, which was large enough to be troublesome to him. He showed it to Sir Everard Home, who advised him to have it removed by an operation. His majesty... expressed to Sir William Knighton that he wished the operation to be performed by myself... [with] Sir Everard... present, and Knighton was commissioned to [tell] me... In the meantime the subject... was mentioned to Lord Liverpool, who was then Prime Minister. Lord Liverpool... urged that nothing should be done without Sir Astley (then Mr) Cooper being first consulted, and that, if an operation was determined on, Sir Astley should perform it...
>
> Accordingly Sir Everard Home, Sir Astley Cooper, and myself were summoned to Windsor; when, after examining the tumour, we agreed that nothing but an operation could be of any service, and that it should be performed when the king returned to London. Mr Cline was consulted afterwards, who confirmed the opinion which we had given. Eventually the operation was performed by Sir Astley Cooper, in the presence of Sir Everard Home, Mr Cline,[13] Sir William Knighton, the king's physicians Sir Henry Halford, Sir Matthew Tierney, and myself, making indeed a very large assembly for so small a matter.
>
> After this attendance, Cooper was created a baronet, Sir Everard Home was comforted by being appointed to the office of surgeon to Chelsea Hospital, vacated by the death of Mr Thomas Keate.[14]

Sir Astley Cooper received his baronetcy as a reward for removing the sebaceous cyst from the scalp of King George IV. (RCS)

Clift's account of Home's successful pleading is contained in

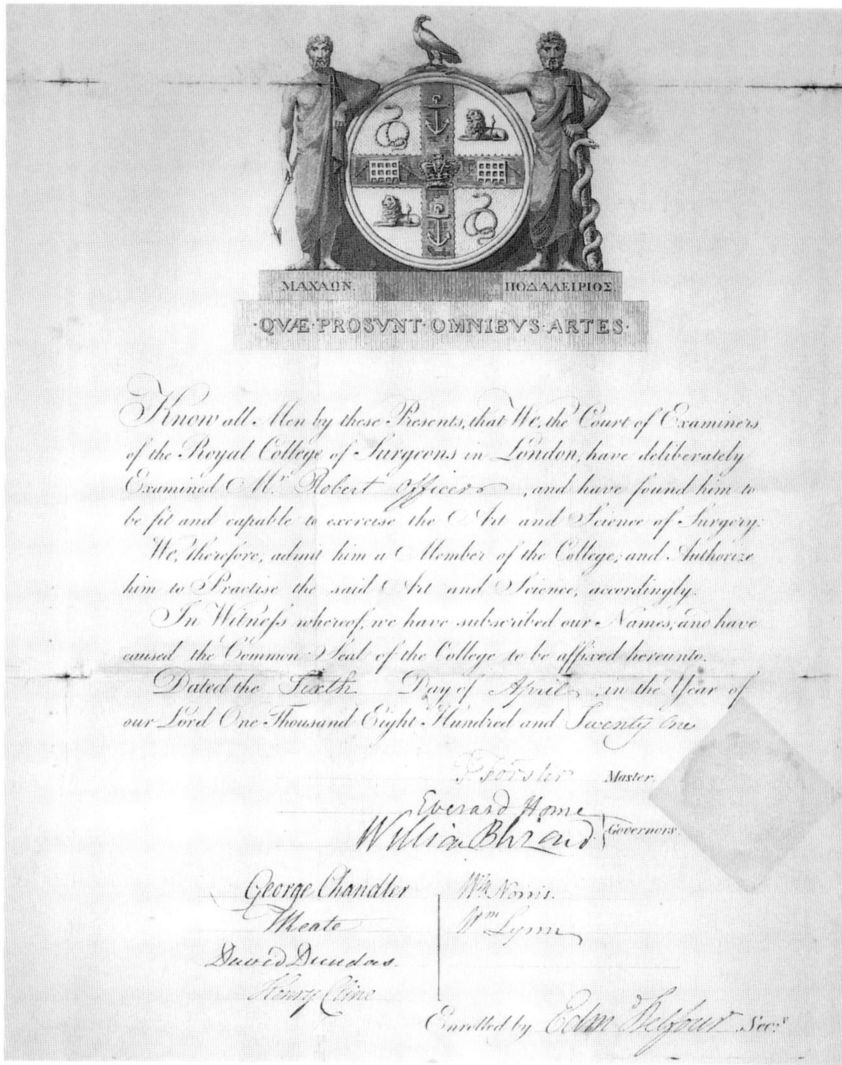
ΜΑΧΑΩΝ ΠΟΔΑΛΕΙΡΙΟΣ

QUÆ PROSUNT OMNIBUS ARTES

Know all Men by these Presents, that We, the Court of Examiners of the Royal College of Surgeons in London, have deliberately Examined Mr Robert Officer, and have found him to be fit and capable to exercise the Art and Science of Surgery. We, therefore, admit him a Member of the College, and Authorize him to Practise the said Art and Science, accordingly. In Witness whereof, we have subscribed our Names, and have caused the Common Seal of the College to be affixed hereunto. Dated the Sixth Day of April, in the Year of our Lord One Thousand Eight Hundred and Twenty One

T. Forster Master

Everard Home
William Blizard Governors

George Chandler
T. Keate
David Dundas
Henry Cline

Wm Norris
Wm Lynn

Enrolled by Edm Belfour Secy

This membership diploma was awarded in 1821 to Robert Officer (whose namesake and descendant would serve on the Council of the Royal Australasian College of Surgeons 1955-59). It will be noted that it is inscribed under the original (unofficial) arms of the English College, and signed by T. Forster as Master, and Everard Home and William Blizard as Governors. The following year Home became Master, to be re-styled President under the new Royal Charter. The two Governors became the Vice-Presidents. The signatures of Thomas Keate (who died soon after), Henry Cline and the secretary Edmund Belfour are also to be noted. (RACS).

jottings made by Richard Owen, of his conversations with his chief soon after his appointment as second assistant in the Museum. So is the intriguing observation that Sir Everard 'usually came drunk to the Council and addressed them with bullying rudeness... The Council begged Mr Clift to expostulate with him'. The council's faith in Clift's superior ability to discipline Home, as compared with their own, is quite touching. At any rate, either in spite of his bullying (or perhaps because of it) the council elected Home as Hunterian Orator for 1822. His oration is in essence a eulogy of his old friend Sir Joseph Banks; it contains an account of the occasion when Banks the schoolboy formed a sudden resolution to devote his career to the study of natural history – which may be true – and the assertion that, even after his withdrawal from Cook's second voyage, Banks did all he could to promote the success of the expedition, which is not.

But in the course of the ceremony Home was able to

The acquisition of a formal grant of arms by the Royal College of Surgeons (still, at this time, 'of London') was a further consequence of the 1822 Royal Charter.

announce the award of a Royal Charter, of date 13 February 1822, under which his title as Master was replaced by that of President and the Court of Assistants became the Council – and moreover that His Majesty had resolved to mark the event with the gift of a Mace.

Young William Home Clift had, by this time, reached the age at which his career became a matter for decision – he showed even greater artistic potential than his father and had already undertaken the odd commission for the college. In 1822 he set out to destroy a rumour that reflected on the man whose name he had been given, writing to the *Morning Herald* on the subject of a supposed mermaid that had been exhibited:

> It having been asserted, both privately and in the public prints that an inspection of the creature now exhibiting... had satisfied Sir Everard Home of its reality, I unfortunately happen to know that that distinguished anatomist has never hesitated to express his conviction... that this representation of a creature of the Poet's brain is no more than a clumsy composition, consisting of the head, arms and trunk of one of the monkey class joined to the lower extremity of a fish.

An interesting phenomenon, the defence of a baronet anatomist by a nineteen-year-old. But young Clift went on, exhibiting, it may be felt, a mature understanding of the Hunterian philosophy:

> If... the violation of that universal law of Nature, by which the form and organisation of each animal are determined according to the element in which it is destined to exist, be for a moment considered, the most simple will have little difficulty in arriving at the conclusion that the existence of a mermaid is universally denied by Naturalists.

Whether the letter was inspired by Clift senior is impossible to tell, but in August 1822 he wrote to his son, holidaying at

Littlehampton, that he might help Home with his researches into the lug-worm;[15] if he 'could get three or four fine ones and let them die either in fresh water or in the air – and then put them in weak spirit for some hours and afterwards into stronger', then he 'would please him by shewing zeal' ('although I do not think much more can be made of the subject', he conceded.)

The combination of William Home Clift's talents – and zeal – and his father's reputation (and efforts on his behalf) bore fruit in January 1823, when young Clift was appointed Assistant Conservator at a salary of £150. Four months later his father was elected to Fellowship of the Royal Society, no small achievement for a man whose scientific education depended largely on his twenty months with Hunter and his own, often solitary, dedication thereafter. Brodie referred to 'the great esteem which [he had] always had for his general character' but observed of him:

> Clift's early education had probably not extended beyond reading and writing, but he had a vast desire of acquiring knowledge... He had great sagacity, great powers of observation, and great memory, but he wanted that method which a better early education would have afforded him; and his knowledge, though extensive, was of a very desultory kind.

Despite these limitations, Clift had already contributed two papers to the *Transactions*: in 1815, one on 'experiments to ascertain the influence of the spinal marrow on the action of the heart in fishes'; and in the year of his election, a 'description of some fossil bones found in the caverns at Oreston'.

His sponsors included a battery of presidents of the college – Home, Blizard, Cline, Abernethy, Astley Cooper; William Buckland whose son Frank would achieve the ultimate tribute to

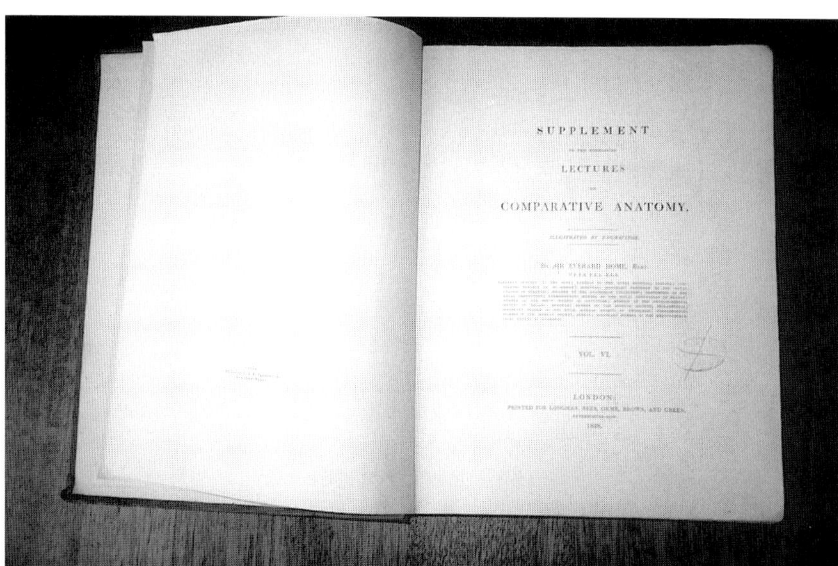

The title page of the final volume of Home's Lectures on comparative anatomy; this copy is in the historical collection of the Royal Australasian College of Surgeons.

John Hunter; Matthew Baillie of course; Babington of the Chemical Society. Davy of that same group, now PRS, used his influence to secure Clift's admission before a new scale of higher admission fees came into operation.

Then, suddenly, all was Dead Sea fruit. On 26 July 1823, when they were driving out to Kew, Home blandly informed Clift that he had burned John Hunter's manuscripts. All the delays in addressing the matter of the catalogue were explained, and all Clift's shadowy apprehensions took on a sudden clarity. So did Home's reason for the deed – for his multitudinous publications in the *Philosophical Transactions* proved, on examination, to be mostly plagiarised, along with a large part of the *Lectures on Comparative Anatomy* that Home had published from 1814 onwards.[16] (The final supplementary volume of 1828 is in the Gordon Craig Library of the Royal Australasian College of Surgeons;[17] and there will be more to record concerning the Antipodean distribution of the series.)

A spectacular correlation exists between lecture 2 in the first volume of Home's 'work' and Hunter's 'Observations on the structure and oeconomy of Whales', published in the *Philosophical Transactions in 1787.* A brief extract from each will suffice:

> HUNTER
> The situation of the teeth, when first formed, and their progress afterwards, as far as I have been able to observe, is very different from those of the quadruped. In the quadruped the teeth are formed in the jaw, almost surrounded by the alveoli, or sockets, and rise in the jaw as they increase in length; the covering of the alveoli being absorbed, the alveoli afterwards rise with the teeth, covering the whole fang; but in this tribe the teeth appear to form in the gum, upon the edge of the jaw, and they either sink in the jaw as they lengthen, or

> HOME
> The situation of the teeth when first formed, and their progress afterwards, so far as I have been able to observe, is very different from those of the quadruped. In the quadruped, the teeth are formed in the jaw, surrounded by the alveoli, or sockets, and rise up as they increase in length; the alveoli afterwards rise with the teeth, inclosing the whole fang: but in this tribe the teeth appear to form in the gum, upon the edge of the jaw, and the alveoli rise to enclose them, increasing the depth of the jaw, and making the teeth appear to sink

Other passages in the *Lectures* correspond with portions of copies made by Clift, from Hunter's notes, during his solitary years at Castle Street and before the transfer of the manuscripts to Sackville Street in 1800. Moreover Brodie, who had helped Clift in the early days when he himself was Home's protégé, (and who remained remarkably, but not blindly, loyal to Home), detected passages – claimed as Home's own original observations – in Home's 'works' which he recognised as being 'lifted' from the Hunter documents.

It is perhaps significant that Brodie, in his reminiscences, ends his account of Home's fall from grace by mentioning that the attempted assassination of the Duke of Cumberland 'first introduced him to the Prince Regent', and goes on

> The Prince found his society agreeable, and used to invite him frequently to dinner, treating him with much familiarity.

I think the juxtaposition of the two accounts, of Home's disgrace and Prinny's 'familiar' treatment, is significant, as providing an explanation of Home's conduct. He was, I suggest, an alcoholic of the truculent sort in his later years: it is a familiar personality, and association with the Prince Regent was well calculated to bring it out.

A view of the avenue leading to the pagoda in Kew Gardens. Here Banks was instrumental in finding employment for Francis Bauer, who became friendly with Everard Home and contributed illustrations for the fourth volume of the infamous Lectures on comparative anatomy.

It is of passing interest that Francis (Franz) Bauer,[18] who contributed to the illustrations of the fourth volume of *Comparative Anatomy*, was a natural history artist who came to London from Austria and was 'head-hunted' by Banks, over dinner the night before his intended return in 1790, to become flower painter at Kew on an attractive salary which Banks himself paid. Bauer and Home in turn became close friends, and Home's concern for Kew led him to pay frequent visits to Bauer's gatherings at his home on Kew Green.

For Clift the revelation of the burning was profoundly distressing:

almost a blasphemy against his revered master, a sad reflection on the man to whom he had tried to transfer his loyalty, but who had now proved so undeserving of it and – worst of all – a major blow to his plans for establishing and cataloguing the museum in the way Hunter would have wished. He fretted over the matter for some while, so disturbed as to produce 'a visible alteration in his appearance', then shared the information with the chairman of the Board of Curators, Sir William Blizard. Blizard was equally nonplussed, and it was not until a board meeting on 26 February 1824 that Clift was interviewed 'relating to the Materials for the Formation of the Catalogue'. The following week, on 5 March, a letter to Home was drawn up:

William Blizard succeeded Home as President, in time to become embroiled in the controversy over the latter's destruction of Hunter's manuscripts. (RCS)

> Sir
>
> I am directed by the Board of Curators of the Museum of the Royal College of Surgeons in London to inform you that they have learned that at the time of Mr Hunter's death there were a great number of manuscript Books and Fasciculi explanatory of the Preparations in the Collection, which Manuscripts came into the Possession of his Executors. As the Board are anxiously engaged in preparing the Catalogue and it appearing to be impossible to describe the Preparations of the Hunterian Collection equally well without reference to such Manuscripts, I am ordered to request that you will direct that the same be forthwith transmitted to this College.
>
> I am, Sir,
> Your most obedient humble Servant
> Edmund Belfour, Secretary.

Home's reply, four days later, was not easy for the board to cope with - but may not have been easy for Home to devise, since he jotted down a note: 'My mind worried on account of an Attack by the Board of Curators claiming Mr Hunter's Manuscripts. My urine nearly resembled fluid blood.'

> Sir
>
> I beg that you will acquaint the Board of Curators that Mr Hunter desired that after his Death, his Manuscripts should not be entrusted to any body, but were to be destroyed, being in too imperfect a state for the public Eye. With a view to affording every material that would assist in the formation of the Catalogue, I spent my leisure Hours in the Museum for ten Years, taking every assistance these Papers could afford, and at the end of thirty years, my own health becoming precarious, I closed my executorship by destroying them.
>
> I am, Sir
> Yours truly
> Everard Home.

The part that asserted Hunter's intention that the papers should be burned was, to say the least, surprising; the claim to have spent ten years of leisure time in the museum difficult to allow. The Board responded on 19 March:

> Sir,
> I am directed by the Board of Curators of the Museum of this College to acknowledge the receipt of your Letter of the 9th Inst. in reply to mine of the 5th Inst. and to inform you that they are so much astonished at such a Reply that they cannot believe it actually means that which the Words seem to imply. They cannot possibly conceive that the Directions of Mr Hunter's Will could have any other meaning than that the Collection was to be preserved entire – that no part was to be separated when sold. He therefore could not intend that the Histories and Descriptions of the Preparations should be destroyed, without which the Collection could be of, comparatively, little Utility. They consider the voluminous Descriptions which Mr Hunter left as much a part of the Collection as any of the Articles contained therein, and that they are in fact by far the most valuable part, because no Individual can supply the loss of those Dissections, with the Observations and Reflections thereon which it is well known Mr Hunter was in the habit of recording... The Board cannot refrain from expecting that the greater part of this most invaluable Collection of Manuscripts is still in existence, and that you will immediately deliver them to this College.

Home was unabashed. On 27 March the Board received his reply, in which he contended that in the agreement between the Government and Hunter's executors, no mention was made of manuscripts,

> ... nor was it possible there should since it would have been directly in contradiction to Mr Hunter's verbal Instructions with which I have already made the Board acquainted. Having proved that neither the Board of Trustees nor the Board of Curators can claim any right in these Manuscripts, I have only to repeat that I employed ten Years in giving the catalogue every advantage it could derive from them, and retained them ten Years longer, that they might be referred to if necessary, and then according to my Instructions, destroyed them. Whether Mr Hunter acted wisely in giving these Instructions, I have not attempted to judge. He made me two requests, the one that his Body should be opened, the other that his Manuscripts should be destroyed. I have complied with both.

It is necessary to admire, if not the man's character, at least the consistency and ingenuity of his protestations up to this point. (To continue to claim reliance on Hunter's instructions, while now taking leave to doubt their wisdom, is devilish ingenious.) Moreover, Home's bold intransigence had the board at a disadvantage. On 6 April Belfour wrote again:

> Sir,
> I am directed by the Board of Curators of the Museum of the College, in reply to your letter of the 22nd ultimo, to state that they cannot conceive it possible for Mr Hunter to have directed that *all* his Manuscripts should be destroyed before a Catalogue had been made

> of the Articles contained in his Collection, without which a great part must be useless. They therefore require particularly to know how they are to obtain Descriptions of the numerous Preparations of diseased Parts in the Hunterian Collection. The Board have good reasons for believing that you are still in possession of the Descriptions of such diseased Parts; and, therefore, they desire to know whether you mean to refuse the Use of them to the Board of Curators, which your letter would seem to imply.

The Royal Society's portrait of the older Everard Home was done in 1829 by the same Thomas Phillips who had, almost two decades earlier, painted Sir Joseph Banks at Home's request. (RSoc)

Home was dismissive; he begged 'to decline all further Communication with the Board of Curators on the Subject of Mr Hunter's Manuscripts'. Thus outwitted, the board brought its dilemma to the Hunterian Trustees; but these gentlemen were even more timorous than the board had been. They proposed that the board should ask Home to help with the catalogue, relying on his memory of what he had destroyed and handing over whatever remained; they advised the Curators to ask for surviving documents as a favour rather than a right. The board saw several weaknesses in this strategy; after chewing over the trustees' advice for some while, they recorded on 3 August

> that they are unable to reply to [the Trustees'] Recommendation of the 1st of May last, because the Board cannot conceive what Sir Everard Home could now do towards the completion of the general descriptive Catalogue of the Hunterian Collection. The Curators deeply lament the Destruction of those Papers which would have elucidated those Preparations which were intended by Mr Hunter for the Demonstration of the Diversities of healthy Structures in Animal Creation. And the Board assert *their right to require that all the existing papers* [my italics], explanatory of morbid appearances, be consigned to the College for the use of the Board of Curators: the Board would thereupon cause to be extracted from them whatever Parts appeared to be essential to the illustration of the Hunterian Collection and which would promote the scientific Purposes of the College; and they would, afterwards, return those Papers to Sir Everard, *as an Act of Courtesy* [my italics again: the Board was inverting the Trustees' counsel] – all which might have been done with those Manuscripts which Sir Everard states he has destroyed.

The board's letter proceeded to demolish Home's pleadings in defence of his actions:

> Sir Everard Home cannot doubt the liberal Sentiments of every Member of the Board of Curators relating to the posthumous Fame of Mr Hunter: the Board, indeed, are now moving in Defence and Extension of the Character of that illustrious Person. And with regard to the Conservator, who, as the Organ of the Board, would, necessarily, make the Extracts from the Manuscripts, Sir Everard must be convinced that Mr Hunter would never have wished that any part of his Writings, which have reference to his Collection, should after his Death, be concealed from him to whose Inspection they were always open during the Life of Hunter; from him, who, while he should be

employed in promoting the Ends for which the Collection was designed, would be animated by the Consideration that he was instrumental in augmenting the Reputation of his repected and admired Patron.

And then, to put resolve into the trustees:

> Should the Delivery of the claimed Manuscripts be refused, the Board respectfully submit, the Trustees ought, on the Part of the Nation, to demand them for the explained Purposes of the Board of Curators.

The board's temper can be gauged from the crescendo of capital letters.

Home's next move was not until 27 November, and when it came it was mildly surprising, even to those at the college who believed that not all Hunter's papers had been destroyed. More significantly, it demolished the substance of Home's earlier pleadings.

> Sir Everard Home, fully to meet the wishes of the Board of Trustees, has sent all the Records in Morbid Anatomy left by Mr Hunter, that they may be deposited with the Collection, *where it has ever been Sir Everard's Intention that they should ultimately be placed* [my italics yet again] .

With the letter came a sealed parcel which proved to contain a manuscript volume of 322 pages together with 86 fasciculi. Plainly this was not a complete 'set' since there were page and other references that went well beyond the volume itself. The trustees interviewed Clift who was able to give details of just how incomplete – the museum, for instance, contained 1,673 morbid anatomy (pathology) specimens, of which fewer than a hundred were documented in the recently obtained material. Home was invited to comment on the record of this February 1825 meeting; he responded with a further bundle of manuscript and a testy letter:

> The Board has heard the severest Censures against me for having destroyed the unfinished Manuscripts which Mr Hunter considered unfit to be laid before the public; but my unceasing Labours to uphold his posthumous Fame, by endeavouring to complete the Investigations that remained imperfect at his Death, most of which are now brought to a successful Issue, are passed over in Silence.

In pursuit of the principle of 'shoot the messenger' he went on

> The Conservator felt himself so outraged at my having destroyed these Papers that when I told him of it, some months after I had done it, he not only complained to the Board of Curators, but declared to me 'that in my whole Life I had never done him one Act of Kindness'.

The board, reporting – apparently for the first time – to the council

William Clift saw Home's actions as an affront to the memory of John Hunter, whom he revered. I believe that this profile of him (far left; drawn by his son) is a deliberate counterpoint to the drawing of Hunter (left), done in 1793 by Nathaniel Dance (Sir Nathaniel Dance-Holland) and given to the College in 1849 by Hunter's nephew, Captain Sir James Everard Home RN, but now in the British Museum. (RCS;BM)

of the college, acknowledged that it had been remiss in delaying its demand for the return of Hunter's papers. It pleaded that it had not, until 1817 (when it commissioned Clift to prepare the full catalogue because Home was producing nothing), appreciated the existence of papers essential to the production of the catalogue. But that, of course, does not excuse the six years of subsequent inactivity, especially since it seems the burning did not take place until shortly before Home's announcement of it,[19] and resolute action in 1817 could have averted tragedy.

Clift calculated that Hunter's writings would have amounted to roughly eight times the recovered amount – but he himself had earlier accomplished one small act of salvage. On a visit to Home's house he retrieved the greater part of Hunter's manuscript *Treatise on the Venereal Disease* (published in 1786) from the water closet. 'The conclusion,' he recorded,

> has gone towards Old Father Thames. I offered to supply as much whity-brown in exchange, but Sir Everard honestly objected to that, and declared that I was welcome to what remained; as he considered the manuscript of a work that had gone through the press of no value. I thought differently, on account of the few MS fingermarks of John Hunter.

The ineffectual behaviour of the trustees, illustrious as they were, is hard to fathom, until we refer to the records of their meetings. Home himself was appointed a trustee in 1817, in succession to the recently deceased Bishop of Llandaff, who had managed to avoid attending a single meeting in the sixteen years or so of his membership.[20] In August 1823 Home alone attended, and the election of a successor to Matthew Baillie had to be deferred until February 1824, when Robert Peel was appointed. At that meeting a catalogue committee was appointed: Lords Spencer, Colchester, Grenville and St Helens, Davies Gilbert (then treasurer, subsequently president of the Royal Society), Sir Humphry Davy PRS and Sir Everard Home – three to be a quorum.

The committee reported in May: that the Board of Curators required neither help nor funding. In August only two members were present, and the meeting was adjourned. The November meeting learned from the Board of Curators that it 'could not conceive what Sir Everard Home could now do towards the completion of the... catalogue' (which was true enough, if not especially helpful!).

On 27 November, the letter and parcel were received from Home, who did not attend meetings on 5 and 19 February 1825, but on the latter date sent another parcel. In May the trustees received the thanks of the Board of Curators, with the comment that much was still missing. On 5 November Home was present, and in February 1826 he was the only trustee to attend.

It seems plain that he was, throughout, in a position to manipulate a group of mostly absentee trustees into inactivity.

Sir Benjamin Brodie was loyal to his old chief, Everard Home, but was not blind to his defects. (RCS)

We have to ask, looking at the destruction of Hunter's papers: why did Home do it? - and, having done it, how did he imagine he could get away with such clumsy lies? In the first place, I believe he found it necessary (from his point of view) to resort to plagiarism in order to bolster his standing, both as Hunter's executor and as a considerable and ambitious figure in the college. Having done so he was, by a natural enough progression of deceit, prompted to get rid of the evidence. As to lying, the development of propaganda as a weapon has illustrated the effectiveness of the big lie - and doubtless Home felt that his reputation (at which, as we know, his council would quail) would allow him to get away with the bluff about meeting Hunter's dying wish by his destruction.

He was probably, by this time, in out of his depth in two respects: intellectually and financially. Even with Hunter's papers, he was floundering, unable to understand enough of his brother-in-law's concepts to let him build on them. And he was competing socially with the big spenders of Prinny's circle, and here Brodie's observations are, I believe, relevant to Home's dilemma. Of his early days as Home's pupil, Brodie wrote:

> At this time Mr Home was the leading surgeon at the west end of London. He was looked up to with something like veneration by all the hospital pupils.

But this did not translate into financial success for, as Brodie wrote later:

> Mr Home never had a very large practice, such as at all corresponded to his reputation. One year, and that was before I knew him, he had received about £6,700 in fees. This was much less than what Mr Cline, or Sir Astley Cooper, or myself have received since; but his income while I knew him never, I imagine amounted to £5,000, and... he had a large family and lived expensively.

Here is the picture of a man striving to keep up appearances and willing to stop at nothing to bolster his standing.

Clift, on the other hand, was the little man of humble origins with truth on his side; and truth did prevail on this occasion, even if rather late in the day. All that remained for Home was to take a parting swipe at Clift in his letter. His alcoholic excesses doubtless influenced matters, both in making his behaviour more erratic and in blunting the shrewdness of his reactions.

I do not accept Cushing's view (quoted by Oppenheimer)[21] that Clift 'may have acquired an unnecessary and undeserved grudge against' Home; nor am I convinced (any more than Oppenheimer was) by Sir Arthur Keith's suggestion that Home 'may have destroyed the manuscripts as an act of piety, to save Hunter the onus of being judged unorthodox'. But I do see in the story elements of Shakespearian tragedy, in which a flaw in the hero's character leads to his ultimate destruction: for Home had been a distinguished character in his time, and his weaknesses destroyed his good name.

Young William Home Clift produced a number of cruelly inspired sketches of his godfather: this is perhaps the most accomplished. (RCS)

What remained for Clift, of course, was to get the catalogue under way with such resources as remained. He had already established the framework of a catalogue that would do justice to Hunter's thesis, and he wrestled with the challenge of devising a numbering system that would prevent any loss of the logical sequence demanded by Hunter's approach, should specimens be disarranged. 'This very kind of removal of preparations in the gallery from one series to another without due consideration by Sir E. Home in 1817, in a few days caused me more than 2 years labour to correct and has never yet been completely remedied,' he complained. He had the help of his son – that is, when young William was not producing cruelly inspired caricatures of Home! – and, from 1827, of another young man, Richard Owen.

John Abernethy (who had, in his time, been one of Hunter's pupils) taught Richard Owen at St Bartholomew's Hospital. In such ways was the Hunterian tradition handed down. (RCS)

Owen was born in 1804, the son of a prosperous Lancashire merchant (also Richard) and his wife Catherine, a member of a Huguenot family. He began a surgical apprenticeship in Lancaster, spent a year in medical school in Edinburgh, then studied under John Abernethy at St Bartholomew's Hospital in London. Abernethy had been a pupil of John Hunter and became president of the Royal College of Surgeons in 1826, the year in which Owen became a Member of the college.[22] Owen practised, not very profitably, from a house in Carey Street, Lincoln's Inn Fields (the street runs from behind the college to behind the Law Courts), but was soon invited – at Abernethy's suggestion – to join the staff of the museum, where he began work at a salary of £30 a quarter and was set to assist with the cataloguing of the physiology specimens.

His arrival was opportune, for a new medical periodical had lately been established by the combative Thomas Wakley, and the College of Surgeons became one of *The Lancet's* principal targets. Stung by Wakley's barbs, the Hunterian Trustees began to chivvy Clift for his failure to produce a definitive catalogue within the first year or two of his formal commissioning into the task. The story of Home's behaviour had been kept remarkably quiet by the college, and even Wakley's sharp nose had not sniffed out the reason for the lack of a fully-catalogued museum; but a correspondent in *The Lancet* was quite ready to complain that

> the College of Surgeons has been fully occupied in framing an excuse for the long period of the year during which the Hunterian Museum is closed, or achieving an explanation of their plan for rendering it nearly useless when open, notwithstanding the kind and communicative attention of the conservator, Mr Clift.

It was, of course, the demand for 'kind and communicative attention' from Clift to a succession of visitors - over 1,500 in 1823

Caroline Clift and Richard Owen were not permitted to marry until Mrs Clift became convinced of Owen's financial reliability. (RCS)

- that denied him the time to work at the catalogue as much as he would have wished.

Owen was called from his work in the college to look at Caroline Clift when, in September 1827, she fell from a ladder while installing a pair of bell-pulls she had made, stunning herself. Their friendship blossomed after this encounter and they were soon engaged. Clift raised no objections, but Mrs Clift doubted Owen's financial reliability and it was not until 1835 that he received her endorsement as a prospective son-in-law and he and Caroline were married.

On 31 August 1832 the Court of Examiners was in session at the

College,[23] when news was received of the death, that morning at his house in Chelsea Hospital, of Sir Everard Home. He had been in indifferent health for a few years, though the Royal Society portrait which Thomas Phillips painted in 1829 shows quite a well-preserved subject. The *London Medical and Physical Journal* recorded that 'his habits, together with his advanced years, had led to considerable bodily infirmity'. *The Lancet* was, naturally, more blunt: 'Always partial to the bottle, he became at last a regular sot and never went to bed sober.'[24] It was a dubious epitaph for a man who had enjoyed so many opportunities and had seemed to have achieved so much. Only the Duke of Sussex (Cumberland's younger brother), as president of the Royal Society, delivered – in his presidential address at the anniversary meeting of 30 November 1832 – a eulogy so generous and inaccurate as to make Clift wonder if Home had written the account himself.

Clift did not let Home's death interfere too much with his holiday plans. By 11 September he was in Brighton when young Clift, travelling in a cab which turned too rapidly from the Strand into Chancery Lane, was thrown from the vehicle and suffered a head injury from which he died six days later in St Bartholomew's Hospital where he had been admitted under Owen's care. It had not been possible to contact his father earlier, and Owen went down to Brighton immediately after young William's death. The return journey on 19 September must have been, for Clift, an awful

The growth of the College and its Museum compelled the replacement of George Dance's original building, the portico of which was 'side-stepped' to allow its incorporation in a larger building designed by Charles Barry, who went on to design the Houses of Parliament. (RCS)

reminder of the occasion in 1793 when Matthew Baillie brought the Hunter family back from Brighton to where a young man grieved over his dead master.

From Hunter's daughter. the former Lady Campbell, now Mrs Charlewood, came a letter of condolence. Acknowledging it, Clift wrote:

> What he has done and what I have done will remain on record for others to judge of without prejudice hereafter: but much yet remains to be accomplished and I shall sadly miss his assistance, whose whole heart and mind were perhaps too severely taxed for its continuance. What remains of my own life will, I trust, be dedicated to the same service, in the hope of still retaining your good opinion.

Young Clift had been accepted as his father's likely successor. After his death no additional appointment was made, but Owen's salary was raised to £300 per year, and in 1834 he was also promoted to become the first Professor of Comparative Anatomy at Bart's (where he had earlier secured a lectureship to augment his meagre £120 from the college). His election to Fellowship of the Royal Society in December 1834 established his credentials to Mrs Clift's satisfaction. The growth of the museum necessitated almost a complete rebuilding of the college, this time to a design by Barry which involved 'side-stepping' Dance's portico to balance the frontage of the new building, into which was incorporated a flat for the Owens after their marriage on 20 July 1835.

To young James Everard Home, now the second baronet, had fallen the task of sorting through his father's effects. His search – which must have been conducted even as Clift's son was dying – brought to light eleven further manuscripts of John Hunter's, which he brought round to the college and handed to the immediate past president, Robert Keate, nephew of the Thomas Keate who had angered John Hunter so many years before. Keate passed them to Clift in October 1832. It was strange if agreeable consolation for the loss of his son – for along with his love for his family, Clift's reverence for Hunter and his vision was the ruling force in his life.

There is an intriguing counterpoint to the college's relieved acceptance of the Hunterian writings retrieved by the younger Everard. It is this: Bauer's anatomical drawings, commissioned by Everard senior and presumably those which illustrated his *Lectures in Comparative Anatomy*, were declined by the College of Surgeons. They were subsequently purchased by the Duke of Cumberland, by this time King of Hanover and, in January 1842, they were presented by him to the University of Göttingen.[25]

NOTES

1 Widowed during the Moscow campaign of 1812, the Grand Duchess had come to London with a view to a dynastic remarriage. But she found the Royal Dukes uncouth – and for the Prince Regent she developed an intense dislike. To her brother, the Czar, she wrote, 'Handsome as he is, he is a man visibly used up by dissipation. His much-boasted affability is the most licentious, I may even say obscene, strain I ever listened to.' She further complained of his 'brazen way of looking where eyes should not go'. When her brother came to London to celebrate the peace of 1814, therefore, the two of them upstaged Prinny at every oppportunity.

2 *Royal Society Catalogue of Portraits,* p.174. Indeed, in the period 1790-1829 (including 1793, when he replaced Hunter after the latter's death) he appears in the society's records on 20 occasions as Croonian lecturer.

3 Collingwood, commanding the lee division of the fleet, transferred his flag to *Euryalus* (after the masts of *Royal Sovereign* were shot away) because, under the command of Capt. the Hon. Henry Blackwood, she enjoyed the reputation of having the most efficient signalling in the fleet. It was Blackwood, a frigate captain of distinction, who had fetched Nelson from Merton to take up his command six weeks before the battle.

4 Dobson, J. *op. cit.* (from which much of the documentation of this chapter, concerning the events after the burning, is derived).

5 Brodie, B.C.; quoted in O'Brian, P. (1987) *Joseph Banks - a life.* London, Collins Harvill.

6 Royal Society Council minutes, 1807. Home's Copley medal was awarded 'for his various Papers on Anatomy and Physiology printed in the Philosophical Transactions'. With the benefit of hindsight, it is possible to see the irony of the award.

7 Fara, P. (1997) Personal communication.

8 Banks was a massive man, weighing some 16-17 stone (about 100-110 kgs); the ladies in the household, his wife Dorothea (née Hugessen) and his unmarried sister Sarah Sophia were of similar build.

9 O'Brian, P. *op. cit.*

10 Two other children of John and Anne's died in infancy, and there were no children from either of Agnes's marriages, so that the direct line died out when John Banks and Agnes died in 1838.

11 Thomas Keate, who beat Home for the surgical appointment at St George's in 1792 and was Master of the College in 1802, 1809 and 1818.

12 Apart from James Everard and his younger brother, there were four daughters.

13 Henry Cline was another of Hunter's pupils, who became surgeon to St Thomas's Hospital; he was Master of the College in 1815 and President in 1823. Astley Cooper was Cline's pupil and later his colleague at Thomas's; he became President in 1827 and again in 1836.

14 Brodie, B.C. (arr. Hawkins, C., 1865) *The works of Sir Benjamin Collins Brodie.* London, Longman Green Longman Roberts & Green.

15 Burrowing marine worms of the genus *Arenicola*; the species *A. Marina* is popular as fishing bait.

16 Vols I (text) and II (plates by Clift) were published in 1814, Vols III & IV (plates by Bauer & Clift) in 1823, and the two volumes of supplementary plates in 1828.

17 The title page of this volume (which contains 68 engravings of subjects as diverse as the stomach of the alpaca and the female organs of the duck-billed platypus, *Ornithorhynchus*) lists Home's credentials:
Vice-President of the Royal Society, Fellow of the Society of Antiquaries, Fellow of the Linnean Society
Serjeant-Surgeon to the King;
Surgeon to the Royal Hospital, Chelsea;
Consulting Surgeon to St George's Hospital;
Honorary Professor to the Royal College of Surgeons;
Trustee to the Hunterian Collection;
Proprietor to the Royal Institution;
Corresponding Member of the Royal Institution of France;
Member of the Royal Society of Göttingen;
Member of the Physico-Medical Society of Erlang;
Honorary Member of the Medical Society, Philadelphia;
Honorary Member of the Royal Medical Society of Edinburgh;
Corresponding Member of the Medical Society, Dublin;
Honorary Member of the Medico-Chirurgical Society of Inverness.
The Göttingen appointment is a reflection of the close links that existed prior to the separation of the British and Hanoverian monarchies in 1837; that in Philadelphia of Home's friendship with Philip Syng Physick, 'the father of American Surgery', who was a resident pupil of Hunter when Home was living in Leicester Square.

18 Bauer's younger brother Ferdinand was with Matthew Flinders on the *Investigator's* voyage. The names of the brothers are confused in O'Brian's biography of Joseph Banks (see p. 306 and index) and, for that matter, in a codicil to Banks's own will, in which Francis becomes 'Frederic'.

19 It is held likely that the burning took place once the proofs of the final volume of the *Lectures in Comparative Anatomy* had been returned to the printer.

20 Richard Watson (1737-1816) became Bishop of Llandaff in 1782. He had previously occupied the chairs of chemistry (1764) and divinity (1771) at Cambridge; in 1774 he made a discovery which led to the development of the black bulb thermometer, and in 1787 his advice to the government on the improvement of gunpowder was calculated to have saved the country £100,000 a year. Plainly a busy divine, he may well have treated his commitments as a Hunterian trustee rather lightly.

21 Oppenheimer, J.M. (1946) *New Aspects of John and William Hunter.* New York, Henry Schuman.

22 Owen was one of the original batch of Fellows of the College when this category came into existence in 1843.

23 A couple of months earlier had occurred a curious event, recounted by Hibbert (*Wellington: a personal history*, pp. 303-4). The Duke of Wellington had persuaded his Tory colleagues 'to refrain from further opposition to the Reform Bill which, Grey having returned to office, became law on 7 June 1832'; but 'The Duke remained a bogy to the mob. Wherever he went in London he was as likely to be hooted as cheered, and even attacked.'

> On 18 June, Waterloo Day, the Duke was threatened by a large mob as he rode back with his groom to Piccadilly from the City... When he emerged into Lincoln's Inn Fields, he was pursued by the mob again. A man on the steps of No. 41 shouted out, 'Waterloo! Waterloo!', a cry which seems to have imposed a brief pause for thought upon the crowd.

One might long to identify Clift, with his well-developed sense of fair play, as the person who, on that anniversary day, spoke out for a proper recognition of the achievement of the man who had been Britain's idol 17 years earlier, and who now needed equal courage to ride through the unthinking fury of a London mob. But sometimes truth gets in the way of a good story, and from Guedalla (in *The Duke*) we learn that it was 'an excited gentleman named Martin Tupper'.

24 *Lancet* (1836-7) i: 646. The comment appears in an anonymous letter, purporting to be from a former assistant of Home's offering advice to a young colleague. Its publication in this form is in character for the journal in Wakley's time, as his coverage of the 1834 enquiry shows so plainly. There a footnote explodes: 'LIAR as well as THIEF, - double, treble, quadruple liar, - as the further evidence will too truly prove.'

25 Desmond, R. (1995) *Kew: the history of the Royal Botanic Gardens*. London, Harvill. p.410.

Inside the lid of John Hunter's tankard a silver plate records that it 'was presented to the Royal College of Surgeons of England by his nephew – Captain Sir Everard Home, Bart, R.N.' (RCS)

4

HOME ON THE DEEP

Britannia needs no bulwarks,
No towers along the steep;
Her march is o'er the mountain waves,
Her home is on the deep.

Thomas Campbell (1777-1844): *Ye Mariners of England.*

By the time of his father's death, young Everard's naval career was well advanced. It will be recalled that his first posting afloat – 14 April 1810 to 5 March 1811 and again 15 April 1811 to 13 August 1812 – was to the *Euryalus,* which had so distinguished herself at Trafalgar a few years before he joined and was now under the command of Captain the Hon. George Lawrence Dundas. Too frail to lie in the line of battle, frigates were too fast to fear much from the ponderous battleships. They were therefore ideally suited to the task of watching enemy ships in port, reporting by flag signals on their movements – the skill that *Euryalus* under Blackwood had so conspicuously acquired – sometimes even enticing them out to the open sea, where a battle fleet could get its teeth into them.

On occasions they would qualify for a spell of independent activity, and although life aboard was cramped and wet, and fluctuated between the tedium of blockade and the frenzy of action, it was well calculated to appeal to a young man, even if 'the midshipmen's berth was governed partly by the strong arm and partly by certain laws designed to give an air of justice to the cruelty they recommended'. Here lived the senior midshipmen – many were men entering middle age, too dull to qualify for promotion and resentful of youngsters who might soon outrank them – with the master's mates, the captain's clerk and in some instances the assistant surgeon. As a result, the 'midshipmen's mess was not a pleasant place'.[1]

Young Everard's next posting, from 14 August 1812 to 20 July 1814, was to the 80-gun battleship *Malta.* Formerly the French *Guillaume Tell,* she was one of only two French battleships to escape capture or destruction at the battle of the Nile in 1798, but her liberty was brief and she was captured off Toulon three years later. It was a fortunate appointment. As Masefield puts it, 'The French treated shipbuilding as an imaginative art' – and he goes on, 'A French 80-gun ship at the close of the eighteenth century was bigger, more roomy, faster and a finer ship in every way, than our 98-gun ships.' (At Trafalgar *Téméraire, Neptune, Prince* and *Dreadnought* were of 98 guns, and only the two flagships, *Victory* and *Royal Sovereign*, larger at 100.)

Young Home must certainly have thought himself lucky to enjoy the benefits of French shipbuilding here and in his next ship, *Tonnant*, also of 80 guns and indeed a Nile prize. In his commanding officer he was arguably even luckier, for in both *Malta* and *Tonnant* – where he served from 15 June 1815 (the very week of Waterloo) to 31 August 1817 – Everard served under the flag of Sir Benjamin Hallowell, who was one of the 'characters' in a Navy rich in vivid personalities.

Admiral Sir Benjamin Hallowell was an imposing example to a young man embarking on a naval career. (NPG)

Born in Boston and brought up in Canada, Hallowell was a giant of a man and jovial to match his size.[2] He was two years younger than Nelson and, like many an oddly assorted pair, the two men were good friends. They served together at the siege of Calvi in the operation to attempt the capture of Corsica in 1794 which saw Hallowell 'much reduced, poor fellow' by fever and Nelson wounded by rock splinters so that the sight of his right eye was lost. Four years later Hallowell was in command of *Swiftsure* in the fleet that Nelson took on two sweeps across the Eastern Mediterranean after de Brueys escaped from Toulon. The first was fruitless, the second brought Nelson to Abu Qir Bay, where on the afternoon of 1 August 1798 he found de Brueys' fleet at anchor along the western wide of the bay. Decent charts of the bay were not to be had, but Hallowell had taken a rough sketch out of a French prize a few days earlier and (arguing that, where there was room for a ship to swing at her anchor, there was also room for an attacker to pass) Nelson elected to make a night attack.

His first five ships passed inshore of the French line, engaging enemy vessels that had their guns on the shore side stowed and surrounded by stores. The rest went for the centre from the seaward side. *Culloden*, hastening from escorting a prize to join the fray, went aground at the entrance to the bay, but *Swiftsure*, returning from scouting duty, was able to profit from *Culloden's* misfortune, avoid the sandbar and charge into the middle of things. Ahead of her *Bellerophon*, dismasted and drifting, escaped Hallowell's broadside only because he held his fire until sure of a target – de Brueys' flagship *L'Orient*. A massive vessel of 120 guns, she had been comfortably engaged in a repaint when the British force appeared, and was soon alight aft. Concentrated fire from *Swiftsure* and her consorts thwarted all efforts to bring the flames under control, and just after 10pm she blew up. The noise of the explosion was heard ten miles away at Rosetta.

Hallowell secured a portion of her mainmast, and from this he had constructed a coffin which he later presented to his admiral with the message:

> My Lord
>
> Herewith I send you a coffin made of part of L'Orient's Main mast, that when you are tired of this life you may be buried in one of your

Under Hallowell, *Swiftsure* played a major part in the destruction of the French flagship, *L'Orient*, at the Battle of the Nile. (NMM)

own Trophies - but may that period be far distant, is the sincere wish of your obedient and most obliged servant,

Ben Hallowell,
Swiftsure.

May 23rd, 1799.

The provenance of the wood was certified on a paper on the bottom of the coffin. Nelson was delighted. He kept the coffin upright behind his chair in *Foudroyant*, moving it later to *Vanguard*; he then lodged it with Peddieson the upholsterer in London, whom he charged to have the certificate engraved on the lid. Before Trafalgar he reclaimed it, having an idea that it might be needed. It sounds a macabre business, but it was a gesture calculated to appeal to Nelson's sense of humour.

Ironically, Hallowell himself was absent from Trafalgar. Now commanding *Tigre*, he was with the group under Admiral Louis that had been sent off to Gibraltar to resupply before the combined French-Spanish fleets emerged from Cadiz. (When Louis expressed his dismay at being first to be detached from the vigil off Cadiz, he was reassured that he would be the first to return fully battle-worthy!)[3]

After the battle Infernet, under whose command *Intrépide* had doubled back from the combined van to join the melée and performed gamely there, found himself a prisoner - or more precisely an honoured guest - aboard Codrington's *Orion*. Here Hallowell, 'although not in the action, insisted on sending him a trunk with two dozen shirts, stockings, a bed, and some cloth to make a coat, and a draft for £100, as an acknowledgment of the civility he met with from Ganteaume[4] and his officers when a prisoner'.

A man who combined resolution, judgment and kindness as Hallowell was able to do was plainly a good commander for a young man to serve under, and Home's subsequent career would indicate that he learned well from his giant mentor. After Home's time with him in *Tonnant*, which ended with the ship based at Cork, Hallowell went on to become commander-in-chief at the Nore in 1821 and full admiral in 1830. He died in 1834. To qualify for an inheritance from a cousin, he took the additional name of Carew.

By the end of his time in *Tonnant* young Everard had completed the necessary six years of service, and on 5 November 1817 he presented himself for the promotion examination to lieutenant. The record of his examination attests that

> He produceth journals kept by himself in the *Malta, Caledonia, Royal Sovereign* and *Tonnant*, and certificates from Captains Dundas, Inglefield, Sibley, Hawke, Brenton and Tailour

and in place of the traditional certificate as to his ability to 'calculate the Tides...' and so on down 'to his competence in the matter of Azimuths and Amplitudes' appears the new-fangled phrasing 'and has passed the necessary examination at the Royal Naval College' – this, no doubt, during September and October, between the end of his time in *Tonnant* and his appearance before the examining board: Captains Dickson of *Rochfort*, Alexander of *Vengeur* and Davis of *Tiber*.[5]

Having satisfied the board, he was commissioned lieutenant on 14 July 1818. The erroneous date of 1814 has crept into most of the records since O'Byrne's *Naval Biographical Dictionary* of 1849 got its 18s and 14s mixed up. (It occurs, for instance, in Home's obituaries in the Australian newspapers.) The *Navy List* provides the correct date. His luck held; and he travelled out forthwith to the West Indies in the *Sybille* frigate, yet another French prize (from 1794, which retained the French spelling of her name) – and flagship of yet another notable figure in the Navy of the time.

Home Riggs Popham was four years younger than Everard senior and, like both Homes, educated at Westminster (which may have had something to do with his taking young Everard under his wing) - though Popham did go on to Cambridge, before entering the Navy in 1778. Nine years later he obtained leave to enter the Far East trade, but in 1793 his vessel, the *Etrusco*, was seized on the pretext that he was trading without a licence from the East India Company – this despite his having obtained the consent of the governor-general in council. He himself was close to ruin, but he recovered to serve with the Duke of York's unhappy Flanders expedition in 1794 and to attract the favourable attention of the Czar at Kronstadt in 1799.

He then pursued a political career for a time, being member of parliament variously for Yarmouth (Isle of Wight), Shaftesbury in Dorset, and Ipswich; and during this period he managed to have his system of naval signalling adopted. This employed a code book in which numbered hoists of signal flags represented common words, while less common words could be spelled out. His code was employed at Trafalgar, where Nelson's display of expectation, rather than confidence, derived from the fact that 'expects' could be represented by the numerical group 269, while 'confides' would have had to be spelt out.[6] (In the event – and ironically – only the final word, 'duty', required individual hoists: 4, 21, 19 and 24.) In its essentials, Popham's code resembled the International Code of today, though with the distinction that it was based on ten numerals rather than a full alphabet.

Sir Home Popham was responsible for the system of signalling at sea that Nelson employed before Trafalgar. (NMM)

After Trafalgar Britain stood alone as the remainder of Europe – including the Dutch – submitted to occupation by, or alliance with, Napoleonic France. Rather, then, than have the Cape route compromised by a hostile power, the hard-pressed British government assembled an expeditionary force under Sir David Baird. Popham commanded the naval escort and, in the month of Pitt's death, the transports landed their 6,000 men with the loss of 36 drowned and one killed by enemy fire. A week later the Highland Brigade led Baird's force into Cape Town to receive the Dutch governor's surrender.

Finding himself without gainful employment in Cape Town, Popham prised a regiment – the 71st Highlanders (later the Highland Light Infantry and, from 1959, the Royal Highland Fusiliers) – from Baird's garrison, picked up a further 400 men from St Helena and joined William Carr Beresford to capture Buenos Aires, 'liberating' a million dollars from the public treasury which he sent back to England, 'announcing his high-handed act', as Bryant has written, 'in a flamboyant circular to the merchants of London. Though the Government sternly censured the irregularity, the country – particularly the commercial community – was thrilled.'[7]

Popham was court-martialled and reprimanded (Beresford and his force were later captured by the Spaniards) but was able to take part in the second Copenhagen expedition of 1808. By 1812 he was commanding a small amphibious force which harried the northern coast of Spain, prevented the French from paying full attention to Wellington's Peninsular campaign and, by capturing Santander and the seaports on the Asturian coast, provided a base for resupply as Wellington approached the passes into Navarre.

Made KCB in 1815, Popham was appointed commander-in-chief on the West Indies station in the rank of rear-admiral in 1817, and young James Everard's journey out with him must once again have been a stimulating episode in his naval upbringing. (It is distressing to record that Popham retired in broken health in 1820 and died later that year.)

In his new rank it is recorded by O'Byrne that Home served under Captain Abraham Lowe in the 20-gun *Larne,* a sloop of 1814, and later in the larger *Pique* of 36 guns, under Captain John MacKellar. *Pique,* the second of that name in the Royal Navy was a prize, ex *Pallas,* taken in 1800 and sold in 1819. After a further eight months on the Home station, O'Byrne states (Marshall, in his *Royal Naval Biography* of 1835 gives the date as 17 May 1821) James Everard was posted to the tiny *Helicon* (10 guns, Commander W.R. Dawkins).

Then, O'Byrne records a trifle waspishly, young Everard 'succeeded in obtaining a second promotal commission' on 28 January 1822. Presumably, the first 'promotal commission' is the one to lieutenant (which O'Byrne's own dating error credits Everard with achieving at the tender age of fifteen-and-a-half!). The timing of the second, the circumstances of which were evidently unknown to O'Byrne, relates to the wen on King George IV's scalp! For Brodie, describing how Everard senior 'was comforted by' his appointment at Chelsea, goes on:

> and by his son, who was then a very young lieutenant in the navy, being advanced rather prematurely to the rank of commander.

It is likely that the Admiralty was displeased by the royal caprice – because, as O'Byrne and Marshall agree, Everard 'did not go afloat again' until 1834. To be sure, this was a period of peace and

The removal of George IV's wen led to young Everard's accelerated promotion to Commander; it seems that the Admiralty was 'not amused' because he was denied any sea time for over a decade. (RColl)

naval retrenchment, but plainly the Navy made certain that young Everard had quite some time 'on the beach' between postings, time in which he was able to attend to his late father's affairs in 1832 (and, it will be recalled, to restore the eleven manuscripts to the college).

Finally, in February 1834, when the Admiralty doubtless felt that his age had 'caught up with' their requirements, and in any case the Navy was being kept active as the Spanish empire disintegrated and the slave trade came under increasing scrutiny,[8] he was given his first command – the 18-gun sloop *Racehorse.* In 1835, at the outbreak of the civil war in Brazil, he was involved, with a Brazilian squadron, in the siege of Pará (present-day Belém, near the main shipping entrance to the Amazon system).[9] Here, for several days, he was engaged in a contest with the shore batteries.

Even as his naval career advanced, he was acquiring a reputation as a natural historian, and on 20 January 1825 (two years after William Clift) he was admitted to Fellowship of the Royal Society – at the age of 27, not quite as young as Banks (who joined that august company at the age of 23 and with no track record in science behind him) but a little earlier in life than his father, and at a much younger stage than either Hunter or that other naval Fellow, James Cook. Unlike his father – who was one of his 16 sponsors – he was not a prolific contributor to the *Philosophical Transactions*; but then he did not have his father's access to ready-made sources! One of his earliest papers, an *Account of a Luminous Animalcule,* was published in the *Quarterly Journal of Science* in 1828.

In 1834, when he was joining *Racehorse,* his father's misdeeds were once again a matter of discussion. In February of that year a parliamentary select committee was appointed to 'enquire into and consider the Laws, Regulations and Usages regarding the Education and Practice of the Various Branches of the Medical Profession in the United Kingdom'. In this may be seen a first step along the way that would lead to the 1858 Medical Act which established the General Medical Council – under the chairmanship of Everard senior's former assistant, Sir Benjamin Brodie. (Such was his standing in the medical community that he was able, as probably no other man of his time could have been, to carry the opinion of his profession into accepting registration requirements that would otherwise have been rejected as draconian.)

In April 1834 George James Guthrie, president of the College of Surgeons, was interviewed – over a period of three days – on subjects as diverse as the method of election to the council, the working of the Anatomy Acts and the administration of the Hunterian Museum. Guthrie mentioned the problems of cataloguing the collection that had resulted from Home's incendiarism, but referred to the value of Clift's earlier transcripts

Home's act of incendiarism took place at the Manor House in Ham.

in limiting the extent of the loss. Accordingly, Clift was called before the committee. In the course of his evidence he described Home's first account of the fire:

> Sir Everard began by telling me, that an accident had very nearly occurred at his house; that it had been nearly on fire, that the engines came, and the firemen insisted on taking possession of his house. They saw the flames coming out of the chimney. He did not wish to admit them, but they insisted upon being admitted. I asked him, how it happened; and then he told me, that it was in burning those manuscripts of Mr Hunter.

This was the Manor House at Ham in Surrey, a little distance upstream from Richmond. The house, the lease of which was secured by Everard senior from the estate of one Joseph Bradney in 1818, stands in the avenue leading to the even more splendid Ham House (nowadays a National Trust property). After his father's death in 1832, young Everard kept up the property until 1850, when the Manor House passed to Lord Dudley Coutts Stuart, a son of the Marquis of Bute.

Clift further stated that he knew Sir Everard to have used the contents of the papers in the composition of the works published under his own name, and he recalled that, some five or six months after the burning, Home had again stated that the papers 'were not fit to be submitted to the public eye' whereupon he (Clift) had remarked that he did not consider his eye the public eye. He went on to record Home's statement, in the same conversation, that Hunter when dying had asked him to destroy the papers. This he knew to be false as Home was not present at Hunter's death.

The bombing of the College in 1941 destroyed much of the Hunterian Museum, but left Richard Owen's bust defiantly intact. (RCS)

In the month of Clift's evidence, the museum was closed to allow the rebuilding of the college, to the design by Barry which has survived to this day, albeit with somewhat topheavy extensions and despite the attentions of the Luftwaffe in 1941, which destroyed much of the Hunterian collection. Official predictions were of a twelvemonth of closure; Clift's own prediction, that more than double this period would be needed, proved accurate, and it was not until Hunter's birthday in 1837 that the museum, enlarged by a generous new wing, was reopened.

The younger Everard was promoted captain in December of that same year, and paid a return visit to Lincoln's Inn Fields two years later. Clift recorded that

> On the day of the delivery of the Hunterian Oration, February 14th, 1839, at the entrance of the visitors and Council, Mr Keate [Robert Keate, in office for his third term as president] put into my hands a thin volume, desiring me to look at it *afterwards.* Mr Keate had doubtless (or probably) just received it from Captain Sir Everard Home, who was among the visitors. The volume had evidently been lately bound in calf, and contains a portion of Mr Hunter's manuscript introduction to a history of fossils, and consists of seventy-two leaves written on one side; and numerous additions on the opposite or blank pages. It is evidently only a *part* of the manuscript by the catchword at the foot of the last page.

Home also – at some point in his naval career, and quite possibly at this visit – presented to the college a tankard that had belonged to his uncle John; this silver tankard bears the hallmark of George II 1738 and was made in London by George Wickes. Inside the lid a silver plate has been affixed, bearing the inscription: 'This tankard, the property of John Hunter, was presented to the Royal College of Surgeons of England by his nephew – Captain Sir Everard Home, Bart., R.N.' The date of its presentation is not stated but, if Everard's rank is a valid indicator, must have been after 1837.

An oval shield on the front bears the heraldic device of two hunting horns (stringed, i.e. shown as if hung from a supporting cord) to the dexter side, and three greyhounds in pale (i.e. one above another) to the sinister. A small tree is depicted as a crest.

The shield incorporates the same devices – hounds and horns – as in the arms granted by the Lord Lyon to John's older brother William in 1752 (and shown, unjustifiably, on John Hunter's memorial brass in Westminster Abbey), but there is nothing to indicate how this particular arrangement of these symbols came to be applied to Hunter's tankard.

From a study of the newly repatriated manuscript Clift was able to date it to the last year or so of Hunter's life, since a number of the pages were in Clift's handwriting, but some of these bore Hunter's own insertions. (The remainder had been taken down by Bell before his ill-fated East Indies posting.)

A second volume in the possession of the English College contains a transcription of the material in the gift volume (with a note by Clift 'End of Capt. Sir E. Home's volume brought Feb. 14th, 1839, collated so far, March 13th, 1839. W.C.'). It carries on the narrative, evidently from a copy made by Clift between 1793 and 1800 – since it can fairly be assumed that the elder Home acquired both parts of the original when he took possession of

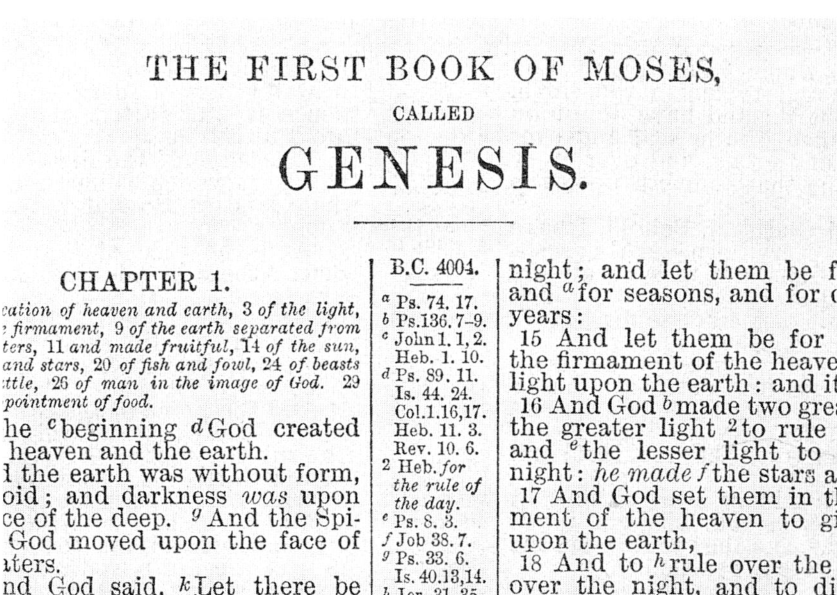
THE FIRST BOOK OF MOSES,

CALLED

GENESIS.

CHAPTER 1.

cation of heaven and earth, 3 *of the light,* *firmament,* 9 *of the earth separated from* *ters,* 11 *and made fruitful,* 14 *of the sun,* *and stars,* 20 *of fish and fowl,* 24 *of beasts* *ttle,* 26 *of man in the image of God.* 29 *pointment of food.*

he [c]beginning [d]God created
heaven and the earth.
l the earth was without form,
oid; and darkness *was* upon
ce of the deep. [g]And the Spi-
God moved upon the face of
ters.
nd God said, [k]Let there be
and there was light.

B.C. 4004.
[a] Ps. 74. 17.
[b] Ps.136. 7–9.
[c] John 1. 1, 2. Heb. 1. 10.
[d] Ps. 89. 11. Is. 44. 24. Col.1.16,17. Heb. 11. 3. Rev. 10. 6.
2 Heb. *for the rule of the day.*
[e] Ps. 8. 3.
[f] Job 38. 7.
[g] Ps. 33. 6. Is. 40.13,14.
[h] Jer. 31. 35.
[i] Ps. 33. 9.

night; and let them be fo
and [a]for seasons, and for da
years:
15 And let them be for l
the firmament of the heaver
light upon the earth: and it
16 And God [b]made two grea
the greater light [2]to rule t
and [e]the lesser light to r
night: *he made* [f]the stars al
17 And God set them in th
ment of the heaven to giv
upon the earth,
18 And to [h]rule over the
over the night, and to div
light from the darkness: a

Bishop Ussher's date for Creation, 4004BC, was retained in the margin of family bibles into the twentieth century.

Hunter's papers. But the curious history of Hunter's writings on geology goes even further.

It appears that, on the completion of part 1 of the work, Hunter sought to publish. Everard senior told Clift that Hunter sent it to the Royal Society, and he further claimed that it was the society that referred the work to Major Rennell for his opinion.[10] There is in existence a transcription (by Clift, that assiduous transcriber – of course!) of Rennell's response, but it is addressed to Hunter, not to the society, and in the society records there is no evidence of receipt of Hunter's manuscript.

Rennell's comments related to Hunter's observation on 'extraneous fossils', that 'many retain some of their form for many thousand centuries'.[11] Hunter's observations of fossils in the rocks of the Alentejo plateau in Portugal, at the end of 1762, had persuaded him that these rocks had been below the sea more than once and that one 40-day flood could not have covered the earth long enough to allow 'such quantities of sea-productions on its surface'. At that time it was considered unseemly, even heretical and hence dangerous, to question the chronology established by Bishop Ussher of Armagh - which held, on the basis of the genealogies in the Old Testament, that creation had occurred in 4004 BC. (He – or perhaps his colleague Lightfoot – indeed calculated the time and date within that year: 9am on Sunday 26 October!) Rennell pointed out to Hunter that 'very numerous persons... will dislike any mention of a specific period that ascends beyond 6,000 years' and urged the substitution of 'years' for 'centuries'. Very numerous persons indeed – at that time all orthodox clergymen and their adherents accepted, as literal truth, Ussher's chronology, which continued to be inserted marginally in family Bibles even into this present century.

Both the surviving manuscripts contain the word 'years' in place of 'centuries' – which indicates several things. In the first place, Hunter was evidently pusillanimous enough to withdraw from – or at least to blur – his original scale of geological time; in the second the older Home's further assertion, that despite Rennell's opinion Hunter stuck to his guns and withdrew the paper, is untenable (but then, Home's reliability as a witness has already been destroyed by other events in this narrative); and finally, it is plain that neither of the college volumes can be the original manuscript that was referred to Rennell.

What thus emerges from the Hunter manuscripts is that, a century before Darwin published his *Origin of Species*, Hunter had perceived that a time scale widely at variance with Bishop Ussher's was necessary to explain his observations. In other insights, that also originated in his Portuguese fossicking, he anticipated the geological research of other men by almost 80 years – he observed, for instance, that 'calcareous earth' (which he had recognised as of animal origin) could be contained 'as a constituent element' in granite; and the view expressed by de Luc in 1779, that granite

In John Hunter's portrait by Sir Joshua Reynolds, there is evidence of his appreciation of much that Darwin would postulate a century later. (RCS)

was the ancient basis of the earth's crust, upon which all other formations must be superimposed, was only exploded by Lyell in 1838.

Doubtless because of his recognition of the true immensity of geological time, he acquired a fair glimpse into the evolution of characteristics that anticipates much of Darwin. It is interesting that the open book at his elbow, in the celebrated Reynolds portrait, shows a progression of skulls and extremities – and, as Wood Jones pointed out, it demonstrates correctly that the human hand is a 'generalised' form, the horse's hoof a highly specialised one.[12]

Unfortunately for the advancement of human knowledge the manuscript that the younger Everard handed in to the college in 1839 did not achieve publication at the time, because (even though circumstances had prevented Hunter's findings from becoming generally known in the 1790s) as late as 1840 they would still have been seminal in the development of scientific understanding. But as it was, they did not see the light of day for another 20 years, and then in controversial circumstances. In March 1855 Richard Owen (Clift's son-in-law and, by this time, his successor as Conservator of the Museum) gave three Hunterian lectures on Hunter's contributions to geology and palaeontology, reading the 1839 gift volume in the second and discussing it in the third. He was, at the time, well advanced with the preparation of the catalogue of Hunterian fossils and had, in the previous month, applied for permission to incorporate the Hunter manuscript as an introduction to the catalogue.

In 1856, however, Owen left to take up the post of natural history superintendent at the British Museum; the catalogue was thereafter edited by John Morris, professor of geology at University College, and was published later in the year, but without the Hunterian manuscript. Three years later, on 25 October 1859, Owen enquired 'as to its publication, since he was anxious to include it among the papers he was arranging for his work on "John Hunter's Essays and Observations on Natural History"'. The Council of the Royal College informed Owen that his request was 'under consideration' but thereupon hastened to publish the volume in question, approving their museum committee's recommendation to that effect on 24 November. Then, on 8 December, J.F. South informed the Council that 'the attention of the Museum committee had been drawn to a second Hunterian Manuscript on the same subject', and the printing of both volumes proceeded with remarkable haste, so that *Observations and Reflections on Geology* appeared before Christmas. A copy went to Owen, but the preface to this printed volume included the statement that

> This Introduction, on which Mr Hunter had bestowed so much time and labour to within a short time of his death, revising and correcting it from time to time, was not prefixed as he intended to the Catalogue of his Collection of Fossils and is neither mentioned nor alluded to, in either [*sic*] of the three volumes of the Descriptive Catalogue of Fossil Organic Remains in the College Museum, published respectively in 1845, 1854 and 1856. It is greatly to be regretted that it was not brought under the notice, either of the Museum Committee, or of the Council of the College. The attention of the Council was, however, unexpectedly drawn to it in 1856 [*sic*] when it was read from the chair by the then Hunterian Professor.

Owen, never one to welcome criticism, lodged a formal protest on 29 December. In it he pointed out that the use of the wrong date for his Hunterian lectures had misled the council into charging him with a breach of trust, and he demanded a retraction.

Receiving only a holding letter (with a promise to recall the offending publication) on 31 December, he wrote again on 2 January 1860, drawing the council's attention to 'a paragraph in the "Lancet"... giving all the publicity to the libel on me which its authors intended' and demanding 'redress' within a week – otherwise, he stated, he would 'be compelled to appeal for it through those laws which have been provided for cases of such unprovoked injury'. The council drafted a reply which included an apology and acknowledged that the confusion of dates had been responsible for the unfortunate statement, but rebuked Owen for threatening legal action so hurriedly – 'especially as you were assured' of the recall of the 'few copies' that had been distributed – while authorising him, if he wished, to publish its letter.

But the letter that was in fact sent to Owen contained only the apology and an assurance that the volume would be printed with the offending material deleted. *The Lancet*, for its part, took the opportunity afforded by its printing the council's letter, to aim another swipe at the council of the college, which had been a regular target since the inception of the journal. The source of its information – given that only two copies were known to have been distributed (one to Owen direct, the other through his successor as conservator, John Thomas Quekett) – remains a mystery. The Quekett copy, however, is in the Natural History Museum, which evolved out of the natural history department of the British Museum, and contains annotations which indicate that it was the one used by Owen when he prepared his *Essays and Observations* for publication in 1861, while several copies of the 'revised edition' are extant.

James Everard's gift of 1839 came to the college as a reminder of past havoc – 20 years later it retained its ability to create havoc. But how it came to be overlooked for those 20 years is still as much a mystery as the source of *The Lancet's* 'leak'.

Richard Owen's statue looks out over the entrance hall of the Natural History Museum in Kensington.

NOTES

1 The conditions of the time are well described by John Masefield, who served before the mast as a young man and went on to become Poet Laureate, in *Sea Life in Nelson's Time* (1905).

2 It is recorded that, in the opening moves of the battle of St Vincent in 1797, Sir John Jervis's flag-captain aboard *Victory*, the unhappy Sir Robert Calder, was reporting to his admiral as the Spanish vessels loomed out of the morning mist, while Hallowell, aboard *Victory* after his own ship was wrecked in a gale, listened to the dialogue:

> There are eight sail-of-the-line, Sir John.
> Very well, Sir.
> There are twenty sail-of-the-line, Sir John.
> Very well, Sir.
> There are twenty-five sail-of-the-line.... twenty-seven, Sir John.

At which point Jervis, with sixteen ships at his disposal, exploded:

> Enough, Sir; no more of that, Sir! The die is cast and if there are fifty sail, I will go through them. England badly needs a victory at present.

Whereupon he found himself struck on the back with a giant hand, and reassured:

> That's right, Sir John, that's right. And, by God, we shall give 'em a damned good licking!

3 But Hallowell's *Swiftsure* was at Trafalgar - under the French flag! She had been captured off the Barbary Coast in 1801, and retained her name as a member of the Combined Fleet. The Royal Navy had meanwhile built a replacement *Swiftsure*, and when the original was recaptured at Trafalgar, she was taken back into the Navy as *Irresistible*.

Tonnant was also present, and performed well in Collingwood's column where, much the better sailer thanks to her French shipbuilders, she was well up with her flagship *Royal Sovereign.* She savaged the Spanish *Monarca,* then engaged the French admiral Magon's *Algéciras* at such close range that, as one of her midshipmen recorded, 'we had actually our fire-engine playing on her broadside to put out the fire caused by the flame of our guns'.

4 Ganteaume first achieved prominence by spiriting Napoleon away from Egypt in his frigate some months after the battle of the Nile had marooned him there. He subsequently commanded the Brest squadron which, if things had gone as planned, was to have joined Villeneuve in the West Indies.

5 P.R.O. ADM 6/114.

6 Nelson's original intention was to signal: 'England confides that every man will do his duty.' His signal lieutenant, John Pasco, obtained permission to substutute 'expects'. Hibbert records:

> According to one report the signal was greeted 'with three cheers in every ship'; Captain Blackwood averred that its reception was 'truly sublime'. Collingwood's response was down to earth. 'What is Nelson signalling about?' he demanded with grumpy irritation. 'We all know what we have to do.' Between decks in the *Victory,* the response to the signal apparently echoed Collingwood's...

7 Bryant, A. (1944) *Years of Victory, 1802-1812.* London, Collins.

8 The Monroe doctrine, in terms of which the United States warned the European powers to keep at arm's length from the struggle for independence by the various Spanish territories of Latin America, was proclaimed in 1823; slavery was abolished in British possessions ten years later.

9 The Portuguese royal family was evacuated to Brazil when the French invaded Portugal in 1807; Rio de Janeiro became the Portuguese capital and Brazil was taken into full partnership. In 1821 King John VI returned to Portugal, leaving his son Pedro as regent; and when Portugal sought to relegate Brazil to colonial status Pedro supported a revolt and was crowned emperor of Brazil in 1822. Four years later he renounced his claim to the Portuguese throne in favour of his daughter; but his absolute rule in Brazil eroded his popularity and in 1831 he abdicated in favour of his six-year-old son Pedro II. Conflict between supporters of the two Pedros, father and son, led to virtual civil war by 1835.

10 James Rennell (1742-1830) went from the Navy into the service of the East India Company in 1763, became surveyor-general of Bengal the following year and, in preparing his survey of the province over the next 13 years, became an authority on land forms.

11 Jones, F. Wood (1953) John Hunter as a geologist. *Ann. Roy. Coll. Surg. Engl.* 12:219.

12 The subject was addressed, in a lecture in 1928 (*Brit. med. j.* I:205), by Sir Arthur Keith - who expressed his own reservations about Wood Jones's assessment of the place of the human hand. The background details in the portrait, and the fact that the open book and the two volumes in front of it (entitled *Natural History of Vegetables* and *Natural History of Fossils*) were among those burned by the older Everard Home, are described by Lord Brock (*Ann. Roy. Coll. Surg. Engl.* 1971; 48:219).

Everard Home was appointed to the command of the frigate *North Star* in time to take part in the Opium War.

5

HOME FROM SEA

This be the verse you grave for me:
Here he lies where he long'd to be;
Home is the sailor, home from sea,
And the hunter home from the hill.

Robert Louis Stevenson (1850-1894)
Underwoods, I,xxi: Requiem

After handing over the geology manuscript in 1839, Home returned to the Navy and the Royal College to its routines. So far as the museum was concerned, these increasingly involved Richard Owen, whose standing was much enhanced after an occasion, later in 1839, when a Dr John Rule brought him a six-inch bone fragment which he had obtained from New Zealand. Owen was preparing a lecture at the time and was almost dismissive of the gift, asking Rule to put it clear of where he was working on his papers and agreeing to examine it when he had time. But when that time came, he formulated a case for the fragment's having come from a giant flightless bird, to which he gave the name *Dinornis novaezelandiae.*[1] At first his claims were sniffed at,

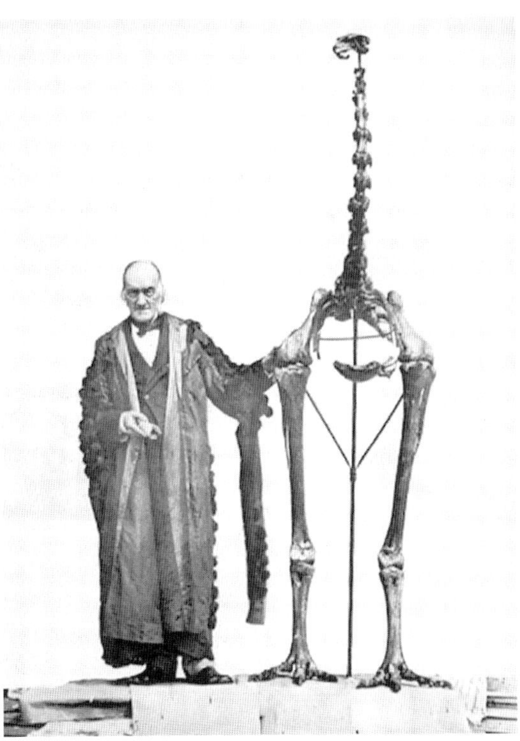

Richard Owen's reputation was established by his reconstruction of the moa. In this photograph taken many years later, he is holding the bone fragment from which he deduced the characteristics of the bird, and standing alongside a complete skeleton.

but, as additional and more complete samples became available, his opinion was vindicated and – of even more importance to him, for he was an opinionated man with a tendency to patronise his colleagues – he was viewed with a respect that bordered on awe.

This is not to suggest, however, that Clift had become irrelevant. He himself had made a significant contribution to the understanding of Antipodean prehistory with his study of fossil marsupial remains in Australia, and in 1831 he published a paper which pointed out the resemblances between these and the surviving Australian marsupials.[2] In 1833-34 he served on the council of the Royal Society. On 14 February 1839 he was on hand to receive the precious geology manuscript from Keate the president, and he continued to receive specimens and curiosities for the museum – now, in the rebuilt college, better able to cope with them.

On 13 September 1841 he received from Dr Gideon Mantell a letter in which Mantell recalled having given to the older Everard Home the antlers of a castrated deer, as a gift for the museum. He had been less than delighted to learn that Home – 'that gentleman' he called him – had presented the specimen in his own name, omitting all reference to Mantell.[3] It seemed that Home's meanness of spirit still haunted the place.

In that same year, 1841, the younger Everard was appointed to command the sixth-rate frigate *North Star*. Of 26 guns, she was of a type then known as 'donkey frigates'[4] – if the name had referred to a lack of beauty, contemporary drawings of *North Star* would suggest it was a well-chosen term. Her first deployment under Home was in China, where the so-called Opium War had broken out in 1839 in consequence of China's attempt to enforce an embargo on the import of opium, upon which depended India's prosperity. At a time when the use of opium – not least by creative artists, but not only by them[5] – was widespread, and the potential of the drug for addiction (and of its trade, for corruption and evil) was grossly underestimated, Britain as a trading nation claimed rights that have, a century and a half later, been considered untenable given the character of the trade. 'The British government,' writes Inglis, 'became addicted to the revenue in the same way that the Chinese became addicted to the drug.'[6]

Farr and Nolan, in their continuation of Hume and Smollett's *History of England*, provide a useful if partisan contemporary account of the war, which

> arose out of the contraband traffic in opium. The government of China resolved to put an end to the commerce altogether, and with this in view an imperial commissioner arrived at Canton... demanding that every particle of opium on board the ships should be at once delivered up to the government to be destroyed.... In the event of any opium being thereafter brought, the goods were to be confiscated,

The archaic spelling of place names has been used

> and the parties were to submit to death. Should the foreigners fail to comply with these requisitions, Commissioner Lin threatened that they would be overwhelmed by numbers and sacrificed. The whole foreign community was thrown into a state of the deepest distress at these demands; and the chief superintendent, Captain Elliot, considered it his duty to take his own countrymen into his protection.

Elliot ordered the surrender to his keeping of all the English opium on the coast, but 20,000 chests were, in fact, delivered to Lin. Some merchants were imprisoned, then released; and once his countrymen were all at liberty, Elliot sent a report to the governor-general of India, seeking naval support from the Indian station. This might have sufficed, but an affray at Macao with some English sailors saw a Chinese villager killed. Lin demanded 'that the homicide should be given up' and, when this was refused, ordered an embargo on supplies to the British in Macao.

> The British superintendent subsequently removed his residence to Hong Kong, off which lay the *Volage* frigate, commanded by Captain Smith. At the latter end of the year 1839 Commissioner Lin issued an edict against the importation of any British goods,... and gave all foreigners to understand that it was no use to deceive the Chinese; for there were skilful translators and interpreters among them... In this state of affairs, Captain Elliot sent a petition... for the restoration of the trade with Canton, until he received further advice from England. The commissioner replied by a haughty refusal; enumerating all the offences of which, in the eyes of the 'great pure dynasty,' the British had been guilty.

Even as tensions were easing, one British captain agreed to Lin's terms; and Lin was thereby prompted to demand compliance by all other British ships.

> Matters now proceeded to extremities... Finding that the inhabitants of the celestial empire were preparing to attack the fleet, and that Admiral Kwan lay in considerable force near Chuenpee, two British frigates, the *Volage* and the *Hyacinth*, were removed to that neighbourhood... an imposing force of war-junks and fire-vessels was collected... and their attitude became so menacing that Captain Smith resolved to compel them to return to their former anchorage. A brief action took place, which told with terrible effect on the celestials: one war-junk blew up at a pistol-shot distance from the *Volage*, three were sunk and several others water-logged. In about half-an-hour Admiral Kwan and his squadron retired in great distress to their former anchorage, no obstruction being offered to their retreat.

By the end of 1839 the British government had decided to send a punitive expedition to 'compel the great pure dynasty to acknowledge the principles of international law'. This force, under Admiral Elliot, of 'eight ships of war, with frigates, transports, and steamers' – rather a modern force, this, to include steamers in 1840! – gathered in Singapore in April. The first arrival in the Canton river was *Alligator*, on 9 June; three weeks later a blockade of the river and port of Canton was declared by Commodore Sir Gordon Brewer, who then sailed north to capture Chusan. The two Elliots pressed on to Pe-che-lee, arriving on 9 August, and entered into negotiations with Keshen (number three in the Chinese hierarchy) which were later transferred back to Canton.

> It was so evident from the establishment of Chinese artillery and the sinking of blockships that the Chinese commissioner was insincere, that hostilities recommenced on the 7th of January 1841 . Two of the Bogue forts were reduced, and Keshen then offered to adjust matters without delay.

However, the agreement worked out with Keshen (which provided for the cession of Hong Kong, an indemnity payable to Britain over six years, the resumption of normal relations, and the opening of Canton) was rejected by Whitehall. The unfortunate Captain Elliot was recalled and Sir Henry Pottinger 'appointed plenipotentiary in his stead'. Sir William Parker was appointed to command the naval force. But before these gentlemen could reach China, there had been another flurry of fighting in February. Howqua's fort at Canton was captured and, while Brewer and General Gough were preparing to attack the remaining strongpoints Kwang-Chow Foo, the prefect of the region, arrived to report that Keshen had been disgraced, and that

> The Emperor,... looking upon the English "as dogs and sheep in their dispositions," and considering that "both gods and men were indignant at their conduct, refused to ratify a treaty with them; and Keshen was ordered to be delivered over to the board of punishment."

Thus both peacemakers had been disgraced and their treaty repudiated. The Chinese were reckoned to be contemplating further hostilities, and the British therefore resumed their advance on the remaining Canton forts. All were captured, but before the city itself could be taken there was another truce, during which Pottinger and Parker arrived, Pottinger published his credentials and the two of them took themselves to Hong Kong. The unfortunate Elliot left on 24 August, two weeks after his successor's arrival. It was in this stage of the conflict that Home and *North Star* came on the scene together. *North Star's* battle honours are for CHINA 1839-42, but this commission is recorded as 1841-46,[7] which suggests that she and Home may have formed part of – may even have brought out – the 'replacement' party. Thereafter, as Farr and Nolan record,

> the British troops still pursued an inglorious war... Sir Henry Pottinger and Sir W. Parker... sailed from [Hong Kong] and anchored on the 25th [August] in the harbour of Amoy... The Chinese fancied the place to be impregnable. Amoy, however, wanted a brave and skilful garrison; and lacking this, the place was soon captured... without the loss of a man on the part of the British.

The expeditionary force, delayed by bad weather at the end of the month, moved northwards on 5 September, reaching the Chusan group of islands two weeks later. Tinghae was soon captured with only two men killed and 24 wounded; Chinghae was as readily reduced, as was Ningpo.

Early in 1842 Yuydo, Tsikee and Funghwa were captured and a Chinese attempt to recapture Ningpo was repulsed. On 16 May Chapoo was taken.

> Sir H. Pottinger, who had recently been to Canton rejoined the squadron before it sailed from Chapoo; and its subsequent operations

In 1841 Stokes took command of *Beagle* , in which FitzRoy and Darwin had circumnavigated the world over a five-year period in the 1830s. (NMM)

Wickham went off sick in March 1841. His survey of Bass Strait ended with his return to England in 1843 to write up and publish his findings. He was promoted captain in July 1846 and given command of *Acheron* in October 1847; in her he conducted a survey of the New Zealand coasts 1848-51 – the first comprehensive survey since Cook's circumnavigation and one which yielded charts that remained in use until the 1930s.

Home, who reached Sydney from Port Phillip on 17 July 1843, was soon to become acquainted with New Zealand as well. The settlers about Cook Strait had become alarmed by the activities of Te Rauparaha, and after news of the 'Wairau massacre' of 17 June reached Sydney the colonial governor, Sir George Gipps, despatched Home to provide support for the colonists. He wasted no time, sailing on 1 August; with him in *North Star* he took Captain Bell, Lieutenant Ormsby and 50 other ranks of the 80th Regiment, and assistant surgeon Galbraith of the 90th. *North Star* grounded briefly at Port Macquarie, but arrived in Wellington on 31 August.

What is now described as the 'Wairau affray' occurred when Rauparaha, the noted Ngati Toa chief born in about 1769 – the year of Cook's first sighting of New Zealand – and his nephew, Te Rangihaeata, sought to prevent surveyors from subdividing land in Marlborough, and matters got out of hand. But the diminutive Rauparaha had made his mark over many years prior to 1843. He was indeed born into violence: soon after his birth his father was murdered and the killer boasted that the infant would make

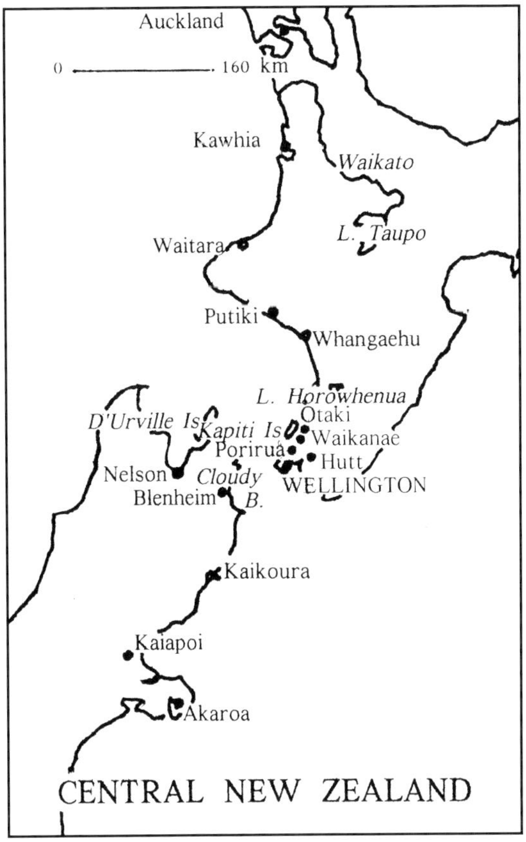

a tasty garnish for the convolvulus-like *rauparaha* plant that grew in profusion in the Kawhia area.

In 1819 Rauparaha and his nephew joined a group of Ngapuhi raiders from the north, who were travelling the length of the North Island to test the value of their newly acquired muskets (the party included Nene, who will return to the story a generation later). Rauparaha saw the military potential of Kapiti island, off the coast at the north-eastern portal to Cook strait, and courted the Ngati Awa people of the area. On his return to Kawhia, almost three hundred miles north, he found that his wife had been killed by Te Wherowhero and, seeking revenge, he became embroiled in an unsuccessful war against the Waikato tribes.

His luck appeared to have turned when he succeeded the chief of the Ngati Raukawa and married his widow, by whom he had a son Tamihana Te Rauparaha. In 1820, however, his Waikato and Maniapoto enemies besieged Kawhia, and only by the assistance of a Maniapoto kinsman was he able to escape. In 1821, therefore, he led the remnants of his people south towards their 'promised land' – Kapiti. They were attacked near Waitara but drove off their attackers; at Ohau they were accepted by Muaupoko, the local chieftain. Then Rauparaha killed one of the local women, and a plot was hatched to dispose of him.

Te Rauparaha, the diminutive Ngati Toa chieftain, was born into violence, and was a challenging figure over much of central New Zealand in his time. (WCA)

He learned of the plot and took a harsh revenge. His 'hosts' were for the most part killed, and the survivors who took refuge on islands in Lake Horowhenua were treated simply as a reserve stock of animal protein, until such time as the Ngati Toa were ready to move on to Kapiti. Their new stronghold was attacked from the sea in 1825 but proved impregnable. However, when their vassal neighbours, Ngati Awa and Ngati Raukawa, began squabbling, Rauparaha resettled them well apart, at Waikanae and near the Whangehu river mouth eighty miles to the north. His Ngati Toa were then able to spill over to Mana island and on to the mainland at Porirua.

Now established as the paramount chief in the lower North Island, Rauparaha began to covet the greenstone (nephrite, jade; *pounamu* to the Maori) of the South Island, and when in 1828 the Ngai Tahu chief Rerewaka boasted that, if Rauparaha set foot in Ngai Tahu territory, he would be sliced up with a shark's-tooth knife, matters came to a head. Rauparaha landed first on D'Urville Island (across the strait from Kapiti) and worked round through Marlborough to Kaikoura. He turned back long enough to redress a Ngati Raukawa grievance by sacking the Putiki *pa* [fortified village] near Wanganui, then returned to avenge Rangihaeata his nephew, cuckolded by a Ngati Ira chief who had then taken refuge with the Ngai Tahu of the South Island. Bringing reinforcements picked up from Kapiti, he landed first at Akaroa, then sacked the large Ngai Tahu *pa* at Kaiapohia (present-day Kaiapoi, to the north of Christchurch). The 'rigour' of the punishment he meted out here became legendary.

The arrival of Ngai Tahu reinforcements from further south forced him to retreat, and after he attempted to make a stand at Cloudy Bay and was defeated, he had to swim for it, out to his canoes. His last tribal fight was in 1834, when he and Te Heu Heu intervened in another squabble between Ngati Raukawa and Ngati Awa.

In 1840 he signed the Treaty of Waitangi, while holding reservations about its implications in terms of land tenure. While Rangihaeata, always the impulsive one, obstructed surveyors, the

Kapiti, Rauparaha's stronghold, crouches like a sleeping lion just off the coast north of Wellington.

Two years before Home's visit, Charles Heaphy painted the scene looking north along the foreshore of the infant settlement of Wellington. (WCA)

wily Rauparaha built a strong *pa* at Plimmerton, a little north of Porirua, moving himself to Otaki. Here he proclaimed his intention of blocking settlement of the Hutt Valley by Europeans (who believed that they had secured possession of the land from Te Puni a few years earlier when that chieftain, feeling beleaguered and in need of support from these new allies, sold off land to the New Zealand Company's advance party – land to which his own title was at best dubious!).

In April 1843 Rauparaha and Rangihaeata blocked a survey party attempting to subdivide land just north of present-day Blenheim The differences escalated into violence when an attempt was made to arrest them for arson, and some 22 Europeans and a few Maori were killed. The dead included Arthur Wakefield, one of the family that was instrumental in establishing Company settlements in the middle portion of the country. It was to his brother William (who had led the advance party into Wellington) that Te Puni had so obligingly sold land, and Rauparaha shrewdly moved to incite his Ngati Awa dependents to attack Wellington.

Into this tense situation, at the end of August, came Home and *North Star*. The settlement's solitary newspaper, the *Gazette*, recorded Home's arrival with evident relief, expressing regret that *North Star's* captain had been injured by a falling boom while entering harbour. However, two days after this report Home was sufficiently recovered to address to Rauparaha advice that could be offered with advantage to activists in any century:

> Her Majesty's ship North Star, Wellington,
> 11 September 1843.
>
> Friend Rauparaha,
>
> It has come to my knowledge that you are collecting the tribes around you, because you expect that I am going to attack you. Those who told you so said that which is not true.
>
> It was to keep peace and not to make war that I came here. You know that where many men meet together, and continue without employment, that they will find something to do. Take care that they do not get into mischief. They had best go home.
>
> J. Everard Home.[11]

And they did go home – for this proved to be Rauparaha's final exploit. He withdrew himself to Otaki, where he professed Christianity and renounced war. The settlers were much heartened by Home's presence and wished it to be prolonged. The *Gazette* of 27 September published an open letter from Home to the mayor of the young town, William Guyton, in which Home agreed to receive a deputation if desired but stressed that his stay must be curtailed by two factors: his need to get back to Sydney to resupply and his obligations elsewhere in the area.

Before leaving, however, he undertook one further inspired activity. Under the heading 'PIC-NIC' the *Gazette* of Wednesday 4 October reported that 'on Friday last' (postponed from Monday on account of bad weather) he and 'his gallant officers... gave an elegant entertainment at the Hutt'. The function was held, not in Wellington under the guns of *North Star*, but in the very area of

To celebrate the removal of Rauparaha's threat, the citizens of Wellington joined Home and his 'gallant officers' in a picnic at Burcham's Aglionby Arms in the Hutt valley. (WCA)

contention, at Burcham's Aglionby Arms, the local equivalent of a coaching inn on the road (or track) into the disputed hinterland. There was, reported the *Gazette*, 'dancing till late'.

Either on 5 October or the following Monday (the *Gazette* reports are contradictory) *North Star* sailed for Nelson, the settlement from which the fatal surveying foray to the Wairau plain had been mounted. From here he reported to Willoughby Shortland, acting governor since the death in office of William Hobson a year earlier (and this report indicates how objective he could be and disinclined simply to 'put the natives in their place'):

> From all that I have been able to see, I am of opinion that none of the settlements, in the parts of New Zealand which I have lately visited, have anything to fear from the natives, so long as they are fairly dealt with. At Nelson a force is wanted, not to repel the attacks of natives, but to restrain and keep in subjection the English labourers brought over by the New Zealand Company, who have, I believe, been in open rebellion against their employers more than once.
>
> At that place also, the general feeling appears to be more inclined to revenge the death of their friends, than to wish impartial justice to be done; and vengeance and revenge are words I have heard used when speaking of that affair. It appears that there are gentlemen at Nelson who look more coolly on the circumstances, and have confidence in the government; they did not attend the meeting, nor were they given to understand that it was about to take place.
>
> I have to apologize to you for the length of this letter, but I consider it proper that I should make your Excellency acquainted with all that has taken place since I left this port.
>
> I have, &c.
> J. Everard Home, Captain.
> His Excellency Willoughby Shortland,
> &c. &c. &c.[11]

From Wellington *North Star* sailed to Nelson, where Home reported that a force was wanted, 'not to repel the attacks of the natives, but to restrain... the English labourers'. (ATL)

Home called at Auckland on his way back to Sydney, where he

arrived on 27 November. Once again he wasted no time and on 9 December *North Star*, her stores replenished, set out for Wellington once more.

Hobson's replacement as governor took up his office on Boxing Day 1843: none other than Darwin's old companion from the *Beagle* voyage, Robert FitzRoy. He and Home soon inspected the settlements in Wellington and Nelson, and prior to *North Star's* departure from New Zealand FitzRoy wrote to Home:

FitzRoy expressed his gratitude to Home before *North Star* returned to Australia in 1844. (ATL)

Wellington, 24 February 1844.

Sir,

As you are about to sail from New Zealand, in Her Majesty's Ship "North Star" under your command, I think it my duty, as the Governor of the colony, to endeavour to express to you how much service your repeated visits to the principal settlements, and to many other places in New Zealand, have rendered to Her Majesty and the public.

It is my firm conviction that, to your extremely judicious conduct at a most critical period, and to your prompt assistance in any measure likely to be really beneficial, we are indebted, under Providence, for the peace and comparative tranquillity which now prevail in New Zealand.

To myself personally your ready and most friendly support and co-operation have been invaluable.

I have, &c.

Robert FitzRoy, Governor.

Captain Sir Everard Home, Bart.,
Her Majesty's Ship "North Star,"
Wellington.[12]

Just 12 days earlier FitzRoy had met Te Rauparaha at Waikanae, exculpating him for the Wairau affray and extracting from him a promise to desist from his Hutt Valley threats in return for a grant of £200 each, to him and his impulsive nephew. FitzRoy's action gained him little respect from a number of the settlers, and the land issue meanwhile smouldered on. The Treaty of Waitangi had obliged Maori to dispose of land only to the Crown, which would on-sell it. Settlers who had bought land in good faith found their title uncertain, and Maori for their part were eager to sell land on the open market

FitzRoy's efforts to get round these problems by giving up the Crown's right of pre-emption, then reducing the levy payable on direct transactions, simply gave ammunition to his critics. Moreover, the Maori of the north had become disaffected as other parts of the country became settled and, it seemed to them, prosperous at the expense of the tribes round the Bay of Islands (where pre-treaty trade and prosperity had been centred). To one in particular, Hone Heke, the flagstaff at Russell became a symbol of oppression, and on 8 July 1844 he cut it down. Later in the month Heke and Nene met at Bishop Selwyn's house and Heke

Hone Heke saw the flagstaff at Kororareka (today's Russell) as a symbol of oppression, and took to cutting it down. (ATL)

was persuaded to write a (somewhat equivocal) letter of apology to FitzRoy, which might have forestalled the later conflict had not the governor, before receiving it, come north with such troops as he had at his disposal.

Tamati Waka Nene (who had been a leader of the 1819 expedition that gave Rauparaha his first glimpse of Kapiti) shared some of Heke's concerns but undertook to keep Heke in order and to re-erect the flagstaff. FitzRoy thereafter enjoyed Nene's support, while also asking the Colonial Office to send military reinforcements to New Zealand. But he was already under attack by various factions in both New Zealand and Britain, and in May 1845 he was superseded.[13] By that time events had moved on, and a good deal was to happen before his replacement arrived. On the night 9-10 January 1845 Heke cut down the flagstaff a second time and ten days later yet again. His fourth attack came on 11 March. This time Kawiti, who shared Heke's mistrust of British policy and its effects, helped by creating a diversion. Kororareka was sacked, and some of Pomare's men from across the bay at Otuihu helped themselves to a share of the spoils, though Pomare himself had taken a neutral stance because of a recent quarrel with Kawiti.

Home and *North Star* were shortly on the scene; and Nene threw his weight behind FitzRoy. On 4 April, Home prepared to sail down to Auckland,[14] taking with him a party gathered by the missionary Henry Williams (a former naval officer himself, who had played a major part in drafting the treaty that has led to so much misunderstanding over a century and a half). Robin Fisher, in the *Dictionary of New Zealand Biography*, describes Williams's situation: 'having failed to prevent hostilities he assisted the wounded and helped evacuate the beleaguered settlers'. Home wrote to Williams on the eve of departure:

> North Star
> Friday Apr 4 1845
> Bay of Islands
>
> My Dear Sir
>
> The things are all off. If you will collect the persons going with me, I will send for them. I sail tomorrow morning as arranged.
>
> The Dr. at Kororareka I find writes upon a sheet of paper
>
> "Rt Rev. Dr Pompallier"
>
> Will you hasten our friends.
>
> I am My Dear Sir
> Faithfully yours
> Everard Home[15]

Williams himself stayed on amid the wreckage of his hopes. On 12 April he wrote to his friend Mair at Whangarei:

> The recent disasters here have totally brought our work to a stand. It is a serious distressing affair... Since the destruction of Kororareka I have scarcely been out of the settlement not having anything to say. They trampled on my advice and must now follow their own.[16]

Having delivered Williams's party to Auckland, Home returned to the Bay of Islands, bringing troops from the 58th and 96th Regiments[17] (mostly arrived only recently from Sydney) in *North*

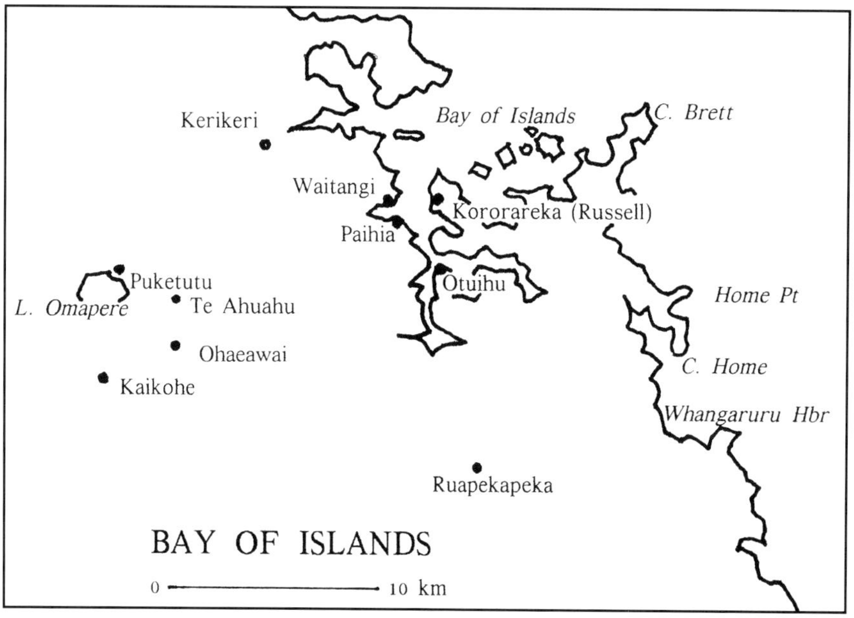

North Star was support ship when Pomare's pa was burned at the end of April 1845. This impression was long attributed to Major Cyprian Bridge, but is now considered to be the work of Sgt J Williams. (ATL)

Star and *Slains Castle*. *North Star* acted as support ship for the operation on 30 April, in which Pomare's *pa* was burned – *pour encourager les autres*, as it were – his people scattered and he himself arrested and taken to Auckland. At Nene's urgings he was shortly released, and he even put together a force to support Nene and the British against Heke; but he was to hold back from the attack on Ohaeawai in July rather than compromise his neutrality yet again.

Meanwhile Heke had moved off, first to his *pa* Te Ahuahu near Lake Omapere. He then constructed a new set of fortifications nearby at Puketutu, where a British attack on 8 May was seen off with help from Kawiti's skirmishers, who fell on the attackers' rear. Heke withdrew in good order to Te Ahuahu before moving with Kawiti to build yet another pa, this time at Ohaeawai. While Ahuahu was undefended, it was taken by an ally of Nene – to Heke's fury. He and Nene fought at Whatitiri and Heke was so badly wounded as to miss the engagement that followed.

The next contingent of troops from Sydney included Lieutenant-Colonel Henry Despard who assumed overall command, but the Ohaeawai position proved to be as defensible as Puketutu had been, although the defenders were outnumbered by six to one – and the colonel's tactics were as unimaginative as those of his predecessor Hulme. His preliminary bombardment was ineffectual, and his attempt to storm the *pa* on 1 July resulted in the loss, killed or wounded, of more than a third of his force. Having seen off his attack, the defenders awaited their opportunity and then, on 11 July, melted away in the night, to establish a new strongpoint towards the south-east.

Cyprian Bridge (or perhaps Williams) also depicted the assault on Ruapekapeka in January of the following year. (ATL)

Not surprisingly, a pause of several months ensued. FitzRoy's proposition that Heke and Kawiti should surrender some land as the basis of a settlement was received with derision, and on 18 November FitzRoy's successor assumed the office of governor. This was George Grey, transferred from South Australia, where he had antagonised many of the settlers but had brought a measure of prosperity with the establishment of wheat-growing and copper-mining. He wasted no time: Heke and Kawiti were given five days to respond to the peace offer that was 'on the table' when he arrived. Meanwhile he prepared for an assault on the new *pa* that Kawiti had constructed, some miles to the south of Pomare's old *pa*.

Here Kawiti had devised a system of underground bunkers, able to withstand the artillery bombardment to which the fort was subjected in December, the defenders sheltering in the gloom like bats in a cave – hence the name, Ruapekapeka. Once again *North Star* (supported by *Calliope*, *Castor*, *Elphinstone* and Home's first command, *Racehorse*)[9] acted as support ship for the attacking force, which struck on 11 January 1846 – to find the complex almost deserted apart from a few of Kawiti's men. Heke had withdrawn his force into the bush behind, ready to mount an ambush, but the British had learned enough about guerrilla tactics not to blunder too far into an environment where the Maori was so much at home.

By the end of January Kawiti and Heke met at Pomare's (new) *pa* and, with Nene acting as intermediary, made peace. Grey issued what he termed a pardon, without trying to extract reparations. (He then addressed concerns at the other end of the island, seizing Rauparaha at Porirua on 23 July and holding him under house arrest in Auckland for a couple of years. Heke kept out of Grey's way for as long, declining to appear as a suppliant.)

With the approach of peace, Home was relieved by *Castor* (36 guns, Captain Charles Graham) and took *North Star* to Sydney

At Well Manor, in the north-eastern corner of Hampshire, James Everard found a place to call home – for almost the first time in his life. Prior to his time there, the original Tudor house had been given a Georgian extension.

for a refit, before sailing on 25 February 1846 for Portsmouth, where he arrived on 22 August, the vessel paying off on 8 September 1846. NEW ZEALAND 1845-47 (*sic*) was duly added to *North Star*'s list of battle honours.

During his shore time Home disposed of the lease of the Manor House at Ham, basing himself instead at Well Manor in Hampshire. His father had taken on the lease of this property, with its surrounding farm, in 1812. (Not until 1824 did the land tax returns for the parish of Long Sutton catch up with the older Everard's baronetcy; and even then the spellings failed to achieve accuracy or even consistency.)

The house still preserves an appearance (from the road that separates it from the well which gave its name to the village) little altered from Everard's day. The original Tudor dwelling had already been extended towards the north by a Georgian wing, and subsequent extensions have been at the back of the house. Well was on the "drovers' way" that ran along a shallow ridge between the Hampshire Downs and the Hog's Back; and the Manor was

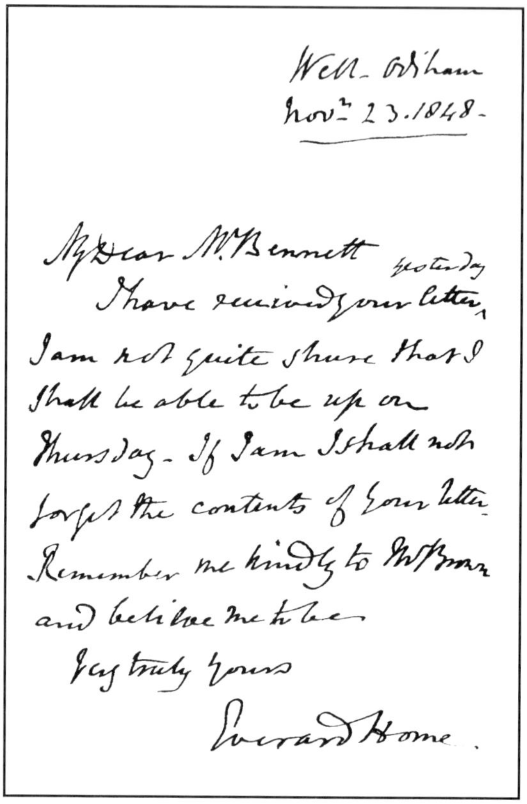

Well – Odiham
Novr. 23. 1848.

My Dear Mr. Bennett yesterday
I have received your letter,
I am not quite shure that I
shall be able to be up on
Thursday. If I am I shall not
forget the contents of your letter.
Remember me kindly to Mr. Brown
and believe me to be
Very truly yours
Everard Home.

From Well, he was able to keep in touch with the natural history community, by letters such as this one to Bennett of the British Museum staff, and by visits. Robert Brown, referred to in the letter, was naturalist in *Investigator* with Flinders, then Banks's librarian, and subsequently Keeper of Botany, a post later held by Bennett himself.

ideally placed for James Everard, about halfway between his naval commitments at Portsmouth and his natural history interests in and around London. It was probably one of the few places he was able to regard as home.

On 28 November 1850 he was appointed to the command of *Calliope*, another wooden 6th rate frigate of 26 guns. Built in 1837 at Sheerness, she was a little larger than *North Star* at 720 tons, with a length of 130 feet on the gundeck and a complement of 175 men.[18]

As *Calliope* was being towed out of Devonport to begin her commission, Home – accident-prone, it must seem, remembering his entry into Wellington in 1843 – suffered a major head injury when a capstan bar flew off and struck him. Not until 2 March 1851 did he get away, and even then, it appears, he was far from fit. Back in Sydney on 20 July, he relieved *Havannah* (Captain Erskine) and set out on a cruise which took him to New Zealand, then far south to the Auckland Islands, where the Great Southern Whale Fishery Company had been established, and back to Sydney by way of Tasmasnia. (Charles Enderby, whose name was given to one of the satellite islands of the Auckland group, was 'lieutenant-governor' – a prestigious title, indeed. The venture was wound up in 1852.)

His next cruise took him to Norfolk Island, Tonga, Fiji and the New Hebrides, returning to Sydney on 19 December 1852. But his health had been poor on this voyage and did not improve after his return, so on 16 March 1853 he put to sea again. He called first, between 30 March and 3 April, at Melbourne, where he doubtless met James Palmer who had published the first edition of his uncle's works in 1837, shortly before migrating to Australia ('to cultivate sheep pastures... Poor fellow. But he may be most at home,' commented William Clift, with unusual asperity.)[19] His next port of call was Adelaide, the capital of the fairly recent colony of South Australia; and his cruise then took him west to King George Sound, in which is the port of Albany, popular then (and indeed until after the First World War) because it saved westbound traffic the need to go 'round the corner' to Fremantle on the Swan River. Eastwards again, to Hobart Town and Port Arthur, site of a notorious penal settlement – and, in 1996, of an equally notorious massacre of tourists by a crazed gunman – and then once again to New Zealand.

He arrived at Wellington, proceeded north to Auckland and then (reported the *Melbourne Argus* of 5 November) *Calliope* 'returned to Sydney somewhat earlier than anticipated, in consequence of the severe indisposition of Sir Everard Home'. A memoir by Captain J.H. Watson, published in the *Sydney Star* on 21 June 1910, reports that Home was 'stricken by paralysis' in New Zealand. The *Argus* goes on to record *Calliope's* arrival in Sydney on 29 October;[20] her captain died on 1 November 1853.

The town came to a standstill for his funeral three days later. To the accompaniment of minute guns from *Calliope* the ship's barge brought the coffin to Circular Quay, from where the cortege left at 10.30am. It was led by a detachment of mounted police, of

FUNERAL PROCESSION OF SIR EVERARD HOME AT SYDNEY, 1853.

The *Illustrated Sydney News* followed up its account of Sir Everard's funeral with an illustration of the funeral procession.

whom the following day's *Illustrated Sydney News* remarked: 'we must in common justice to this highly respectable troop pay them a compliment on their clean and soldier-like appearance and bearing'. Then came men of the 11th Regiment (later the Devonshire Regiment) followed by staff officers and the gun carriage, drawn by *Calliope's* sailors. It was, said the *News*, 'a sad and imposing though novel sight to witness these noble fellows with downcast looks dragging' the carriage.

Behind the carriage came the chief officers and members of the clergy, and following them the crews and marines of *Calliope*, *Fantome* and *Torch*. The general in chief, on foot for the occasion, with his staff and Captain FitzRoy 'in splendid artillery dress' came next, then the mayor and other civic dignitaries, another troop of mounted police and numerous carriages – in which were the governor-general, the colonial secretary, the Speaker of the legislature, members of the consular corps and 'many wealthy merchants and residents'.

The procession made its way to Christ Church for a brief service conducted by the Rev. Canon Walsh, before proceeding to the Camperdown (or New Town) cemetery, where the burial service was conducted by *Calliope's* chaplain, the Rev. G. Carwithen. In its way it was as imposing an event as Nelson's own funeral almost half a century earlier, and a reflection of the respect in which Home was held.

Tributes poured in. Home was, according to the *News*, 'thoroughly devoted to his profession, and by his kindness and urbanity had endeared himself to his officers and men and indeed to all with whom he came in contact'. The *Sydney Morning Herald*

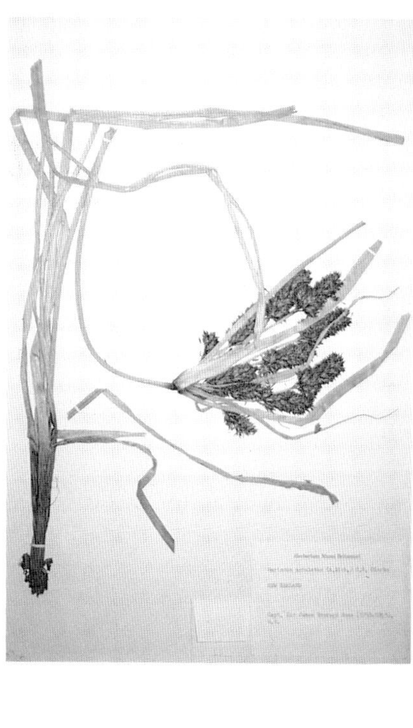

Specimens sent back by Home are still in the herbarium of the Natural History Museum. From New Zealand came *Mariscus ustulatus*, the coastal cutty-grass; and from the Isle of Pines in New Caledonia (as late as December 1852) the eponymous sandalwood, *Santalum homei SEEM.*

commented, 'Sir Everard's tastes decidedly inclined to the study and the library. He was a good and zealous botanist... We believe he made valuable contributions of specimens to scientific institutions at home.'

This was indeed the case. His China specimens were augmented by a prodigious 1286 plants from Australia and the Pacific which went to the British Museum, and additional specimens which found a home at Kew. The plant species *Santalum homei* SEEM[21] and *Geranium homeanum* TURCZ were named in his honour. He corresponded with Sir William Hooker,[22] who went from the Regius chair of botany at Glasgow to become director of Kew Gardens, and with Robert Brown who was Banks's librarian. To Hooker he proposed that officers of ships about to sail to foreign countries should be instructed to make collections of plants. His letters recorded observations on the condition of the Norfolk Island pines, and one of them was published in 1847 in the *Proceedings of the Linnean Society.*

He expressed the opinion that flowers and fruits in New Zealand had not so sweet a perfume or so rich a flavour as the same varieties in England, 'nor have the bees the same venom in their sting'.

A shared interest in natural history and in books brought him into friendship with Grey. (Indeed, he was one of the few in his time to have been friendly with both FitzRoy and Grey, who had tended to split the colonists into opposing camps.) His friendship with Grey was also facilitated by the fact that they were part of the circle of natural historians which included Richard Owen. It will be recalled that Owen was already well established at the College of Surgeons when Home paid his two visits (in 1832 and 1839), and Grey's natural history interests brought him into association with Owen even before he set out for Australia in 1836, so that he began sending specimens back to Owen when he made his forays into the Western Australian hinterland. It was a process which would continue. In May 1839 Owen wrote from the College of Surgeons:

George Grey was friendly both with Home and with Richard Owen. Home, for his part, managed to be friendly both with Grey and with his predecessor FitzRoy - which only a few achieved, since the two governors tended to polarise opinion. (ATL)

> My dear Grey
> I cannot tell you how much I was gratified to receive your two cases, and your welcome letter, and sincerely hope you may receive this at Swan River after a successful conclusion of your enterprise [Grey's expedition in Western Australia] All the specimens you sent were new to us, or of great rarity, and what is more to the point, of much utility. I shall soon commence a monograph on the muscles and other parts of the hooded lizard; your note on the action of the hood is a new and interesting fact in its history... Darwin's zoology has gone on steadily. All the mammalia, many of the birds, and three fasciculi of the fossils from the Beagle voyage are now described... I have finished my preparation of the foetal wallaby; it is now before me, thanks to your care... Mrs Owen sends her kind remembrances...

> Our little boy thrives. I will retain this red notebook, and birdskin till you come home, when you will be welcomed by none more sincerely than by
>
> Your faithful friend,
>
> Richard Owen
>
> Lieutenant George Grey
> Swan River
> Australia.

And in July 1844, when Grey was about to move from South Australia to New Zealand:

> I have received some most interesting fossils from Melbourne district, Darling Downs, and Wellington Valley. From each locality have come remains of the diprotodon, a genus indicated by a single inferior incisor in Sir T. Mitchell's 'Australia'. They establish the fact of the former existence of a marsupial type of pachyderms, equalling the largest rhinocerous [*sic*] in bulk, and combining characteristics of the existing kangaroo and wombat [Owen's father-in-law William Clift had also written on these resemblances] with peculiarities of its own – altogether by far the most extraordinary and interesting form that has yet come under my notice... I conclude that you have taken possession of your new Government, and entertain so confident a hope of your being able to maintain Auckland against General Heke [Owen was evidently unaware of the distance between Auckland and the Bay of Islands, though already well enough acquainted with the threat represented by Heke] as to direct this letter to the capital of your present island... I have to thank you for several valuable contributions from your last seat of Empire, and I send the accompanying memoirs, in the hope that should any opportunity occur of contributing for the materials towards completing the history of the apteryx and dinornis (more especially the latter, in respect of its head and beak) you may, amidst your more important and pressing avocations, act and advise in the interest of your anatomical friend.

That Grey was not alone in contributing to Owen's collection emerges from a letter of January 1848:

> You have given me abundant proof that the more immediate and arduous cares of Government will not divert you from that one encouragement of the collection of the materials for the natural history of your colony. The collection of the remains of the great extinct birds of New Zealand, which the laborious son of my eminent and esteemed friend, Dr Mantell, has just transmitted to this country, are the most valuable and instructive that have reached us.

But Grey certainly played his part, and it was appreciated. On 8 June 1850 Owen wrote to him:

> You have given me very great pleasure by the transmission of the box of specimens of the remains of the dinornis, from the cavern at

The notornis or *takahe*, about which Owen wrote to Grey, did indeed 'still exist' - though it was not until 1948 that it was rediscovered.

> the base of Tongariro... The great skull is a magnificent specimen, and there is a fragment of one of a younger bird of the same species, very interesting from the sutures being retained[23]... Your collection contains remains of a large short-winged water rail (notornis), which may, perhaps, still exist in some parts of New Zealand; and also indubitable leg bones of the apteryx, or kiwi, and these to all appearances as old as the bones of the gigantic birds. The kiwi seems, therefore, to have survived, by virtue of its smaller size and nocturnal habits, those causes of destruction which have extirpated its larger congeners...

At the time of Home's death, his own friendship with Grey was sufficiently close for him to make a significant bequest.[24] The *New Zealander* of 24 December 1853 recorded:

> The Governor expresses his deep regret in announcing the death of Sir Everard Home and directs the publication of an extract from that lamented officer's will, containing a list of valuable books which Sir Everard bequeathed to His Excellency to be taken as part of a Public Library which he trusted would be established at the seat of Government in New Zealand.

Home's generosity probably set the pattern for Grey's own later gifts, whose habit it became thereafter, when he completed a vice-regal term,[25] to take with him only his most prized volumes, leaving the remainder of his acquisitions to form the basis of a public library. The Home volumes were duly transferred to Auckland, then the capital of New Zealand.[26] They found their way into what is now the Auckland Institute and Museum, where the accessions register for 1854 lists:

20 vols Journal of the Geographical Society, no.1 being the index
6 vols Home's lectures on comparative anatomy
1 vol Collins English colonies in New South Wales
1 vol Oxley's Journal in New South Wales
7 vols Linnaeus – translated by Turton
1 vol Sweet Hortus Britannicus
1 vol Berwick's Quadrupeds
2 vols Smith's Grammar of Botany
    and Introduction to Botany
3 vols 2 Flinders' Voyage to Terra Australis
    1 Flinders' charts
3 vols Vancouver's Voyage
4 vols Burney's South Seas Discoveries
5 vols Sprengeles (*sic*) Linnaeus
2 vols Ellis on Zoophytes
    Ellis on Corallines
1 vol Brown's Prodromus

In this list, of course, it is possible to identify one of the plagiarised Hunter works; regrettably, the six volumes on comparative anatomy are no longer in the possession of the museum. (In a letter dated 13 January 1993 to his colleague Donald Kerr, a specialist in the subject of the Grey bequests, the then museum librarian Peter Hughes comments: 'Our records suggest that [they] must have been deaccessioned in the dim dark past.') But the bequest of such a series to a new land, half a world away, provides an intriguing coda to the story of a plagiarist father and his bibliophile son.[27]

James Everard Home used a heraldic bookplate with a Victorian teardrop-shaped shield; this lacked the red hand of his baronetcy, but did ornament the lion's head crest with the label that had been awarded to his father in 1812.

NOTES

1 The fragment was from the lower femur. The bird was the *moa*, and the specimen first examined by Owen was from one of the larger species. Since New Zealand lacked indigenous mammalian predators, a number of flightless birds came to occupy what would elsewhere have been mammalian niches in the country's ecology. Only the giant Haast's eagle *Harpagornis moorei* and the large harrier *Circus eylesi* – both also now extinct – preyed on the *moa* : the eagle on adults, the harrier on chicks. But the arrival of the Maori provided a predator, and the *moa* had been hunted to extinction (or destroyed in the burning of forest and grassland) by the time of European settlement. The most complete sets of bones came to be recovered from swamps or from caves in limestone country, into which the birds were apt to fall. Eleven species have been distinguished by recent research.

2 Clift, W. (1831) On the fossil bones found in the bone-caves and bone-breccia of New Holland. *Edinburgh New Phil. Journal.* p.394.

3 Gideon Mantell (1790-1852), surgeon and geologist, had published *The Wonders of Geology* the previous year. He played a leading role in the discovery and classification of dinosaurs. He had become FRS in 1825, along with the younger Home and, in 1844, he was one of the first honorary Fellows of the Royal College of Surgeons. His son Walter (1820-95) gave up a medical course to emigrate to New Zealand, arriving in the infant settlement of Wellington in the *Oriental* in 1840. He brought his inherited interest in palaeontology, and soon discovered fossil remains of two flightless birds – the *moa* and the rail *takahe.* (Four live specimens of the latter, *Notornis mantelli,* were discovered in the second half of the nineteenth century. It was then believed extinct until 1948, when Dr G.B. Orbell located a small family in the depths of Fiordland, from which a breeding population has been derived by careful husbandry.) It was from Walter Mantell that Owen secured many of the *moa* bones that confirmed his initial assertions.

4 A stage in the transition to steam, these vessels were still wind-propelled but had a 'donkey engine' to perform the heavier tasks and hence could manage with smaller crews. *North Star* was built at Woolwich in 1824; of 501 tons, she had a length on the gundeck of 113 feet 9 inches, and carried a complement of 165 men.

5 De Quincey wrote of his addiction, Coleridge was both inspired and destroyed by his; but even John Hunter would take '20-30 drops of laudanum' to steady his nerves before an inaugural lecture, while Gideon Mantell died of an overdose of opium taken to relieve the pain of an old back injury.

6 Inglis, B. (1976) *The opium war.* London, Hodder & Stoughton.

7 *North Star's* two later commissions involved her in Arctic exploration: in 1849-50 under the command of Captain Saunders, and under Pullen in 1852-54. She was broken up in 1860.

8 Canton: present day Guangzhou; the name of Shang-hae has changed little, to Shanghai. The other so-called 'treaty ports' now bear the names Xiamen, Fuzhou and Ningbo.

9 Sainsbury, A.B. (?1994) *The Royal Navy day by day.* London, Ian Allan.

10 Moorehead, A. (1969) *Darwin and the Beagle.* London, Hamish Hamilton.

11 GBPP, 1844 (556) App 272.

12 GBPP, 1845 (137): 34.

13 That is to say, announcement of FitzRoy's dismissal was made in the Commons on 5 May; but the despatch to FitzRoy was dated 30 April, he heard unofficially during September and received the despatch itself on 1 October. Such were the problems of communication in the 1840s. C.S. Forester built the first Hornblower novel round just such a problem, and has described its ramifications in *The Hornblower Companion.*

14 Just south of the Bay of Islands, on the sea route to Auckland, Home was commemorated by Cape Home, which forms the northern entrance to Whangaruru harbour (recent maps show it renamed North Head – a change which, like that in Victoria, is unkind to Home, and insipid into the bargain! – But near the base of the promontory Home Point still projects into the sea like an appendix awaiting the surgeon. It may be felt that this atones in part for the loss of Cape Everard from the map of Victoria.

James Palmer made a distinguished career for himself in Melbourne, and is commemorated by a tablet in the Royal Melbourne Hospital, whose original foundation stone he laid in 1846.

15 Williams papers MS91/75 (252). ATL. Jean Baptiste François Pompallier (1801-71) referred to in the letter, was chosen by Rome as first vicar apostolic of Western Oceania and consecrated titular bishop of Western Oceania in 1836. He arrived in New Zealand in 1838. His episcopal status was not well received by Protestant clergy in this country, such as Williams, and this doubtless underlies Home's remarking on Pompallier's form of address, in what is otherwise a very brief business-like letter.

16 Lee, J. (1983) *I have named it the Bay of Islands...* Auckland, Hodder & Stoughton.

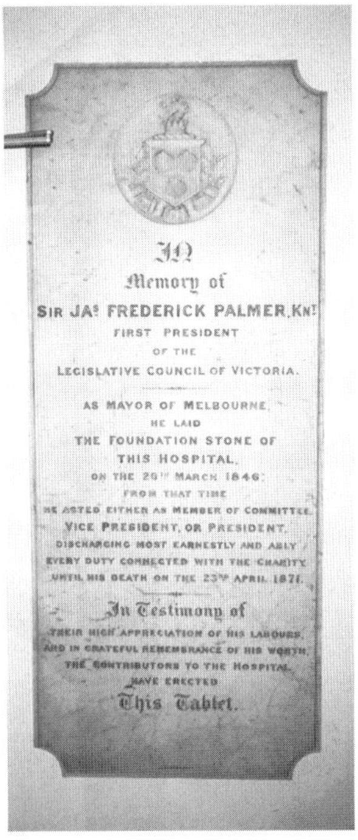

17 The 58th later became the Northampton Regiment and, in 1964, part of the Royal Anglian Regiment; their fellows of the 96th were merged into the Manchesters and became part of the King's Regiment in 1958.

18 It was the successor to this *Calliope,* a 2770-ton 3rd class light cruiser of 1884, that achieved fame first by surviving the Apia hurricane of 1889, and then by opening the naval graving dock in Auckland that was given her name.

19 James Palmer was one of Hunter's successors at St George's, and his edition of Hunter's works was published in four volumes, with a biographical sketch by Drewry Ottley, which recapitulated many items of legend, to Clift's annoyance. Despite Clift's reservations, Palmer was highly successful in Melbourne, turning from medicine to business, becoming mayor in 1846 and in that capacity laying the foundation stones of the first Melbourne Hospital and the original Prince's Bridge – all on one morning! He became Speaker in the Victorian legislative council, was knighted in 1857 and was chairman of the hospital at the time of his death in 1871.

20 Before the seriousness of Home's condition was fully appreciated in Sydney, the *Melbourne Argus's* correspondent foresaw that 'a number of the seamen from *Calliope* will be employed dismantling the batteries from Pinchgut, Bradley's Head and Coogie'. They found themselves hauling a gun carriage instead.

21 Home's specimen of the sandalwood *Santalum homei* was obtained on the Isle of Pines, at the southern tip of New Caledonia, in the course of the 1852 cruise. If we bear in mind that Cook almost came to grief in *Resolution* in September 1774 – Midshipman Elliott called it 'a most anxious, and perilous night' – while trying to prove to the Forsters that they were looking at trees, not stone pillars, we can admire Home's botanical zeal in collecting his specimen. The tremulous handwriting in which it is labelled may be taken as evidence of his deteriorating health.

22 Hooker's even more famous son, Sir Joseph Dalton Hooker, went as naturalist with Sir James Clark Ross's Antarctic expedition of 1840-42, spending three months in New Zealand during a southern winter. He explored extensively and produced a two-volume *Flora Novaezelandiae* in 1852-54, followed by handbooks on the Australian and New Zealand flora, the latter in 1867. He became a member of the Order of Merit in 1907. (Like another more recent OM, the late J.C. Beaglehole, he also edited Banks's *Endeavour Journal*.)

23 The sutures are the wavy fibrous lines of junction between individual bones of the vault of the skull, present in young creatures; as growth becomes complete, the bones interdigitate so as to form virtually a continuous casing.

24 They had maintained their correspondence – mainly on matters of natural history, but not exclusively – during Home's time at Well Manor after *North Star* paid off. Early in 1848 (as G.J. Tee, an Auckland polymath, points out to me) Home wrote to Grey:

> ...Owen is very well. He is most anxious to obtain the head and beak of the moa, and Captain Erskine [of the *Havannah*, whom Home would relieve when he brought *Calliope* out three years later] has directions from him where to seek for bones. It is below high water at the mouths of certain rivers in the sand... A week ago the Ministers were ordered to be in readiness to attend at Buckingham House upon the Queen, who is expected to be brought to bed.

Queen Victoria's fourth daughter (and sixth child), the Princess Louise, later Duchess of Argyll, was born on 18 March 1848.

On 6 June 1850 Home wrote to Grey and once again gave him news of Owen:

> Professor Owen considers the burning of your house [Grey's Government House in Auckland had been destroyed by fire on 23 June 1848] with the collections in natural history as a national loss... I have no doubt the moa will be found alive in some part of the Middle or South Island... Sir William Hooker... wanted to know if you had commenced anything yet of a botanical garden... He thought... the Government and the Admiralty at least seem desirous of encouraging officers... in collecting, and in sending their collections to the public establishments.

Within six months of writing this letter Home would receive his poisoned chalice, the command of *Calliope*. At the time he would have rejoiced, since it is obvious how preoccupied he was with the natural history of the new land to which his Antipodean service had introduced him.

25 Indeed his first New Zealand term ended just one week after the announcement of Home's gift.

26 Writing in *The Turnbull Library Record* (Vol. 30; 1997, at p.78) concerning Alexander Horsburgh Turnbull's 1918 bequest which established the library, Bland observes:

> It was also the last and most important of the principal acts of public benefaction that had established the major research collections in New Zealand. In 1894, Sir George Grey returned to England to spend the last four years of his life there, leaving behind his second collection of books to the people of Auckland... - his first collection he had left in Cape Town in 1861. Then, in 1904, Thomas Hocken offered his library to the people of Dunedin... Three years later the historian Thomas McNab gave a similarly sized collection of printed books to Dunedin Public Library.

But Home's bequest, which Grey passed on to Auckland, antedated all these acts of generosity; and indeed it can be argued that it provided the stimulus for Grey's later bequests, for in 1853 Grey's own munificence was yet to become established. Indeed I am informed by Donald Kerr that, prior to his departure at the end of 1853, Grey auctioned off those volumes from his own library that he did not wish to take with him.

27 James Everard Home died unmarried; the baronetcy passed, according to his Australian obituaries, to his younger brother, the Rev. William Archibald Home, born in 1800. These sources were unaware of the fact, duly recorded in the Westminster School register, that William Archibald had died at Palermo in Sicily on 2 February 1848! The baronetcy thus died with James Everard. I am informed (Bondeson, J; personal communication 1998) that William Archibald's exile was a consequence of his being apprehended for an indecent assault on a footman near Piccadilly in 1835, at a time when (after many years at Oxford) he was Rector of Hertingfordbury.

6

GOING HENCE

Men must endure their going hence,
even as their coming hither.

Shakespeare: *King Lear*, V.ii.9.

The Rev. Dr William Buckland occupied the chair of mineralogy in Oxford, with the subsequent addition of a readership in geology, before becoming Dean of Westminster. He was a great admirer of John Hunter.

Had Hunter's writings on geology been published immediately on their presentation to the English College by the younger Everard Home in 1839, Buckland might have revised his estimate. He was (as befitted his clerical background) a resolute believer in the scientific accuracy of the biblical account of creation and a loyal follower of Bishop Ussher's chronology – and to such men Hunter's views would have been as heretical, even in 1847, as Rennell had apprehended in 1790.

As it was, however, at the Hunterian festival of 1847 Buckland regretted to Richard Owen, who had by then succeeded Clift as conservator of the museum, that there was as yet no proper memorial of Hunter apart from this annual festival (where, at the oration and the dinner that followed, everyone who mattered in the scientific community seems to have met everyone else). Buckland observed that he had himself proposed the insertion of some monument into a vacant niche in Westminster Abbey.[1]

Nine years later St George's Hospital celebrated the centenary of Hunter's entry there as house surgeon, and on that occasion Buckland's son Frank (himself a 'George's man', and hence disposed by heritage and upbringing to hold Hunter in awe) formed his own resolve to do honour to his hero. Within a couple of years his opportunity arose.

He was at Windsor serving as assistant surgeon to the 2nd Life Guards when, in January 1859, he read in the paper of an Order in Council that authorised the clearing of the vaults of St-Martin's-in-the-Fields. He had some leave due and employed it first in verifying (by enquiries of Quekett, the conservator, and a study of Palmer's *Works*) that Hunter's remains had in fact been interred in St Martin's, and then in making a search of the church itself. The burials register gave final confirmation, on 26 January, and at that stage Buckland dared hope that he might achieve success in time for the Hunterian festival on 14 February. But in the vaults were some 3,260 coffins – and, on 22 February, Hunter's was the penultimate one that Buckland examined. On schedule

John Hunter's remains were transferred to Westminister Abbey in 1859. (Far right): A richly ornamented memorial brass in the nave of the Abbey marks Hunter's final resting place.

or not, grimy, probably glad of the wintry conditions of a London February, Buckland was jubilant. (He had probably overstayed his leave, too. Certainly he did not gain his hoped-for promotion to full regimental surgeon. He left the army in 1863, and built himself a second career far more illustrious than his first could have been, as the first scientist of fishery.)[2]

Hunter's coffin was taken to the Abbey on 26 March 1859 and re-interred (between Ben Jonson and Sir Charles Lyell) two days later, in front of a congregation of some 600 persons. Over the tomb a memorial brass, elaborately Victorian in style, records its placing by the Royal College of Surgeons of England 'to record

Their previous situation is recorded on a plaque in the crypt of the church of St Martin-in-the-Fields.

their admiration of his genius as a gifted interpreter of the Divine Power and Wisdom at work in the Laws of Organic Life, and their grateful veneration for his services to mankind as the Founder of Scientific Surgery'. In the border of the tablet is the verse from Psalm 104: 'O Lord, how manifold are Thy works! - in wisdom hast Thou made them all.'[3]

On 14 February 1952 a memorial service was held in St Martin's-in-the-Fields. An address, punctilious in narrative and redolent with classicism, was given by Sir Gordon Gordon-Taylor and a plaque unveiled by Sir Henry Dale:

ERECTED BY
THE ROYAL COLLEGE OF SURGEONS OF ENGLAND
TO RECORD THAT THERE RESTED IN THESE VAULTS
FROM 1793 TO 1859 THE BODY OF
JOHN HUNTER
FOUNDER OF SCIENTIFIC SURGERY
AFTER LONG AND DILIGENT SEARCH INITIATED
AND CARRIED OUT BY **FRANK BUCKLAND** A MEMBER
OF THE COLLEGE THE REMAINS WERE IDENTIFIED
AND TRANSFERRED TO WESTMINSTER ABBEY

It is proper to record that changes in the layout and use of St Martin's crypt have brought about a situation in which the plaque stands adjacent to the door of a games room, and between the restaurant counter and the staff toilets. But Hunter, as a practical man, would undoubtedly welcome the variety of activities going on in a church which is once again – as churches used to be – a community centre, and that in the centre of a major city.

More than forty years after the unveiling occurred a further chapter in the veneration of John Hunter: on 14 September 1993, during the bicentenary commemoration of his death, the President of the College, Sir Norman Browse, and the chairman of the Hunterian Trustees, Sir Reginald Murley, laid a wreath on Hunter's tomb in the Abbey before joining the congregation in a packed St Margaret's next door for a service of thanksgiving. After the service, it was possible for those attending the celebrations to walk into the Abbey and admire the flowers, glowing there against the dull sheen of the brass, in the north aisle of the nave.

On the subject of the last resting place of Hunter's brother-in-law, who let him down, there is widespread reticence. He died on 31 August 1832, it will be recalled, at his house in the Royal Hospital, Chelsea. Five years earlier he had presented his medical books to the hospital, and a mahogany bookcase was designed by Sir John Soane to house them. (The collection is in store at the moment, during a refurbishment programme, so that it is impossible to ascertain how many plagiarised volumes it contains.)

With the aid of the 1842 survey, Major R.A.G. Courage and A/CSM M. Ford locate the tombstone of the older Everard Home.

His remains were interred in the burial ground of the institution, just to the east of the main buildings. Ten years later C.J. Ford, Captain of Invalids, conducted a survey of the burial ground and drew a detailed plan, dated 1 August 1842, of the layout of the various tombstones. He noted that the older Everard's inscription, on tombstone No. 95 in his series, read:

EVERARDUS HOME, BARONETUS
F.R.S. NATUS 6 MAY 1756
DIED 31 AUG 1832

It is well that he did, because time and encroaching lichen have totally obliterated the inscription on the slab which Ford's plan identifies as Home's tombstone.

But half a world away in Australia, you can take a short ride on a suburban Sydney train, and come to the bustling main street of Newtown. Only a stone's throw away, just where the street map says it should be, there is the old Camperdown cemetery. It is a quiet place, though so near the traffic. The mellow golden stone church would not look out of place in an English village, and round it, under the trees, sprawls an unpatterned array of tombs and headstones, of varied date and often barely decipherable. You could wonder if it is possible to find a particular grave – but there by the path is a prominent essay in sculpture, representing the bow of a boat with an incredible frozen bow wave, and you begin to wonder if, after all, you are on the right track.

The upper surface bears no legend, and you look beyond. There is a rusty iron anchor on top of a slab a short distance away, which looks as if it may repay examination, but in working your way round to it you notice a smaller anchor in relief on the end of a tomb, and you pause to examine this in passing. On one side of the tomb is a heraldic shield you recognise from the Home bookplate,[4] and yes – faint, but clear enough under its coating of lichen, the name you have come to find:

SACRED
TO THE MEMORY OF
SIR JAMES EVERARD HOME, BART
C.B., F.R.S.
OF WEL- -ANOR FARM, HANTS
HE DEPARTED THIS LIFE
ON THE FIRST OF NOVEMBER 1853
CAPTAIN OF THE CALLIOPE
AND SENIOR OFFICER
ON THE AUSTRALIAN STATION
AGED 55

In the old Camperdown cemetery, James Everard's tomb displays an anchor at one end; the inscription is faint but can be made out on careful examination. It is a peaceful place.

The surface has flaked off in the middle of the fifth line, but otherwise the inscription is readable enough, even though faint.

Here you can reflect on the man whose remains lie beneath, and then return yet again to the bustle of Newtown (and before catching the train call in to the pub on the corner, where you can replace your fluid loss from all this with a beer – cold in the Australian fashion and welcome because November in Sydney is hot and humid and the undertaking has been a warm one). You never do get as far as examining the iron anchor closely. But you feel the same sense of achievement as Frank Buckland must have done – in his more chilly surroundings.

I think James Everard Home sleeps here in peace; and somehow I think he does not mind being half a world away from his father.

NOTES

1 In the context of monuments and the Rev. Dr Buckland it seems worth noting a stanza from Archbishop Whately's *Anticipatory Dirge on Professor Buckland, the geologist.*

Where shall we our great professor inter,
That in peace may rest his bones?
If we hew him a rocky sepulchre
He'll get up and break the stones,
And examine each stratum that lies around,
For he's quite in his element underground.

Richard Whately (1787-1863) was archbishop of Dublin, 1831-63. He was a prolific writer who edited Bacon and ridiculed Hume.

2 Frank Buckland has a New Zealand connexion, but one seemingly less to his credit. Rabbits were introduced to New Zealand by the early settlers between 1840 and about 1870, at which stage they multiplied abruptly and alarmingly, devastating much of Otago and Southland so that (as the Begg brothers describe in their account of Dusky Bay)

> '... sheep perished from starvation by hundreds of thousands, and it is no exaggeration to say that the majority of the squatters were ruined'... It was in a mood of despair that the incredible folly of the introduction of weasels, stoats and ferrets was perpetrated... the introduction of the predators was a Government venture...
> It was not that the Government had not been warned about the danger these bloodthirsty vermin would present to our defenceless native birds. In 1876, a distinguished scientist from Cambridge, Professor A. Newton, had written anguished letters to Buller, Hector, Hutton, Kirk and others, asking for their help in forcing legislation to prevent the predators from entering New Zealand. He drew attention to the fact that two Invercargill men, Macowie and Cuthbertson, had ordered five pairs of weasels from Frank Buckland, a naturalist in England. Newton managed to block this order, but could see that he might not be so successful in the future. In the blunt but refreshing terms of the day he finished a

> letter to Buller: 'It is too annoying to think that the fate of your fauna should depend on the rash act of the greatest fool that was ever called a naturalist.'

Perhaps it is as well Buckland turned his attention to fish.

3 The brass is ornamented with a coat of arms, which commits the double solecism of displaying William Hunter's arms (three 'Dogs of Chase', silver on a green field; with a silver chief bearing a green hunting horn with red strings; granted by the Lord Lyon in 1752) – arms to which John was not entitled – alongside a rendering of Everard Home's arms, which equally Anne Hunter was not entitled to impale with her husband's. It is amusing in its way, that the down-to-earth John Hunter, who 'might well have considered such a display pretentious', as Harrison points out in a recent paper [Harrison, DFN (1997) *Jl Med. Biog.* 5: 178-185] , has been given posthumous recognition to which he was not entitled.

4 The lion and the piles at least (they look even more like stalactites when carved in stone) are identifiable despite the ageing process.

APPENDIX

THE HOME ANCESTRY

The family tree which follows provides a simplified table of the generations and interrelationships of

1. the Earls of Home
2. the Earls of Marchmont
3. the Homes of Greenlaw

It has been constructed using material from five principal sources:

i: from the Lyon Register, which contains a statement of the ancestry of Everard Home senior, in the preamble to his 1788 grant.

ii: Martine, R. (1987) *Scottish clan and family names.* Edinburgh: Bartholomew.

iii: Gibson, A. (1905) *An old Berwickshire town.* London: Oliver & Boyd, which examines the generations of the Homes of Greenlaw.

iv: Huxford, J.F. (1984) *Honour and arms.* London: Buckland, which documents the career of Patrick Home, first Earl of Marchmont, in the context of his augmentation of honour (yet, curiously, omits reference to Everard's even more unusual augmentation).

v: *The concise dictionary of national biography* (1992) Oxford & New York: Oxford University Press, which has allowed certain lacunae to be filled in.

Successive generations are linked by a continuous line; dotted lines indicate more indirect descent.

* The marital history of Robert Home (1752-1834), the painter, is uncertain. He has been credited (as quoted in my earlier book *Fellowship of Three*) with marrying Susan Delany in 1783. Gibson, on the other hand, claims that he married, first, his teacher Angelica Kauffmann - the DNB does not agree - and later Anne Paterson.

Aldan de Home
c. 1130, took his name from
the lands of Home in Berwickshire

Sir Thomas = Nichola
heiress of Dunglass

Sir Christopher of that Ilk

Sir Alexander
Ambassador to England 1459
Lord Home 1473, d. 1491

Alexander, 6th Lord Home
(1566-1619)
1st Earl of Home 1605

11th Earl became
Baron Douglas 1875

12th Earl
ADC to Queen Victoria 1887-97

14th Earl of Home
renounced title 1963 to become
Prime Minister as Sir Alec
Douglas-Home (later life peer
as Lord Home of the Hirsel)

Sir David of Wedderburn
c. 1413

Sir Patrick, 2nd Baron of Polwarth

Sir Patrick, 1st Bt of Polwarth
d. 1648

Patrick (1641-1724)
Baron Polwarth 1690
Earl of Marchmont 1697

Alexander (1695-1740)
2nd Earl of Marchmont
married Campbell heiress,
took name Campbell

Hugh Hume (1708=94)
3rd Earl of Marchmont

earldom dormant after 1794
(barony of Polwarth descended
through a grand-daughter to
the family of Hepburne-Scott)

Patrick of Coldinghamlaw
?Patrick Home of the law, c.1576

David

Robert (1595-1673) = Agnes Methven

William
of Greenlaw Castle, d. 1703

James

Margaret = George Holiwell
Minister of Polwarth

Sir Alexander Purves, 2nd Bt

William, d. 1743 = Anne, d. 1729
1705
renounced Greenlaw to
Alexander Earl of Marchmont 1738
and purchased Sharplaw (Roxburghshire)

Helen = Rev Dr Alexander Duncan | Elizabeth = John Jack | Jean, d. 1731 | Patrick | William (both died young) | ROBERT BOYNE (1713-86) = Mary

Col Alexander Hutchison

William Hutchison died young | Anne = John Hunter 1771, 1742-1821, 1728-93 | Mary = Robert Mylne 1770 | Robert = * | Helen | Elizabeth

James Tunstall DD

Henry Thompson 1 = Jane = 2 EVERARD
1792
1756-1832

1805
Ann Gosset = William
East India Co

William Duncan | Anne | Emily | LC Rooke RN = Elizabeth

JAMES EVERARD 1798-1853 | William Archibald 1800-48 | Jane = Henry Forbes Capt RN | Mary = CP Rushworth | Harriet Catherine | Charlotte = Bernard Yeoman Capt RN

SELECT BIBLIOGRAPHY

BOOKS AND JOURNALS

Adams, B. (1986) *The flowering of the Pacific.* Sydney: Collins/British Museum (NH).

Archibald, E.H.H. (1984) *The fighting ship in the Royal Navy.* Poole: Blandford.

Badger, G. (1988) *The explorers of the Pacific.* Kenthurst NSW: Kangaroo Press.

Banks, J. (ed.Beaglehole J.C. 1962) *The Endeavour journal of Joseph Banks.* Sydney: State Library of NSW/Angus & Robertson.

Banks, R.E.R. et al. (eds) (1994) *Sir Joseph Banks: a global perspective.* Kew: Royal Botanic Gardens.

Beaglehole, J.C. (1974) *The life of Captain James Cook.* London: A & C Black.

Beasley, A.W. (1993) *Fellowship of three.* Kenthurst NSW: Kangaroo Press.

Beasley, A.W. (1996) *The Club on The Terrace.* Wellington: The Wellington Club.

Begg, A.C. & Begg, N.C. (1966) *Dusky Bay.* Christchurch: Whitcombe & Tombs.

Boswell, J. (ed. Chapman, R.W. 1980) *Life of Johnson.* Oxford: Oxford.

Brodie, B.C. (arr Hawkins, C. 1865) *The works of Sir Benjamin Collins Brodie.* London: Longman Green.

Brooke-Little, J.P. (1973) *Boutell's Heraldry.* London, Warne.

Bryant, A. (1942) *The years of endurance 1793-1802.* London: Collins.

Bryant, A. (1944) *Years of victory 1802-1812.* London: Collins.

Bryant, A. (1986) *Freedom's own island.* London: Collins.

Burney, J. (1975) *With Captain James Cook in the Antarctic and Pacific.* Canberra: National Library of Australia.

Carter, H.B. (1985) *Sir Joseph Banks.* London: British Museum (NH).

Carver, M. (1984) *The seven ages of the British army.* London: Weidenfield & Nicolson.

Cook, J. (ed. Beaglehole, J.C. 1955) *The voyage of the Endeavour.* Cambridge: Hakluyt Society.

Darwin, C. (1859) *The origin of species.* London: John Murray.

Desmond, R. (1995) *Kew: the history of the Royal Botanic Gardens.* London: Harvill.

Dickens, C. (ed. Patten, R.L. 1972) *The posthumous papers of the Pickwick Club.* Harmondsworth: Penguin.

Dobson, J. (1969) *John Hunter.* Edinburgh: Livingstone.

Dobson, J. (1954) *William Clift.* London: Heinemann.

Elliott, J. Memoirs of the early life of John Elliott: in (1984) *Captain Cook's second voyage.* London: Caliban.

Farr, E. & Nolan, E.H. (1860) *The history of England by Hume & Smollett with a continuation to the present time.* London: Virtue.

Forester, C.S. (1937) *The happy return.* London: Michael Joseph.

Forester, C.S. (1964) *The Hornblower companion.* London: Michael Joseph.

Fox-Davies, A.C. (ed. Brooke-Little, J.P. 1969) *A complete guide to heraldry.* London: Nelson.

Gask, G. (1950) *Essays in the history of medicine.* London: Butterworth.

Gibson, R. (1905) *An old Berwickshire town.* London: Oliver & Boyd.

Guedalla, P. (1931) *The Duke.* London: Hodder & Stoughton.

Haswell, J. (1975) *The British army.* London: Thames & Hudson.

Heberden, W. (ed. Heberden, W. jnr 1802) *Commentaries on history and cure of diseases.* London: Payne.

Hibbert, C. (1994) *Nelson: a personal history*. London: Viking.
Hibbert, C. (1997) *Wellington: a personal history*. London: HarperCollins.
Home, E. (1814-28) *Lectures on comparative anatomy*. 6 vols. London: Nicol; Longman Green.
Home, E. (1822) *Hunterian oration*. London: Longman Green.
Hudson, R. (1994) *Nelson and Emma*. London, The Folio Society.
Hunter, J. (1794) *On the blood, inflammation and gun shot wounds*. London: Nicol.
Hunter, J. (arr. Owen, R. 1861) *Essays and observations on natural history, anatomy, physiology, psychology and geology*. London: van Voorst.
Hunter, J. (ed. Allan, E: 1993) *John Hunter's case books*. London: RCS & RSM.
Huxford, J.F. (1984) *Honour and arms*. London: Buckland.
Inglis, B. (1976) *The opium war*. London: Hodder & Stoughton.
Lee, J. (1983) *I have named it the Bay of Islands...* Auckland: Hodder & Stoughton.
Lloyd, C. (1992) *The Royal collection*. London: Sinclair-Stevenson.
Macalpine, I & Hunter, R (1969) *George III and the mad-business*. London: Allen Lane The Penguin Press.
Mahan, A.T. (1980) *The influence of sea power upon history*. Greenwich CT: Bison.
Manning, T.D. & Walker, C.F. (1959) *British warship names*. London: Putnam.
Martine, R. (1987) *Scottish clan and family names*. Edinburgh: Bartholomew.
Masefield, J. (1905) *Sea life in Nelson's time*. Conway Maritime Press.
Moorehead, A. (1969) *Darwin and the Beagle*. London: Hamish Hamilton.
Morton, H. & Johnston, C.M. (1988) *The farthest corner*. Auckland: Century Hutchinson.
Negus, V. (1966) *History of the trustees of the Hunterian collection*. Edinburgh & London: Livingstone.
O'Brian, P. (1987) *Joseph Banks - a life*. London: Collins Harvill.
Oman, C. (1947) *Nelson*. London: Hodder & Stoughton.
Oppenheimer, J.M. (1946) *New aspects of John and William Hunter*. New York: Schuman.
Paget, S. (1897) *Life of John Hunter*. London: Unwin.
Palmer, J.F. (1835-7) The works of John Hunter FRS with notes. Vols 1-4. London: Longman Rees.
Pepys, S. (ed. Latham, R. 1978) *The illustrated Pepys*. London: Unwin.
Pettigrew, T.J. (1817) *Memoirs of John Coakley Lettsom*. London: Nicholls Son & Bentley.
Qvist, G. (1981) *John Hunter 1728-1793*. London: Heinemann.
Robinson, N.H. (1980) *The Royal Society catalogue of portraits*. London: Royal Society.
Russell, K.F. (1979) *Catalogue of the historical books in the library of the Royal Australasian College of Surgeons*. Melbourne: Queensbury Hill.
Sainsbury, A.B. (?1994) *The Royal Navy day by day*. London: Ian Allan.
Smith, B. (2nd edn, 1984) *European vision and the South Pacific*. Sydney: Harper & Row.
Southey, R. (1813) *The life of Nelson*. London: Blackie.
Taylor, S. (1993) *John Hunter and his painters*. London: Royal College of Surgeons.
van der Kiste, J. (1992) *George III's children*. Stroud: Alan Sutton.
Ward, L.E. (1928) *Early Wellington*. Auckland & Wellington: Whitcombe & Tombs.
Warner, O. (1959) *Trafalgar*. London: Batsford.
Weinreb, B. & Hibbert, C. (1983) *The London Encyclopaedia*. London: Macmillan.

Annals of the Royal College of Surgeons of England (and subsequently the College Bulletin, where historical articles are now published)

Australian and New Zealand Journal of Surgery

New Zealand Geographic (No 12: Oct-Dec 1991 - *moa*)

MANUSCRIPT AND ARCHIVAL SOURCES

United Kingdom:

Public Record Office, Kew (Admiralty & Colonial records)
Royal College of Surgeons, Lincoln's Inn Fields, London (Clift & Owen papers; records of Hunterian Museum)
Royal Society, London (Council records, nomination forms)
National Maritime Museum, Greenwich (Navy Lists 1800-20; particulars of naval vessels)
Natural History Museum, Kensington (herbarium specimens and associated documentation))
Hampshire Record Office, Winchester (land tax returns for the parish of Long Sutton to 1832)
Public Register of all Arms and Bearings in Scotland (Lyon Register), Edinburgh
Royal Hospital, Chelsea (Ford burial ground survey)

Australia:

State Library of New South Wales, Sydney (newspaper files)
State Library of Victoria, Melbourne (newspaper files)

New Zealand:

Alexander Turnbull Library, Wellington (newspaper files)

DICTIONARIES OF BIOGRAPHY

Jones, B. & Dixon, M.V. (1981) *The Macmillan dictionary of biography.* London: Macmillan.
Marshall, J. (1835) *Royal Naval biography.* London: Longman Rees.
O'Byrne, W.R. (1849) *A naval biographical dictionary.* London: John Murray.
Oliver, W.H. (ed.) (1990) *Dictionary of New Zealand Biography, Vol. I (1769-1869)* Wellington: Allen & Unwin, Dept of Internal Affairs.
Oxbury, H.F. et al. (1992) *The concise Dictionary of National Biography* (3 vols) Oxford: Oxford University Press.
Westminster School Register.

NOTE ON THE ILLUSTRATIONS

Most of the photographs of places and plaques, cemeteries and churches are my own, and I am grateful to Louise Goossens and Andrew Turner for their assistance in preparing some unpromising material for publication.

An abbreviation in parentheses at the end of a caption will indicate the source of the remainder. For these other illustrations, acknowledgment is offered to

- the Royal Collection (RColl) ©1999 Her Majesty the Queen: for
  Ernest, Duke of Cumberland, by Sir William Beechey (p.56)
  George IV, Coronation portrait by Sir Thomas Lawrence (p.94)

- the Royal Society (RSoc) for
  Sir Humphrey Davy, by Sir Thomas Lawrence (p.68)
  Sir Everard Home, by Thomas Phillips (p.77)

- the Royal College of Surgeons of England (RCS), by permission of the President and Council,
  for the Dance and Barry College buildings (p.12)
  John Hunter, now considered to be by John Zoffany (p.14)
  Hunter's specimen of a lizard, from Belleisle (p.18)
  John Hunter, by his brother-in-law Robert Home jnr (the study with the dog is a copy, by Dorofield Hardy, of the Royal Society portrait (p.29)
  Everard Home as a young man; engraving by William Sharp from the portrait by Sir William Beechey (p.32)
  The Earl's Court house (p.37)
  Plan of the Leicester Square complex, drawn by William Clift (p.42)
  Rhinoceros, painted by George Stubbs (p.45)
  Anne Hunter, by John James Masquerier (p.46)
  Matthew Baillie (p.47)
  Lincoln's Inn Fields, showing Nos 41 & 42 before the building of the College (p.53)
  Bust of Sir Everard Home (p.62)
  Drawing of the interior of the Hunterian Museum by William Clift (p.63)
  Sir Astley Cooper, by Sir Thomas Lawrence (p.69)
  Sir William Blizard (p.75)
  William Clift, by his son William Home Clift (p.79)
  Sir Benjamin Brodie (p.79)
  Caricature of Sir Everard Home, by William Home Clift (p.81)
  John Abernethy (p.81)
  Caroline Clift, Richard Owen (p.82)
  The rebuilding of the College, by Sir George Scharf (p.83)
  John Hunter's tankard (p.88)
  The aftermath of the 1941 bombing (p.97)
  John Hunter, by Sir Joshua Reynolds (p.100);

- the Royal Australasian College of Surgeons (RACS) for
  William Cheselden, copy of the portrait by Jonathan Richardson (p.34)
  Plate XXXVI from the *Osteographia* (p.35)
  which appeared in my book on the College portraits;
  Robert Officer's diploma of membership of the English College (p.70)

which was part of the archival disp lay at the first Cowlishaw symposium;

- to the National Maritime Museum, Greenwich, London (NMM) for
  Belleisle, the full attack, after D. Serres & R. Short (p.17)
  Hon. Augustus Keppel, by Sir Joshua Reynolds (p.38)
  Admiral Lord George Brydges Rodney, after Sir Joshua Reynolds (p.39)
  The Battle of The Saints, by Thomas Whitcombe (p.39)
  The Battle of the Nile, by George Arnald (p.91)
  Sir Home Popham (p.93)
  Nemesis destroying Chinese war junks, by E. Duncan (p.110)
  Beagle in Sydney harbour, 1841, by Owen Stanley (p.112);

- to the National Portrait Gallery, London (NPG) for
  John Burgoyne, after Sir Alan Ramsay, cat. 4158 (p.19)
  Robert Mylne, by George Dance the younger, cat. 1150 (p.27)
  Robert Home jnr, self-portrait, cat. 3162 (p.29)
  Sir Benjamin Hallowell-Carew, by John Hayter, cat. 373 (p.90);

- to the Linnean Society, London (LS) for
  Sir Joseph Banks, by Thomas Phillips (p.67);

- to ©The British Museum, London (BM) for
  John Hunter, by Nathaniel Dance (Sir Nathaniel Dance-Holland) (p.79);

- to the Hocken Library, Uare Taoka o Hakena, University of Otago, Dunedin (HL) for Captain John Lort Stokes 1812-1885 (p.111);

- to the Alexander Turnbull Library, Wellington (ATL) for
  Nelson 1841, by Charles Heaphy (p.117)
  Robert FitzRoy (p.118)
  Kororareka, drawing by Capt Clayton, engraved by W A Nicholas (p.119)
  North Star at the burning of Pomare's pa, by Williams (p.121)
  The assault on Ruapekapeka, by Williams (or Cyprian Bridge) (p.122)
  Sir George Grey (p.127);

- to the Wellington Club (WCA) for illustrations from the Club archives, previously used in my history of the Club:
  Te Rauparaha (p.114)
  Wellington 1841, by Charles Heaphy (p.115)
  Burcham's Aglionby Arms, by Samuel Charles Brees (p.116).

The photograph of Sir Richard Owen and the moa skeleton (p.105) was made available by the editor of *New Zealand Geographic* magazine, and the engraving of the funeral procession of Captain Sir Everard Home (p.125), from the *Illustrated Sydney News* of 12 November 1853, is taken from a copy held in the State Reference Library, State Library of New South Wales.

The portrait of Mrs Nancy Gilbert, by Thomas Hudson (p.42) was published as an illustration in Jessie Dobson's 1954 biography of William Clift, where it is acknowledged to Commander Walter Raleigh Gilbert of Compton Castle, Devon; but I have been unable to establish contact with Commander Gilbert or his heirs.

The portrait of Captain Sir Everard Home (p.104) was made available to me by Peter Hughes, along with a photocopy of Home's bookplate (p.130). The portrait appeared in a 1931 publication of the Royal Horticultural Society, where it was acknowledged to Miss Amy Watson.

To any persons whose copyright may have been unwittingly infringed, I extend my apologies and the hope that the use of their material in this book will be seen as fitting tribute to the subjects concerned.

INDEX

All roads in Abrantes seem to lead up towards the castle, from which the Allied forces watched the discomfiture of the Spanish invaders.

The parish church in Bodmin is dedicated to St Petroc. Here William Clift was baptised on 12 April 1775.

Hong Kong was ceded to Britain in the treaty which ended the Opium War. For a century and a half it was a combined naval base and commercial centre: in this 1970 photograph a destroyer seeking deep water under its keel passes junks heading for the protection of a typhoon shelter.

The statue of John Hunter by Weekes dominates the entrance hall of the Royal College of Surgeons, which celebrated the bicentenary of his Museum and its Board of Trustees in October 1999.

John Crump's painting of Kapiti from the north, in the possession of the Wellington Club, captures the scene that attracted Te Rauparaha to the island on his 1819 journey with a Ngapuhi war party.

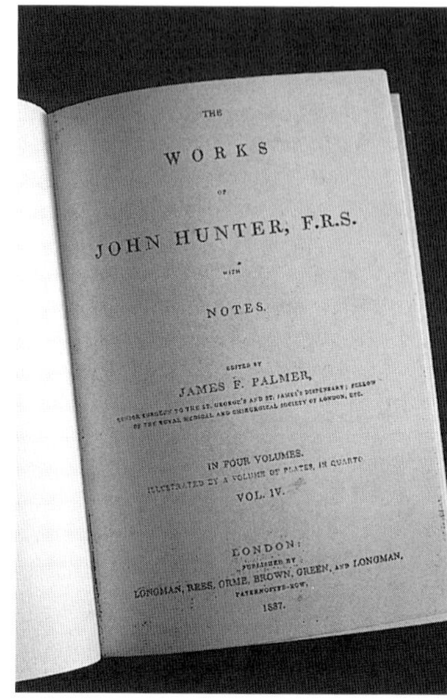

James Palmer published the first collection of the works of John Hunter in 1837, shortly before migrating to Australia.

The appearance of this farmhouse near Punhete is little different from those which greeted John Hunter when he established a 'temporary' in the town in 1762.

John Hunter found Tancos a suitable spot for a forward hospital, despite a heavy workload during August 1762.

SOUPS
BEST-EVER SOUPS RECIPES

SOUPS

BEST-EVER SOUPS RECIPES

maj 2007

bay books

RECIPE PLANNER

Use the following table to select your best-ever Soup recipe. The recipes have been grouped into appropriate classifications and the portion size of each recipe is clearly shown. Choose your soup and then turn to the appropriate page to find your clear and concise recipe together with a large-format picture of the finished dish.

BEEF, LAMB & PORK

RECIPE	PAGE	PORTIONS
Beef consomme	113	4-6
Beef pho	114	4
Chickpea, chorizo and pork rib soup	125	6-8
Grilled Italian sausage and vegetable soup	133	4
Hot and sour lime soup with beef	134	4
Lamb and pasta soup	141	6-8
Long and short noodle soup	145	6
Moroccan lamb, chickpea and coriander soup	146	4-6
Oxtail soup with stout and vegetables	150	4
Pea and ham soup	153	6-8
Pork and buttered corn ramen soup	154	4
Pork congee	157	4-6
Rustic hot pot	158	4
Scotch broth	161	8
Spaghetti and meatball soup	162	4
Spicy lamb soup	166	4-6
Vietnamese beef soup	170	4
Beef and beet borscht	189	4

CHICKEN & POULTRY

RECIPE	PAGE	PORTIONS
Curried chicken noodle soup	35	4
Avgolemono with chicken	110	4
Chicken and couscous soup	117	6
Chicken and galangal soup	118	4
Chicken and vegetable soup	121	6-8
Chicken, mushroom and Madeira soup	122	4
Creamy chicken and corn soup	126	4-6
Duck, shiitake mushrooms and rice noodle broth	129	4-6
Five-spice duck and somen noodle soup	130	4
Thai-style chicken and coconut soup	137	4
Jungle soup	138	4
Lemon chicken soup	142	4
Mulligatawny soup	149	4-6
Spicy chicken broth with coriander pasta	165	4
Tom kha gai	169	4
Miso soup with chicken and udon noodles	182	4

FISH & SEAFOOD

RECIPE	PAGE	PORTIONS
Bouillabaisse	12	4-6
Clam chowder	15	4
Lobster bisque	16	4
Mediterranean fish soup	19	6-8
Prawn gumbo	20	4
Saffron fish soup	23	4
Seafood ravioli in gingery soup	24	4

VEGETABLES & VEGETARIAN

SOUP SUCCESS

There's nothing quite like homemade soup. It's enjoyable and surprisingly easy to make if you follow a few commonsense rules, and can be dressed up or down to suit just about any occasion.

The French quotation states 'soup is to dinner what the gateway is to a building', meaning that the soup should be chosen carefully to lead the diners into the meal. With some soups, such as consommés and light broths, this is still the case, but many others have become delicious, nutritious, flavour-packed meals in their own right. Today there are many different types of soup, varying in preparation, creaminess and consistency. We have broths, chowders, bouillons, consommés, as well as all manner of creamy soups.

The story goes that the most famous soup of all, Minestrone, was first tasted during the Crusades when Italian soldiers boiled up meat in water to make a simple broth, then asked the neighbouring villagers to contribute vegetables and herbs. Such humble beginnings for one of the world's most popular dishes.

STOCK SECRETS

While soup is the ideal vehicle for using up odds and ends from the refrigerator, it is only as good as its ingredients, and the backbone of any good soup is its stock. There are several alternatives when choosing stock. You can use home-made, fresh or frozen stock available from some delicatessens or poultry shops, or tetra packs or cubes from the supermarket. The best stock will be home-made or fresh and, as it can be frozen, it is a good idea to cook up large quantities every time. Tetra packs are convenient, as are stock cubes; however, check the labels and choose cubes made from natural ingredients with no added MSG. Commercial stocks always tend to be much saltier than home-made, so taste the soup before seasoning with salt and pepper. Always season soup at the end of the cooking time, as long cooking concentrates the flavours.

Try to use the flavour stock called for in the recipe. A beef stock would be overpowering in a recipe that calls for chicken stock, although vegetarians might prefer to use vegetable stock in all their soups.

PUREEING AND STRAINING

Many soups are puréed before serving and there is a sensible way to go about this. Let the soup cool a little first, so that it is safe if it

Clear soups can be strained through a sieve lined with damp muslin.

Some soups thicken on standing and need to be diluted when they are reheated.

splashes. Cool it quickly by pouring it into a bowl, then wash the pan to take the puréed soup for reheating. Purée in either a food processor or a blender – a blender will give a finer result, though it tends to aerate the soup slightly. Always purée in batches, never filling the processor above halfway.

Occasionally, recipes ask for the soup to be strained, particularly if making the stock is part of the recipe. A fine sieve (not a colander) is usually adequate. Some clear soups need more than one straining, through a sieve lined with damp muslin. If you don't have muslin, use a clean damp chux (kitchen cloth).

AHEAD OF TIME

Many soups can be made in advance and do, in fact, benefit from overnight refrigeration as the flavours develop. Use commonsense to determine if any of the ingredients will not store well, for example if the soup has cream, add it when you are reheating for serving. The same goes for pasta; for instance, if you add the pasta to Minestrone, then leave it to sit around, it will be unpleasantly soggy. Generally, soups can be kept for up to 3 days in the refrigerator, or frozen in airtight containers or freezer bags for up to 1–3 months. A lot of soups become very thick on standing and need to be diluted when reheated. Use more of the same stock, water or cream, as appropriate. The seasoning will also need to be adjusted.

SIMMERING SOUPS

Most recipes call for a heavy-based pan for making soup. This is so that the pan distributes heat evenly and prevents anything 'catching' on the bottom. A wide, shallow pan will allow too much evaporation. The recipe will state if the pan should be covered. If it is not to be covered the soup will simmer and, as the liquid evaporates off it, it will reduce down and thicken. So, if your soup is still a little thin, simply simmer it uncovered for a while. Most soups are cooked at a gentle simmer, meaning that the surface of the soup is barely moving, while a simmer means the soup will be moving faster but without bubbles breaking the surface. Boiling is when bubbles actively break the surface of the soup. Watch the soup and adjust the heat accordingly. If the recipe says to partially cover the pan, tilt the lid at an angle so that there is a gap for steam to escape.

Bubbles will be breaking on the surface when the soup is boiling.

Tilt the lid at an angle if the recipe calls for a partially covered pan.

Soup is a dish whose sum is definitely greater than its parts. And one of its most important parts is stock. A good stock makes the difference between an ordinary and a spectacular soup, giving full-bodied flavours and a sound base for the other ingredients. If you are looking at these recipes and thinking the cooking times seeming very long and it all looks like too much trouble, think again. It doesn't take long to chop up the ingredients and then you can leave your stock to simmer lazily while you get on with other things.

BEEF STOCK

2 kg (4 lb) beef bones; 2 unpeeled carrots, chopped; 2 unpeeled onions, quartered; 2 tablespoons tomato paste; 2 sticks celery, leaves included, chopped; 1 bouquet garni, 12 black peppercorns

1 Preheat the oven to hot 210°C (415°F/Gas 6–7). Put the bones in a baking dish and bake for 30 minutes, turning occasionally. Add the carrot and onion and cook for a further 20 minutes. Allow to cool.

2 Put the bones, carrot and onion in a large, heavy-based pan. Drain the excess fat from the baking dish and pour 1 cup (250 ml/8 fl oz) of water into the dish. Stir to dissolve any juices; add the liquid to the pan.

3 Add the tomato paste, celery and 10 cups (2.5 litres/85 fl oz) water. Bring to the boil, skimming the surface as required and add the bouquet garni and peppercorns. Reduce the heat to low and simmer gently for four hours. Skim the froth from the surface regularly.

4 Ladle the stock in batches into a fine sieve sitting over a bowl. Gently press the solids with a ladle to extract all the liquid. Discard the bones and vegetables and set aside to cool. Refrigerate until cold and spoon off any fat that has set on top. At this stage you can reduce the stock to concentrate its flavour (dilute before using) and store in the refrigerator for up to 2 days or in the freezer for up to 6 months.

Beef stock, chicken stock, fish stock, vegetable stock

CHICKEN STOCK

2 kg (4 lb) chicken bones; 2 unpeeled onions, quartered; 2 unpeeled carrots, chopped; 2 sticks celery, leaves included, chopped; 1 bouquet garni; 12 black peppercorns

1 Put the chicken bones, onion, carrot, celery and 14 cups (3.5 litres/118 fl oz) of water in a large, heavy-based pan. Bring slowly to the boil. Skim the surface as required and add the bouquet garni and peppercorns. Reduce the heat to low and simmer gently for 3 hours. Skim the froth from the surface regularly.

2 Ladle the stock in batches into a fine sieve sitting over a bowl. Gently press the solids with a ladle to extract all the liquid. Let the stock cool, then refrigerate until cold and spoon off any fat that has set on the top. At this stage you can reduce the stock to concentrate its flavour (dilute before using) and store in the refrigerator for up to 2 days or in the freezer for up to 6 months.

FISH STOCK

2 kg (4 lb) chopped fish bones, heads and tails; 1 stick celery, leaves included, roughly chopped; 1 onion, chopped; 1 unpeeled carrot, chopped; 1 leek, sliced; 1 bouquet garni; 12 black peppercorns

1 Place the fish bones, celery, onion, carrot, leek and 8 cups (2 litres/68 fl oz) water in a large, heavy-based pan. Bring slowly to the boil. Skim the surface as required and add the bouquet garni and peppercorns. Reduce the heat to low and simmer very gently for 20 minutes. Skim the froth from the surface regularly.

2 Ladle the stock in batches into a sieve line with damp muslin sitting over a bowl. To keep a clear fish stock, do not press the solids, but simply allow the stock to strain undisturbed. Allow to cool, then store in the refrigerator for up to 2 days or in the freezer for up to 6 months.

VEGETABLE STOCK

1 tablespoon oil; 1 onion, chopped; 2 leeks, chopped; 4 carrots, chopped; 2 parsnips, chopped; 4 sticks celery, leaves included, chopped; 2 bay leaves; 1 bouquet garni; 4 unpeeled cloves garlic; 8 black peppercorns

1 Heat the oil in a large, heavy-based pan and add the onion, leek, carrot, parsnip and celery. Cover and cook for 5 minutes without colouring. Add 12 cups (3 litres/118 fl oz) of water. Bring to the boil. Skim the surface if required, and add the bay leaves, bouquet garni, garlic and peppercorns. Reduce the heat to low and simmer for 1 hour. Skim the froth from the surface of the stock regularly.

2 Ladle the stock in batches into a fine sieve sitting over a bowl. Gently press the solids to extract all the liquid.

3 Allow the stock to cool, then refrigerate until cold and spoon off any fat that has set on the top. At this stage you can reduce the stock to concentrate its flavour (dilute before using) and store in the refrigerate for up to 2 days or in the freezer for up to 6 months.

If you are preparing soup to serve as a dinner party starter or as a main course meal for the family, liven it up a little by adding bowls of accompaniments in the centre of the table. People can pick and choose what to add to their own bowl of soup. Croutons and Garlic Sippets are a delicious way to add extra texture and interest to just about any soup. Rouille and Aioli are best known as creamy, garlicky toppings for fish soups. Harissa is great for spicing up pumpkin soup and Pesto is perfect on thick vegetable soups. You could try serving toppings with stews as well.

AIOLI

Put 2 egg yolks in a food processor. Add 3 peeled, crushed cloves of garlic and 2 teaspoons lemon juice and process for 20 seconds. With the motor running add 250 ml (1 cup/8 fl oz) light olive oil in a thin steady stream and continue processing until the mixture is thick and creamy. Add 2 extra teaspoons of lemon juice and season to taste. Aioli is served in dollops on top of soups and can be stored in an airtight container in the refrigerator for up to 3 weeks.

GARLIC SIPPETS

Trim the crusts from 3 slices of white or brown bread and cut the bread into small cubes. Heat 60 ml (1/4 cup/2 fl oz) olive oil in a small, heavy-based pan. Add 1–2 crushed cloves of garlic. When the oil is moderately hot add the bread cubes in batches. Cook until golden and crisp, then remove from the pan with a slotted spoon and leave to drain on paper towels while frying the rest. Sprinkle over soup.

PESTO

Put 2–3 cloves of garlic, 60 g (2 cups/2 oz) of fresh basil leaves, 50 g (1/2 cup) of freshly grated Parmesan cheese, 2 tablespoons toasted pinenuts and 125 ml (1/2 cup/4 fl oz) of olive oil in a food processor. Process to form a paste, adding a little extra oil to thin if necessary. Spoon the pesto sparingly over soup in serving bowls. Store in an airtight, screw-top jar. Pack the pesto firmly into the jar and pour in enough extra olive oil to cover the surface. Refrigerate for up to 2 weeks.

ROUILLE

Remove the crusts from 4 thick slices of white bread. Put the bread in a bowl and just cover with water. Leave to soak for 5 minutes then drain, squeezing out the water. Put the bread in a food processor with 4 cloves of garlic, 2 chopped red chillies, 2 egg yolks, salt and pepper. Process for 20 seconds and then, with the motor still running, add 185 ml (3/4 cup/6 fl oz) of olive oil in a thin steady stream. Process until thick and creamy, adding 1 small peeled red capsicum (pepper) if you like. Serve in dollops on top of fish soups.

Hint: To peel a capsicum, cut in half and remove the seeds and membrane. Brush the skin with a little oil and grill (broil), skin side up, under high heat until the skin blackens. Leave to cool under a clean tea towel, then peel away the skin and discard.

HARISSA

Split 100 g (3 1/2 oz) dried red chillies in half and remove the seeds—wear rubber or cotton gloves to do this or later you'll rub your eyes or mouth and find them smarting with hot chilli.

Place the chillies in hot water to soften and rehydrate slightly. Drain the chillies and put them in a food processor or blender with 6 cloves of garlic, 4 tablespoons salt, 50 g (½ cup/1¾ oz) of ground coriander and 35 g (⅓ cup/1¼ oz) of ground cumin. Process for 30 seconds. Add 170 ml (⅔ cup/5¾ fl oz) of olive oil in a thin steady stream, processing as you do so until the mixture forms a paste. Store in an airtight screw-top jar in the refrigerator. Add sufficient Harissa to enhance the flavour of the soup, stirring in a little at a time.

CROUTONS

Discard the crusts from 3–4 slices of white or brown bread. Combine 2–3 tablespoons olive oil and 1–2 peeled, crushed cloves of garlic in a small bowl, then use to brush both sides of the bread. Cut the bread into small cubes and put them on an oven tray. Bake in a preheated 180°C (350°F/Gas 4) oven for 10–15 minutes, or until golden. Allow to cool before serving on top of soups.

Variations: Omit the garlic or add ½–1 teaspoon of any ground spice to the oil for an alternative flavour. Croutons can also be made without using any oil. Simply toast the bread cubes in the oven until golden.

BOUILLABAISSE

INGREDIENTS

4–6 tomatoes
500 g (1 lb) raw king prawns
1 raw lobster tail
1–2 fish heads
1 cup (250 ml/8 fl oz) red wine
3 onions, finely chopped
6 cloves garlic, crushed
3 bay leaves
1/4 cup (60 ml/2 fl oz) olive oil
1 leek, finely sliced
1/4 cup (60 g/2 oz) tomato paste
small piece of orange rind
500 g (1 lb) white fish fillet, cut into small pieces
12 mussels, firmly closed, scrubbed and beards removed
200 g (6 1/2 oz) scallops with corals
1/2 cup (30 g/1 oz) chopped parsley
1/4 cup (15 g/1/2 oz) shredded basil leaves

1 Score a cross in the base of each tomato. Cover with boiling water for 1 minute, plunge in cold water, drain and peel away the skins.

2 To make the fish stock, peel and devein prawns and set shells, heads and tails aside. Shell lobster tail, keeping shell and chopping meat. Put lobster shell, fish heads, prawn shells, heads and tails in a large pan. Add wine, 1 onion, 2 cloves garlic, 1 bay leaf and 2 cups (500 ml/16 fl oz) of water. Bring to the boil, reduce heat and simmer for 20 minutes. Strain through a fine sieve, reserving stock.

3 Heat oil in a large, heavy-based pan. Add leek and remaining onion and garlic. Cover and simmer, stirring occasionally, over low heat for 20 minutes, or until browned. Add the tomato, remaining bay leaves, tomato paste and orange rind and stir well. Remove lid and continue to cook for 10 minutes, stirring occasionally. Add the reserved fish stock, bring to the boil, reduce the heat and simmer for 10 minutes, stirring occasionally.

4 Add prawns, lobster, fish pieces, mussels and scallops. Simmer, covered, for 4–5 minutes. Discard any unopened mussels, the rind and bay leaves. Add the herbs and season to taste with salt and freshly ground black pepper. The Bouillabaisse is shown here with a bowlful of Rouille, a delicious accompaniment.

CLAM CHOWDER

INGREDIENTS

1.5 kg (3 lb 5 oz) fresh clams (vongole) in shell
1 tablespoon oil
3 rashers bacon, chopped
1 onion, chopped
1 garlic clove, crushed
4 potatoes, cubed
310 ml (1 $^1/_4$ cups) fish stock
500 ml (2 cups) milk
125 ml ($^1/_2$ cup) cream
15 g ($^1/_4$ cup) chopped fresh parsley

1 Discard any clams which are already open. Put the remainder in a large heavy-based pan with 250 ml (1 cup/8 fl oz) water and simmer, covered, over low heat for 5 minutes, or until the shells open (discard any clams which do not open during cooking). Strain the liquid and reserve. Remove the clam meat from the shells, discarding the shells.

2 Heat the oil in a clean pan and then add the bacon, onion and garlic. Cook, stirring, until the onion is soft and the bacon golden. Add the potato and stir to combine.

3 Measure the reserved clam liquid and add enough water to make it up to 310 ml (1 $^1/_4$ cups/10 $^1/_2$ fl oz). Add this to the pan with the stock and milk. Bring to the boil and then reduce the heat, cover and simmer for 20 minutes, or until the potato is tender.

4 Uncover and leave to simmer for a further 10 minutes, or until reduced and slightly thickened. Add the cream, clam meat, salt and pepper to taste and parsley. Heat through gently before serving but do not allow to boil or the flavour will be impaired.

LOBSTER BISQUE

INGREDIENTS

400 g (13 oz) raw lobster tail
100 g (3$^1/_2$ oz) butter, softened
7 spring onions, chopped
1 onion, chopped
1 carrot, chopped
4 cups (1 litre/34 fl oz) fish stock
4 sprigs parsley
1 bay leaf
4 peppercorns
$^1/_3$ cup (40 g/1$^1/_4$ oz) plain (all-purpose) flour
1$^3/_4$ cups (440 ml/14 fl oz) tomato paste (purée)
1 tablespoon sherry, optional
$^1/_2$ cup (125 ml/4 fl oz) cream
pinch of nutmeg
2 teaspoons chopped tarragon

1 Cut the lobster tail in half lengthways. Melt half the butter in a pan, add the spring onion and onion and cook for 5 minutes, or until soft but not coloured. Add the carrot and cook for 2 minutes. Add the lobster halves, fish stock, parsley, bay leaf, peppercorns and 2$^1/_2$ cups (600 ml/20 fl oz) of water. Bring to the boil, reduce the heat and simmer for 20 minutes, skimming the surface as required.

2 Remove the lobster from the stock, cool slightly and take the meat from the shells. Crush the shells and return to the pan. Continue simmering for a further 40 minutes. Strain the stock, then strain again through a sieve lined with 2 layers of damp muslin.

3 Cut some thin slices from the lobster to use as a garnish and set aside. In a blender, blend the remaining lobster flesh with a little of the strained stock until smooth. Mix the flour and remaining butter to a paste. Add the puréed lobster to the pan along with the flour paste, tomato purée, sherry, cream, nutmeg and salt and pepper, to taste. Mix well.

4 Add the tarragon and remaining stock and cook, stirring continuously, over high heat until the soup boils and thickens. Reduce the heat and simmer gently for 5 minutes. Season to taste and serve garnished with the reserved lobster and some sprigs of tarragon, if you want.

MEDITERRANEAN FISH SOUP

INGREDIENTS

1 kg (2 lb 4 oz) white fish fillets
60 ml (1/4 cup) olive oil
2 large onions, chopped
1–2 garlic cloves, crushed
4 large tomatoes, peeled, seeded and chopped
2 tablespoons tomato paste (purée)
6 tablespoons chopped gherkins
1 tablespoon chopped capers
1 tablespoon pitted and chopped green olives
1 tablespoon pitted and chopped black olives
750 ml (3 cups) fish stock
250 ml (1 cup) white wine
1 bay leaf
15 g (1/4 cup) chopped fresh basil
60 g (1 cup) chopped fresh parsley

1 Remove the skin and bones from the fish and chop into bite-sized pieces. Heat the oil in a large heavy-based pan and cook the onion and garlic for 8 minutes until soft.

2 Stir in the tomato and paste. Stir for 2–3 minutes, or until the tomato is soft. Stir in the gherkins and half the capers and olives.

3 Add the fish, stock, wine and bay leaf and season. Bring slowly to the boil, reduce the heat and simmer for 10–12 minutes, or until the fish is just cooked. Stir in the herbs. Add the remaining capers and olives. Serve.

PRAWN GUMBO

INGREDIENTS

2 tablespoons olive oil
1 large onion, finely chopped
3 garlic cloves, crushed
1 red capsicum (pepper), chopped
4 rashers bacon, chopped
1 1/2 teaspoons dried thyme
2 teaspoons dried oregano
1 teaspoon paprika
1/2 teaspoon cayenne pepper
60 ml (1/4 cup) sherry
1 litre (4 cups) fish stock
100 g (1/2 cup) long-grain rice
2 bay leaves
400 g (14 oz) can chopped tomatoes
150 g (5 1/2 oz) okra, thinly sliced
850 g (1 lb 14 oz) medium raw prawns (shrimp), peeled and deveined
3 tablespoons finely chopped flat-leaf (Italian) parsley

1 Heat the oil in a large saucepan over low heat. Cook the onion, garlic, capsicum and bacon for 5 minutes, or until soft. Stir in the herbs and spices. Season. Add the sherry and cook until evaporated, then add the stock and 500 ml (2 cups) water. Bring to the boil. Add the rice and bay leaves, reduce the heat and simmer, covered, for 20 minutes.

2 Add the tomato and okra. Simmer, covered, for 20–25 minutes. Stir in the prawns and parsley and simmer for 5 minutes, or until the prawns are cooked through.

SAFFRON FISH SOUP

INGREDIENTS

1 kg (2 lb) white fish bones (heads and trimmings), chopped
2 cups (500 ml/16 fl oz) dry white wine
1 onion, chopped
1 carrot, chopped
1 stick celery, chopped
1 bay leaf
6 black peppercorns
3/4 teaspoon saffron threads
50 g (1 3/4 oz) butter
1/4 cup (30 g/1 oz) plain (all-purpose) flour
12 scallops, trimmed
250 g (8 oz) boneless white fish fillets, cut into cubes
1 cup (250 ml/8 fl oz) cream

1 To make the saffron fish stock, place the fish bones, 3 cups (750 ml/24 fl oz) of water, the wine, onion, carrot, celery, bay leaf and peppercorns in a large pan. Bring to the boil slowly, skimming the surface as required. Simmer, covered, for 20 minutes. Strain and discard the fish and vegetables. Take 4 cups (1 litre) of the hot stock and stir in the saffron threads. (If you have any stock leftover at this stage, you can simply freeze it for use in another recipe.)

2 Melt the butter in a large pan and stir in the flour. Cook, stirring continuously, over low heat for 3 minutes but do not allow the mixture to colour. Remove from the heat and gradually pour in the reserved fish stock. Return to the heat and stir continuously until the mixture boils and thickens slightly. Add the scallops and fish cubes, bring back to the boil and simmer for 1–2 minutes.

3 Stir in the cream and reheat gently, but do not allow the soup to boil. Season to taste with salt and freshly ground white pepper. Garnish with sprigs of chervil, if you want.

SEAFOOD RAVIOLI IN GINGERY SOUP

INGREDIENTS

8 raw prawns (shrimp)
1 carrot, chopped
1 onion, chopped
1 celery stick, chopped
3 spring onions, thinly sliced
6 cm (2½ inch) piece fresh ginger, thinly shredded
1 tablespoon mirin
1 teaspoon kecap manis
1 tablespoon soy sauce
4 large scallops
100 g (3½ oz) boneless white fish fillet
1 egg white
200 g (6½ oz) round gow gee wrappers
⅓ cup (10 g/¼ oz) fresh coriander (cilantro) leaves

1 To make the soup, peel the prawns, reserve 4 for the ravioli filling and chop the rest into small pieces and reserve. Put the prawn heads and shells in a large pan, cook over high heat until starting to brown, then cover with 1 litre water. Add the carrot, onion and celery, bring to the boil, reduce the heat and simmer for 10 minutes. Strain and discard the prawn heads, shells and vegetables. Return the stock to a clean pan and add the spring onion, ginger, mirin, kecap manis and soy sauce. Set aside.

2 To make the ravioli, chop the whole reserved prawns with the scallops and fish in a food processor until smooth. Add enough egg white to bind. Lay half the gow gee wrappers on a work surface and place a rounded teaspoon of filling in the centre of each. Brush the edges with water. Top each with another wrapper and press the edges to seal, eliminating air bubbles as you go. Trim with a fluted cutter. Cover with plastic wrap.

3 Bring a large pan of water to the boil. Meanwhile, heat the stock and leave simmering. Just prior to serving, drop a few ravioli at a time into the boiling water. Cook for 2 minutes, remove with a slotted spoon and divide among heated bowls. Cook the chopped reserved prawns in the same water for 2 minutes; drain. Pour the hot stock over the ravioli and serve, sprinkled with the chopped cooked prawns and coriander leaves.

SMOKED HADDOCK CHOWDER

INGREDIENTS

500 g (1 lb) smoked haddock
1 potato, diced
1 stick celery, diced
1 onion, finely chopped
50 g ($1\frac{3}{4}$ oz) butter
1 rasher bacon, rind removed and finely chopped
2 tablespoons plain (all-purpose) flour
$\frac{1}{2}$ teaspoon dried mustard
$\frac{1}{2}$ teaspoon Worcestershire sauce
1 cup (250 ml/8 fl oz) milk
$\frac{1}{2}$ cup (15 g/$\frac{1}{2}$ oz) chopped parsley
$\frac{1}{4}$ cup (60 ml/2 fl oz) cream (optional)

1 To make the fish stock, put the fish in a frying pan, cover with water and bring to the boil. Reduce the heat and simmer for 8 minutes, or until the fish flakes easily. Drain, reserving the fish stock, then peel, bone and flake the fish. Set aside.

2 Put the potato, celery and onion in a medium pan and pour over enough reserved fish stock to cover the vegetables. Bring to the boil, reduce the heat and simmer for 8 minutes, or until the vegetables are tender. Set aside.

3 Melt the butter in a large pan, add the bacon and cook, stirring, for 3 minutes. Add the flour, mustard and Worcestershire sauce and stir until combined. Cook for 1 minute. Remove from the heat and gradually pour in the milk, stirring continuously, until smooth. Return to the heat and stir for 5 minutes, until the mixture comes to the boil and has thickened. Stir in the vegetables and remaining stock, then add the parsley and fish. Simmer over low heat for 5 minutes, or until heated through. Taste for seasoning and serve with some cream, if you want.

SPICY SEAFOOD AND ROASTED CORN SOUP

INGREDIENTS

2 corn cobs (700 g/1 lb 9 oz)
1 tablespoon olive oil
1 red onion, finely chopped
1 small red chilli, finely chopped
1/2 teaspoon ground allspice
4 vine-ripened tomatoes, peeled and finely diced
1.5 litres (6 cups) fish stock or light chicken stock
300 g (10 1/2 oz) boneless firm white fish fillets (ling or perch), diced
200 g (7 oz) fresh crab meat
200 g (7 oz) peeled raw prawns (shrimp), roughly chopped
1 tablespoon lime juice

Quesadillas
4 flour tortillas (19 cm/7 1/2 in)
85 g (2/3 cup) grated Cheddar cheese
4 tablespoons coriander (cilantro) leaves
2 tablespoons olive oil

1 Preheat the oven to 200°C (400°F/Gas 6). Peel back the husks on the corn cobs (making sure they stay intact at the base) and remove the silks. Fold the husks back over the corn, place in a baking dish and bake for 1 hour, or until the corn is tender.

2 Heat the oil in a large saucepan over medium heat. Add the onion and cook until soft. Add the chilli and allspice and cook for 1 minute, then add the tomato and stock and bring to the boil. Reduce the heat and simmer, covered, for 45 minutes.

3 Slice off the kernels from the corn cobs with a sharp knife, add to the soup and simmer, uncovered, for 15 minutes. Add the fish, crab and prawn meat to the soup and simmer for 5 minutes, or until the seafood is cooked. Stir in the lime juice and serve with the quesadillas, if desired.

4 To make the quesadillas, top one tortilla with half the cheese and half the coriander. Season, then top with another tortilla. Heat 1 tablespoon of the oil in a frying pan and cook the quesadilla for 30 seconds on each side, or until the cheese just begins to melt. Repeat to make the other quesadilla. Cut into wedges.

TOM YAM GOONG

INGREDIENTS

500 g (1 lb) raw prawns (shrimp)
1 tablespoon oil
2 tablespoons tom yam curry paste
2 tablespoons tamarind purée
2 teaspoons ground turmeric
1 teaspoon chopped small red chillies
4 kaffir lime (makrut) leaves, shredded
2 tablespoons fish sauce
2 tablespoons lime juice
2 teaspoons grated palm sugar or soft brown sugar
kaffir lime (makrut) leaves, shredded, extra, to garnish

1 Peel the prawns, leaving the tails intact. Devein the prawns, starting at the head end. Reserve the shells and heads. Cover and refrigerate the prawn meat. Heat the oil in a wok or large saucepan and cook the shells and heads over medium heat, stirring frequently, for 10 minutes, or until the shells turn orange.

2 Add 1 cup (250 ml/8 fl oz) water and the tom yam paste to the pan. Bring to the boil and cook for 5 minutes, or until reduced slightly. Add another 2 litres water, bring to the boil, reduce the heat and simmer for 20 minutes. Strain, discarding the shells and heads, and return the stock to the pan.

3 Add the tamarind, turmeric, chilli and lime leaves to the pan, bring to the boil and cook for 2 minutes. Add the prawns and cook for 5 minutes, or until pink. Stir in the fish sauce, lime juice and sugar. Garnish with shredded kaffir lime leaves.

ASIAN NOODLE SOUP

INGREDIENTS

8 dried Chinese mushrooms
100 g (3 $^1/_2$ oz) dried rice vermicelli
800 g (1 lb 12 oz) Chinese broccoli, cut into 5 cm (2 inch) lengths
8 fried tofu puffs, cut into strips
125 g (4 $^1/_2$ oz) bean sprouts
1 litre (4 cups) vegetable stock
2 tablespoons light soy sauce
1 $^1/_2$ tablespoons Chinese rice wine
3 spring onions (scallions), finely chopped
coriander (cilantro) leaves, to serve

1. Place the dried mushrooms in a bowl, cover with boiling water and soak for 15 minutes. Drain, reserving 125 ml ($^1/_2$ cup) of the liquid. Squeeze the mushrooms to remove any excess liquid. Discard the stems and thinly slice the caps.

2. Soak the vermicelli in boiling water for 5 minutes. Drain. Divide the vermicelli, broccoli, tofu puffs and bean sprouts among the four serving bowls.

3. Place the reserved mushroom liquid, stock, soy sauce, rice wine, spring onion and mushrooms in a saucepan and bring to the boil. Cook, covered, for 10 minutes.

4. Ladle the soup into the serving bowls and garnish with the coriander leaves.

CURRIED CHICKEN NOODLE SOUP

INGREDIENTS

175 g (6 oz) dried thin egg noodles
2 tablespoons peanut oil
2 chicken breasts (about 250 g/9 oz each)
1 onion, sliced
1 small fresh red chilli, seeded and finely chopped
1 tablespoon finely chopped fresh ginger
2 tablespoons Indian curry powder
3 cups (750 ml/25 fl oz) chicken stock
800 ml (27 fl oz) coconut milk
300 g (10½ oz) baby bok choy, cut into long strips
⅓ cup (20 g/¾ oz) fresh basil, torn

1. Cook the noodles in a large saucepan of boiling water for 3–4 minutes, or until cooked. Drain well and set aside. Wipe the saucepan clean and dry.

2. Heat the oil in the dry pan and add the chicken. Cook on each side for 5 minutes, or until cooked through. Remove the chicken and keep warm.

3. Place the onion in the pan and cook over low heat for 8 minutes, or until softened but not browned. Add the chilli, ginger and curry powder and cook for a further 2 minutes. Add the chicken stock and bring to the boil. Reduce the heat and simmer for 20 minutes. Thinly slice the chicken on the diagonal.

4. Add the coconut milk to the saucepan and simmer for 10 minutes. Add the bok choy and cook for 3 minutes, then stir in the basil.

5. To serve, divide the noodles among four deep serving bowls. Top with slices of chicken and ladle in the soup. Serve immediately.

BROTH WITH RAVIOLI

INGREDIENTS

750 ml (3 cups) vegetable or chicken stock
250 g (9 oz) spinach and ricotta ravioli
85 g (3 oz) snowpeas (mangetout), sliced on the diagonal
2 tablespoons chopped flat-leaf (Italian) parsley
2 tablespoons chopped basil
grated Parmesan cheese, to garnish

1 Place the stock in a large heavy-based saucepan and bring to the boil. Add the ravioli and cook for 8–10 minutes, or until the pasta is al dente.

2 Season to taste with salt and pepper, and stir in the snowpeas, parsley and basil. Pour the soup into two bowls and sprinkle with grated Parmesan before serving.

CABBAGE SOUP

INGREDIENTS

100 g ($^1/_2$ cup) dried haricot beans
125 g ($4^1/_2$ oz) bacon, cubed
40 g ($1^1/_2$ oz) butter
1 carrot, sliced
1 onion, chopped
1 leek, white part only, roughly chopped
1 turnip, peeled and chopped
bouquet garni
1.25 litres (5 cups) chicken stock
400 g (14 oz) white cabbage, finely shredded

1 Soak the beans overnight in cold water. Drain, put in a saucepan and cover with cold water. Bring to the boil and simmer for 5 minutes, then drain. Put the bacon in the same saucepan, cover with water and simmer for 5 minutes. Drain and pat dry with paper towels.

2 Melt the butter in a large heavy-based saucepan, add the bacon and cook for 5 minutes, without browning. Add the beans, carrot, onion, leek and turnip and cook for 5 minutes. Add the bouquet garni and chicken stock and bring to the boil. Cover and simmer for 30 minutes. Add the cabbage, uncover and simmer for 30 minutes, or until the beans are tender. Remove the bouquet garni before serving and season to taste.

CAPSICUM, SPINACH AND CHICKPEA SOUP

INGREDIENTS

1 tablespoon olive oil
8 spring onions (scallions), finely sliced
1 red capsicum (pepper)
1 garlic clove, crushed
1 teaspoon cumin seeds
375 ml (1$^1/_2$ cups) Italian tomato passata
750 ml (3 cups) vegetable or beef stock
300 g (10$^1/_2$ oz) tin chickpeas, rinsed and drained
2 teaspoons red wine vinegar
1–2 teaspoons sugar
100 g (3$^1/_2$ oz) baby English spinach leaves

1. Heat the oil in a large heavy-based saucepan and stir in the spring onion. Reduce the heat and cook, covered, for 2–3 minutes, or until softened. Meanwhile, remove the seeds and membrane from the capsicum and finely dice. Add the capsicum, garlic and cumin seeds to the pan and cook for 1 minute.

2. Add the passata and stock and bring the mixture to the boil. Reduce the heat and simmer for 10 minutes. Add the chickpeas, vinegar and sugar to the soup and simmer for a further 5 minutes.

3. Stir in the baby spinach and season to taste with salt and ground black pepper. Cook until the spinach begins to wilt, then serve immediately.

CARROT AND GINGER SOUP

INGREDIENTS

750 ml (3 cups) vegetable stock
1 tablespoon oil
1 onion, chopped
1 tablespoon grated fresh ginger
1 kg (2 lb 4 oz) carrots, chopped
2 tablespoons chopped coriander (cilantro) leaves

1. Place the stock in a pan and bring to the boil. Heat the oil in a large heavy-based pan, add the onion and ginger and cook for 2 minutes, or until the onion has softened.
2. Add the stock and carrots. Bring to the boil, then reduce the heat and simmer for 10–15 minutes, or until the carrot is cooked and tender.
3. Place in a blender or food processor and process in batches until smooth. Return to the pan and add a little more stock or water to thin the soup to your preferred consistency.
4. Stir in the coriander and season to taste. Heat gently before serving.

CHICKPEA, POTATO AND SPINACH SOUP

INGREDIENTS

1 litre (4 cups) vegetable stock
1 1/2 tablespoons olive oil
1 onion, finely chopped
1 large potato, cut into 1.5 cm (5/8 inch) cubes
1 1/2 teaspoons paprika
2 garlic cloves, crushed
400 g (14 oz) tin chickpeas, drained
1 large tomato, cut into small cubes
50 g (1 cup) English spinach, coarsely shredded
25 g (1/4 cup) grated Parmesan cheese

1. Place the stock in a saucepan, then cover and slowly bring to the boil. Heat the olive oil in a large heavy-based saucepan, and cook the onion for 2–3 minutes, or until soft.

2. Add the potato to the onion, and stir in the paprika, garlic and chickpeas. Add the onion mixture to the stock and bring to the boil. Stir in the tomato, and season with salt and cracked black pepper.

3. Simmer for 10 minutes, or until the potato is tender. Add the spinach and cook until wilted. Top with Parmesan, season to taste and serve.

CHILLED GARLIC AND ALMOND SOUP

INGREDIENTS

1 loaf (200 g/7 oz) day-old white Italian bread, crust removed
155 g (1 cup) whole blanched almonds
3–4 garlic cloves, chopped
125 ml (½ cup) extra virgin olive oil
80 ml (⅓ cup) sherry or white wine vinegar
315–375 ml (1¼–1½ cups) vegetable stock
2 tablespoons olive oil, extra
75 g (2½ oz) day-old white Italian bread, extra, crust removed, cut into 1 cm (½ inch) cubes
200 g (7 oz) small seedless green grapes

1 Soak the bread in cold water for 5 minutes, then squeeze out any excess liquid. Chop the almonds and garlic in a processor until well ground. Add the bread and process until the mixture is smooth.

2 With the motor running, add the olive oil in a steady slow stream until the mixture is the consistency of thick mayonnaise. Slowly add the sherry and 315 ml (1¼ cups) of the stock. Blend for 1 minute. Season with salt. Refrigerate for at least 2 hours. The soup thickens on refrigeration so you may need to add extra stock or water to thin it.

3 When ready to serve, heat the extra oil in a frying pan, add the bread cubes and toss over medium heat for 2–3 minutes, or until golden. Drain on crumpled paper towels. Serve the soup very cold, garnished with the grapes and bread cubes.

CHILLI, CORN AND RED CAPSICUM SOUP

INGREDIENTS

1 coriander (cilantro) sprig
4 cobs sweet corn
30 g (1 oz) butter
2 red capsicums (peppers), diced
1 small onion, finely chopped
1 small red chilli, finely chopped
1 tablespoon plain (all-purpose) flour
500 ml (2 cups) vegetable stock
125 ml (1/2 cup) cream

1. Trim the leaves off the coriander and finely chop the root and stems. Cut the kernels off the corn cobs.

2. Heat the butter in a saucepan over medium heat. Add the corn kernels, capsicum, onion and chilli and stir to coat in the butter. Cook, covered, over low heat, stirring occasionally, for 10 minutes, or until soft. Increase the heat to medium, add the coriander root and stem and cook, stirring, for 30 seconds, or until fragrant. Sprinkle with the flour and stir for 1 minute. Remove from the heat and gradually stir in the stock. Add 500 ml (2 cups) water and return to the heat. Bring to the boil, reduce the heat to low and simmer, covered, for 30 minutes, or until the vegetables are tender. Cool slightly.

3. Ladle 500 ml (2 cups) of the soup into a blender and purée until smooth. Return the purée to the soup in the pan, pour in the cream and gently heat until warmed through. Season. Sprinkle with the coriander leaves and serve. Delicious with grilled cheese on pitta bread.

COLD SPICY ROAST CAPSICUM SOUP

INGREDIENTS

4 red capsicums (peppers)
2 teaspoons oil
2 garlic cloves, crushed
4 spring onions (scallions), sliced
1 teaspoon finely chopped seeded chillies
425 g (15 oz) tin crushed tomatoes
125 ml (1/2 cup) chilled vegetable stock
1 teaspoon balsamic vinegar
2 tablespoons chopped basil

1. Cut the capsicums into quarters and remove the seeds and membrane. Place the capsicums skin-side up under a hot grill (broiler) and grill until the skins blacken and blister. Cool in a plastic bag, then peel away the skin and roughly chop the flesh.

2. Heat the oil in a small saucepan, add the garlic, spring onion and chilli, and cook over low heat for 1–2 minutes, or until softened.

3. Transfer to a food processor or blender, and add the capsicum, crushed tomatoes and stock. Blend until smooth, then stir in the vinegar and basil. Season to taste with salt and cracked pepper. Refrigerate, then serve cold.

CREAM OF ASPARAGUS SOUP

INGREDIENTS

1 kg (2 lb) asparagus spears
30 g (1 oz) butter
1 onion, finely chopped
1 litre (4 cups) chicken stock
1/4 cup (7 g/1/4 oz) basil leaves, chopped
1 teaspoon celery salt
1 cup (250 ml/8 fl oz) cream

1. Break off woody ends from asparagus and trim off tips. Blanch the tips in boiling water for 1–2 minutes, refresh in cold water and set aside. Chop the remaining asparagus spears into large pieces.

2. Melt the butter in a large pan and cook the onion for 3–4 minutes over medium-low heat, or until soft and golden. Add the asparagus spears and cook for 1–2 minutes, stirring continuously.

3. Add chicken stock, basil and celery salt. Bring to the boil, reduce heat and simmer gently, covered, for 30 minutes.

4. Check that the asparagus is well cooked and soft. If not, simmer for a further 10 minutes. Set aside and allow to cool slightly.

5. Pour into a processor and process in batches until smooth. Sieve into a clean pan. Return to the heat, pour in cream and gently reheat. Do not allow the soup to boil. Season to taste with salt and pepper.

6. Serve immediately, with the asparagus tips placed on top of the soup.

CREAM OF FENNEL AND LEEK SOUP

INGREDIENTS

30 g (1 oz) butter
2 large fennel bulbs, thinly sliced
2 leeks, thinly sliced
1 litre (4 cups) hot vegetable or chicken stock
2 rosemary sprigs
1/8 teaspoon ground nutmeg
80 g (1/3 cup) sour cream
25 g (1/4 cup) finely grated Parmesan cheese
1 tablespoon oil
1 leek, extra, cut in half lengthways, and cut into 4 cm (1 1/2 inch) lengths
grated Parmesan cheese, extra, to garnish
sour cream, extra, to garnish

1. Heat the butter in a large heavy-based saucepan, add the sliced fennel and leek, and cook, covered, over medium heat for 2–3 minutes, stirring occasionally.

2. Put the hot stock, rosemary sprigs and nutmeg in a saucepan and bring to the boil. Simmer over low heat for about 15 minutes, then remove the rosemary sprigs and add the fennel and leek mixture to the pan.

3. Transfer the soup to a blender or food processor and blend in batches until smooth. Return to the pan, and stir in the sour cream and Parmesan. Reheat over medium heat until hot. Season to taste with salt and cracked black pepper and keep warm.

4. Heat the oil in a frying pan and cook the extra leek for 2–3 minutes, or until soft but not browned.

5. Spoon the soup into six warm soup bowls and top with the fried leek. Garnish with the extra Parmesan and sour cream and serve immediately.

CREAM OF TOMATO SOUP

INGREDIENTS

1.25 kg (2½ lb) tomatoes
1 tablespoon oil
1 onion, chopped
1 clove garlic, chopped
1½ cups (375 ml/12 fl oz) chicken stock
2 tablespoons tomato paste (purée)
1 teaspoon sugar
1 cup (250 ml/8 fl oz) cream

1. Cut a cross in the base of each tomato. Cover with boiling water for 1 minute, plunge in iced water, drain and peel away the skins. Scoop out the seeds and discard, then roughly chop the flesh.

2. Heat the oil in a large pan and cook the onion for 3 minutes, or until soft. Add the garlic and cook for 1 minute longer. Add the tomato and cook for 5 minutes, stirring occasionally, until very soft. Stir in the stock, bring to the boil, reduce the heat and simmer for 10 minutes.

3. Cool slightly, then transfer to a food processor. Process in batches until smooth, and return to the pan. Add the tomato paste and sugar and bring to the boil, stirring continuously. Reduce the heat and stir in the cream but do not allow the soup to boil. Season to taste before serving. Serve with an extra spoonful of cream and chopped parsley, if you want.

CHICKEN AND PUMPKIN LAKSA

INGREDIENTS

Paste

2 birds eye chillies, seeded and roughly chopped

2 stems lemon grass, white part only, roughly chopped

4 red Asian shallots, peeled

1 tablespoon roughly chopped fresh ginger

1 teaspoon ground turmeric

3 candlenuts, optional

110 g (4 oz) dried rice noodle sticks

1 tablespoon peanut oil

250 g (9 oz) butternut pumpkin (squash), cut into 2 cm (1 inch) chunks

800 ml (27 fl oz) coconut milk

600 g (21 oz) chicken breast fillets, cut into cubes

2 tablespoons lime juice

1 tablespoon fish sauce

1 cup (90 g/3 oz) bean sprouts

$^1/_2$ cup (15 g/$^1/_2$ oz) torn fresh basil

$^1/_2$ cup (10 g/$^1/_2$ oz) torn fresh mint

$^1/_2$ cup (50 g/1$^3/_4$ oz) unsalted peanuts, toasted and chopped

1 lime, cut into quarters

1 Place all the paste ingredients in a food processor with 1 tablespoon water and blend until smooth.

2 Soak the noodles in boiling water for 15–20 minutes. Drain.

3 Meanwhile, heat the oil in a wok and swirl to coat. Add the paste and stir over low heat for 5 minutes, or until aromatic. Add the pumpkin and coconut milk and simmer for 10 minutes. Add the chicken and simmer for 20 minutes. Stir in the lime juice and fish sauce.

4 Divide the noodles among four deep serving bowls, then ladle the soup over them. Garnish with the bean sprouts, basil, mint, peanuts and lime.

FENNEL, ASPARAGUS AND PEA SOUP

INGREDIENTS

30 g (1 oz) butter
1½ tablespoons olive oil
1 leek, white part only, sliced
1 fennel bulb, sliced
375 g (12 oz) asparagus, cut into pieces
1 clove garlic, crushed
8 mint leaves, chopped
150 g (5 oz) shelled or frozen peas (400 g/13 oz in pods)
200 g (6½ oz) potatoes, cubed
4 cups (1 litre) chicken or vegetable stock
pinch of cayenne pepper
pinch of ground nutmeg

Mint and garlic croutons

20 g (¾ oz) butter
1 tablespoon olive oil
2 slices day-old white bread, crusts removed, cut into four
mint leaves
2 cloves garlic, sliced, soaked in cold water

1 Heat the butter and oil in a large pan and add the leek and fennel. Cook over medium heat for 8–10 minutes, then stir in the asparagus, garlic, mint, peas and potato. Cook for 1 minute longer.

2 Add enough stock to cover the vegetables, and bring to the boil. Remove 4 asparagus tips, plunge into a bowl of iced water and set aside. Reduce the heat and simmer for 15–20 minutes, or until the vegetables are tender. Cool slightly then purée in a food processor. Return to the pan with the remaining stock, cayenne pepper and nutmeg and season.

3 Preheat the oven to moderately hot 190°C (375°F/Gas 5). To make the croutons, melt the butter and oil and brush on both sides of the bread. Lay on a baking tray. Tear the mint leaves in half, and place on the bread; dry the garlic and place on the mint. Drizzle the remaining butter mixture over the top. Bake for 5–6 minutes, or until the bread is toasted and the garlic golden.

4 Gently reheat the soup and serve garnished with the croutons and the reserved asparagus tips.

FRESH MUSHROOM, SHALLOT AND SOUR CREAM SOUP

INGREDIENTS

2 tablespoons butter
100 g (about 4) French shallots, roughly chopped
3 garlic cloves, crushed
30 g (1 cup) firmly packed flat-leaf (Italian) parsley
315 ml (1 1/4 cups) vegetable or chicken stock
315 ml (1 1/4 cups) milk
600 g (1 lb 5 oz) button mushrooms
1/4 teaspoon ground nutmeg
1/4 teaspoon cayenne pepper
150 g (5 1/2 oz) light sour cream
cayenne pepper, to garnish

1 Melt the butter in a large heavy-based saucepan and add the shallots, garlic and parsley. Cook over medium heat for 2–3 minutes. Put the stock and milk in a separate saucepan and bring to the boil.

2 Gently wipe the mushrooms, then chop and add to the shallot mixture. Season with salt and pepper, and stir in the nutmeg and cayenne pepper. Cook, stirring, for 1 minute. Add the stock and milk, bring to the boil, then reduce the heat and simmer for 5 minutes. Transfer the soup to a blender or food processor and blend until smooth. Return to the pan.

3 Stir in the sour cream, adjust the seasoning and reheat gently. Serve sprinkled with cayenne pepper.

GAZPACHO

INGREDIENTS

750 g (1 1/2 lb) ripe tomatoes
1 Lebanese cucumber, chopped
1 green capsicum (pepper), chopped
2–3 cloves garlic, crushed
1–2 tablespoons finely chopped black olives (optional)
1/3 cup (80 ml/2 3/4 fl oz) red or white wine vinegar
1/4 cup (60 ml/2 fl oz) olive oil
1 tablespoon tomato paste (purée)

Accompaniments
1 onion, finely chopped
1 red capsicum (pepper), finely chopped
2 spring onions, finely chopped
1 Lebanese cucumber, finely chopped
2 hard-boiled eggs, chopped
chopped mint or parsley
Garlic and herb croutons

1 Score a cross in the base of each tomato. Cover with boiling water for 1 minute, plunge into cold water, drain and peel away the skins. Chop the flesh so finely that it is almost a purée.

2 Mix together the tomato, cucumber, capsicum, garlic, olives, vinegar, oil, and tomato paste, and season to taste. Cover and refrigerate for 2–3 hours.

3 Use 2–3 cups (750 ml/24 fl oz) of chilled water to thin the soup to your taste. Serve chilled, with the chopped onion, capsicum, spring onion, cucumber, boiled egg, herbs and croutons served separately for diners to add to their own bowls.

HEARTY MINESTRONE

INGREDIENTS

2 tablespoons olive oil
2 onions, chopped
2 rashers bacon, chopped
1 potato, chopped into large cubes
280 g (9 oz) sweet potato (kumera) , chopped into large cubes
3 carrots, sliced
250 g (8 oz) pumpkin, cubed
400 g (13 oz) cabbage, shredded
280 g (9 oz) yellow squash, sliced
220 g (7 oz) green beans, chopped
2 x 400 g (13 oz) can chopped tomatoes
6 cups (1.5 litres) chicken stock
1 teaspoon dried Italian herbs
1 teaspoon dried oregano
½ cup (80 g/2¾ oz) macaroni
300 g (10 oz) can butter beans
grated Parmesan, to serve

1 Heat the oil and cook the onion and bacon for 3–4 minutes over moderate heat, or until the onion is just brown. Reduce the heat slightly and add the potato and sweet potato. Stir and cook for 1-2 minutes. Add the carrot and pumpkin and cook for a further 1–2 minutes, stirring continuously.

2 Add the cabbage, squash, green beans, tomato, stock and herbs. Increase the heat and bring to the boil. Reduce the heat and simmer gently, cover, for 1 hour.

3 Add the macaroni and butter beans and cook for a further 10–12 minutes, or until the pasta is tender. Season to taste. Serve with Parmesan.

JERUSALEM ARTICHOKE AND ROAST GARLIC SOUP

INGREDIENTS

1 garlic head
2 tablespoons butter
1 tablespoon olive oil
1 onion, chopped
1 leek, white part only, washed and chopped
1 celery stalk, chopped
700 g (1 lb 9 oz) Jerusalem artichokes, peeled and chopped
1 small potato, chopped
1.5 litres (6 cups) vegetable or chicken stock
olive oil, to serve
finely chopped chives, to serve

1. Preheat the oven to 200°C (400°F/Gas 6). Slice the base from the head of garlic, wrap it in foil and roast for 30 minutes, or until soft. When cool enough to handle, remove from the foil and slip the cloves from the skin. Set aside.

2. In a large heavy-based saucepan, heat the butter and oil. Add the onion, leek and celery and a large pinch of salt, and cook for 10 minutes, or until soft. Add the Jerusalem artichokes, potato and garlic and cook for a further 10 minutes. Pour in the stock, bring the mixture to the boil, then reduce the heat and simmer for 30 minutes, or until the vegetables are soft.

3. Purée in a blender until smooth, and season well. Serve with a drizzle of olive oil and some chives. Delicious with warm crusty bread.

MINESTRONE

INGREDIENTS

80 g (1/2 cup) macaroni
1 tablespoon olive oil
1 leek, sliced
2 garlic cloves, crushed
1 carrot, sliced
1 waxy potato, chopped
1 zucchini (courgette), sliced
2 celery stalks, sliced
100 g (3 1/2 oz) green beans, cut into short lengths
425 g (15 oz) tin chopped tomatoes
2 litres (8 cups) vegetable or beef stock
2 tablespoons tomato paste (purée)
425 g (15 oz) tin cannellini beans, rinsed and drained
2 tablespoons chopped flat-leaf (Italian) parsley
shaved Parmesan cheese, to serve

1. Bring a saucepan of water to the boil, add the macaroni and cook for 10–12 minutes, or until tender. Drain.

2. Meanwhile, heat the oil in a large heavy-based saucepan, add the leek and garlic and cook over medium heat for 3–4 minutes.

3. Add the carrot, potato, zucchini, celery, green beans, tomato, stock and tomato paste. Bring to the boil, then reduce the heat and simmer for 10 minutes, or until the vegetables are tender.

4. Stir in the cooked pasta and cannellini beans and heat through. Spoon into warmed serving bowls and garnish with parsley and shaved Parmesan.

PIE-CRUST MUSHROOM SOUP

INGREDIENTS

400 g (14 oz) field mushrooms
60 g (2 1/4 oz) butter
1 small onion, finely chopped
1 garlic clove, crushed
30 g (1/4 cup) plain (all-purpose) flour
750 ml (3 cups) chicken stock
2 tablespoons fresh thyme leaves
2 tablespoons sherry
250 ml (1 cup) cream
1 sheet frozen puff pastry, thawed
1 egg, lightly beaten

1. Preheat the oven to 200°C (400°F/Gas 6). Roughly chop the mushrooms. Melt the butter in a pan and cook the onion for 3 minutes, until soft. Add the garlic; cook for 1 minute. Add the mushrooms; cook until soft. Sprinkle with the flour and stir for 1 minute.

2. Stir in the stock, add the thyme and bring to the boil. Reduce the heat, cover and simmer for 10 minutes. Cool and process in batches. Return to the pan, stir in the sherry and cream and pour into four ovenproof bowls.

3. Cut rounds of pastry slightly larger than the bowl tops and cover each bowl with pastry (use small deep bowls rather than wide shallow ones or the pastry may sag into the soup).

4. Seal the pastry edges and brush lightly with the beaten egg. Bake for 15 minutes, until golden and puffed.

POACHED SEAFOOD BROTH WITH SOBA NOODLES

INGREDIENTS

250 g (9 oz) dried soba noodles
8 raw prawns (shrimp)
1½ tablespoons finely chopped ginger
4 spring onions (scallions), cut on the diagonal
100 ml (3½ fl oz) light soy sauce
60 ml (¼ cup) mirin
1 teaspoon grated palm sugar or soft brown sugar
300 g (10½ oz) boneless salmon fillet, skinned and cut into 5 cm (2 in) strips
300 g (10½ oz) boneless white fish fillet, skinned and cut into 5 cm (2 in) strips
150 g (5½ oz) cleaned calamari hood, scored and cut into 3 cm (1¼ in) cubes
50 g (1¾ oz) mizuna, roughly chopped (see note)

1 Cook the noodles in a large saucepan of boiling water for 5 minutes, or until they are tender. Drain and rinse with cold water.

2 Peel and devein the prawns, reserving the shells and leaving the tails intact. Place the heads and shells in a large saucepan with the ginger, half the spring onion and 1.5 litres (6 cups) water. Bring slowly to the boil and boil for 5 minutes. Strain and discard the prawn heads, shells and spring onion. Return the stock to the pan. Add the soy sauce, mirin and palm sugar to the stock. Heat and stir to dissolve the sugar.

3 Add the seafood to the pan and poach over low heat for 2–3 minutes, or until it is just cooked. Add the remaining spring onion.

4 Divide the noodles evenly among four large bowls. Add the seafood, pour on the stock and scatter with the mizuna.

NOTE Mizuna is a salad leaf with dark green, feathery and glossy leaves. It has a mild peppery flavour. Young leaves are often used in salads or as a garnish, while older leaves are used in stir-fries or in Japanese cooking.

POTATO AND ROCKET SOUP

INGREDIENTS

1.5 litres (6 cups) vegetable or chicken stock
1.25 kg (2 lb 12 oz) desiree potatoes, chopped into small pieces
2 large garlic cloves, peeled, left whole
250 g (9 oz) rocket (arugula)
1 tablespoon extra virgin olive oil
extra rocket (arugula) leaves, to garnish (optional)
50 g (1/2 cup) shaved Parmesan cheese

1 Place the stock in a large heavy-based saucepan and bring to the boil. Add the potato and garlic and simmer over medium heat for 15 minutes, or until the potato is tender to the point of a sharp knife. Add the rocket and simmer for a further 2 minutes. Stir in the olive oil.

2 Transfer the mixture to a blender or food processor and blend in batches until smooth. Return the mixture to the pan and stir over medium heat until hot. Season to taste with salt and cracked black pepper and serve in warmed bowls. Garnish with the rocket leaves and shaved Parmesan before serving.

POTATO AND SWEET CORN CHOWDER

INGREDIENTS

6 cobs sweet corn
2 tablespoons vegetable oil
1 onion, finely diced
3 garlic cloves, crushed
1 celery stalk, diced
1 carrot, peeled and diced
2 large potatoes, peeled and diced
1 litre (4 cups) vegetable or chicken stock
2 tablespoons finely chopped flat-leaf (Italian) parsley

1. Bring a large pot of salted water to the boil, and cook the sweet corn for 5 minutes. Reserve 250 ml (1 cup) of the cooking water. Cut the corn kernels from the cob, place half in a blender with the reserved cooking water, and blend until smooth.

2. Heat the oil in a large saucepan, add the onion, garlic, celery and a large pinch of salt and cook for 5 minutes. Add the carrot and potatoes, cook for a further 5 minutes, then add the stock, corn kernels and blended corn mixture. Reduce the heat and simmer for 20 minutes, or until the vegetables are tender. Season well, and stir in the chopped parsley before serving.

PUMPKIN SOUP

INGREDIENTS

500 ml (2 cups) vegetable stock
750 g (1 ib 10 oz) butternut pumpkin (squash), cut into 1.5 cm ($^{5}/_{8}$ inch) cubes
2 onions, chopped
2 garlic cloves, halved
$^{1}/_{4}$ teaspoon ground nutmeg
60 ml ($^{1}/_{4}$ cup) cream

1 Put the stock and 500 ml (2 cups) water in a large heavy-based saucepan and bring to the boil. Add the pumpkin, onion and garlic and return to the boil. Reduce the heat slightly and cook for 15 minutes, or until the pumpkin is soft.

2 Drain the vegetables through a colander, reserving the liquid. Purée the pumpkin mixture in a blender until smooth (you may need to add some of the reserved liquid). Return the pumpkin purée to the pan and stir in enough of the reserved liquid to reach the desired consistency. Season to taste with nutmeg, salt and cracked black pepper.

3 Ladle the soup into four soup bowls and pour some cream into each bowl to create a swirl pattern on the top. Serve with warm crusty bread.

RED LENTIL, BURGHUL AND MINT SOUP

INGREDIENTS

2 tablespoons olive oil
1 large red onion, finely chopped
2 garlic cloves, crushed
2 tablespoons tomato paste (purée)
2 tomatoes, finely chopped
2 teaspoons paprika
1 teaspoon cayenne pepper
500 g (2 cups) red lentils
50 g (1/4 cup) long-grain rice
2.125 litres (8 1/2 cups) chicken stock
45 g (1/4 cup) fine burghul (bulgar wheat)
2 tablespoons chopped mint
2 tablespoons chopped flat-leaf (Italian) parsley
90 g (1/3 cup) thick natural yoghurt
1/4 preserved lemon, pulp removed, zest washed and julienned

1 Heat the oil in a saucepan over medium heat. Add the onion and garlic and cook for 2–3 minutes, or until soft. Stir in the tomato paste, tomato and spices and cook for 1 minute.

2 Add the lentils, rice and chicken stock, then cover and bring to the boil over high heat. Reduce the heat and simmer for 30–35 minutes, or until the rice is cooked.

3 Stir in the burghul and herbs, then season to taste. Divide the soup among serving bowls, garnish with yoghurt and preserved lemon and serve immediately.

NOTE This soup will thicken on standing, so if reheating you may need to add more liquid.

ROASTED LEEK, GARLIC AND BACON SOUP

INGREDIENTS

1 tablespoon olive oil
20 g ($^3/_4$ oz) butter
2 rashers bacon, chopped
3 leeks, chopped
2 cloves garlic, chopped
1 stick celery, coarsely chopped
2 zucchini, coarsely chopped
2 bay leaves
6 cups (1.5 litres) chicken stock
$^1/_3$ cup (80 ml/2$^3/_4$ fl oz) cream
$^1/_4$ cup (15 g/$^1/_2$ oz) finely chopped parsley
2 rashers bacon, extra, to serve

1. Preheat the oven to warm 160°C (315°F/Gas 2–3). Heat the oil and butter in a large roasting tin. Add the bacon rashers and stir over medium heat for 1–2 minutes. Add the leek, garlic, celery, zucchini and bay leaves and cook, stirring, for 2–3 minutes, without allowing to brown.

2. Transfer the roasting tin to the oven and roast the vegetables and bacon for 40 minutes, turning a couple of times. Cover with foil if starting to brown. Transfer to a large pan, pour on the stock and bring to the boil. Lower the heat and simmer for 30 minutes. Cool slightly, strain and return the liquid to the pan. Remove the bay leaves.

3. Put the vegetables and bacon in a food processor with a ladleful of the cooking liquid and process until smooth, adding more liquid if necessary. Return the purée to the pan with the liquid and add some pepper, the cream and parsley. Reheat gently.

4. To make the bacon garnish, trim off the rind and excess fat from the bacon and grill until crisp. Drain on paper towels, then crumble with your fingers and serve on top of the soup.

ROASTED VEGETABLE SOUP

INGREDIENTS

2 carrots, cut into large pieces
1 parsnip, cut into large pieces
500 g (1 lb) unpeeled pumpkin, cut into large pieces
350 g (11 oz) unpeeled sweet potato, cut into large pieces
1 red capsicum, cut into large pieces
2 onions, halved
4 cloves garlic, unpeeled
3 cups (750 ml/24 fl oz) vegetable stock
sour cream and thyme, to serve

1. Preheat the oven to moderate 180°C (350°F/Gas 4). Put the vegetables in a large greased baking dish and brush lightly with some olive oil.

2. Bake for 1 hour, turning often. Remove the capsicum. Bake for 30 minutes longer; cool the vegetables slightly. Remove the skin from the capsicum; place in a food processor with the carrot, parsnip and onion.

3. Scrape the pumpkin and sweet potato flesh into the processor and squeeze in the garlic pulp. Add half the stock and purée until smooth. Place in a pan with the remaining stock and heat through. Season and serve with sour cream and thyme.

SAFFRON AND JERUSALEM ARTICHOKE SOUP

INGREDIENTS

1 pinch saffron threads
250 g (9 oz) Jerusalem artichokes
2 tablespoons lemon juice
1 tablespoon olive oil
1 large onion, finely chopped
1 litre (4 cups) vegetable or chicken stock
3 teaspoons ground cumin
500 g (1 lb 2 oz) desiree potatoes, grated
2 teaspoons lemon juice, extra

1 Place the saffron threads in a bowl with 2 tablespoons boiling water and leave until needed. Peel and thinly slice the artichokes, dropping the slices into a bowl of water mixed with lemon juice to prevent discolouration.

2 Heat the oil in a large heavy-based saucepan, add the onion and cook over medium heat for 2–3 minutes, or until the onion is softened. Bring the stock to the boil in a separate saucepan. Add the cumin to the onion mixture and cook for a further 30 seconds, or until fragrant. Add the drained artichokes, potato, saffron mixture, stock and extra lemon juice. Bring to the boil, then reduce the heat and simmer for 15–18 minutes, or until the artichokes are very soft.

3 Transfer to a blender and process in batches until smooth. Return the soup to the pan and season to taste with salt and cracked pepper. Reheat over medium heat and serve.

SILVERBEET AND RISONI SOUP WITH GRUYÈRE CROUTONS

INGREDIENTS

30 g (1 oz) butter
1 large onion, finely chopped
1 garlic clove, crushed
2 litres (8 cups) vegetable or chicken stock
200 g (1 cup) risoni
½ baguette, cut into 6 slices
15 g (½ oz) butter, extra, melted
1 teaspoon Dijon mustard
50 g (1¾ oz) Gruyère cheese, coarsely grated
500 g (1 lb 2 oz) silverbeet (Swiss chard), central stalk removed, shredded
30 g (1 cup) basil, torn

1 Heat the butter in a large heavy-based saucepan, add the onion and garlic and cook over medium heat for 2–3 minutes, or until the onion is softened. Meanwhile, place the stock in a separate pan and bring to the boil.

2 Add the stock to the onion mixture and bring to the boil. Add the risoni, reduce the heat and simmer for 8 minutes, stirring occasionally.

3 Meanwhile, place the baguette slices in a single layer on a baking tray and cook under a preheated grill (broiler) until golden brown on one side. Turn the slices over and brush with the combined melted butter and mustard. Top with the Gruyère and grill until the cheese has melted.

4 Add the silverbeet and basil to the risoni mixture and simmer for about 1 minute, or until the risoni is al dente and the silverbeet is cooked. Season with salt and freshly ground black pepper and serve with the Gruyère croutons.

SPLIT PEA AND VEGETABLE SOUP

INGREDIENTS

1 tablespoon peanut or vegetable oil
1 onion, chopped
2 garlic cloves, chopped
1½ teaspoons chopped fresh ginger
1½ tablespoons Madras curry paste
100 g (3½ oz) yellow split peas, rinsed and drained1 large zucchini (courgette), peeled and chopped
1 large carrot, roughly chopped
170 g (6 oz) button mushrooms, roughly chopped
1 celery stalk, roughly chopped
1 litre (4 cups) vegetable stock
125 ml (½ cup) cream

1. Heat the oil in a saucepan, add the onion and cook over low heat for 5 minutes, or until soft. Add the garlic, ginger and curry paste and cook over medium heat for 2 minutes. Stir in the split peas until well coated with paste, then add the zucchini, carrot, mushroom and celery and cook for 2 minutes.

2. Add the stock, bring to the boil, then reduce the heat and simmer, partly covered, for 1 hour. Remove from the heat and allow to cool slightly.

3. Transfer the soup to a blender or food processor and process in batches until smooth. Return to the pan, stir in the cream and gently heat until warmed through. Delicious served with naan bread.

SWEET POTATO AND CHILLI SOUP

INGREDIENTS

1 tablespoon oil
1 onion, chopped
2 garlic cloves, finely chopped
1–2 small red chillies, finely chopped
$^1/_4$ teaspoon paprika
750 g (1 lb 10 oz) orange sweet potato (kumera), chopped into small pieces
1 litre (4 cups) vegetable or beef stock
chopped dried chilli, to garnish

1 Heat the oil in a large heavy-based saucepan, add the onion and cook for 1–2 minutes, or until soft. Add the garlic, chilli and paprika and cook for a further 2 minutes, or until aromatic. Add the sweet potato to the pan and toss to coat with the spices.

2 Pour in the stock, bring to the boil, then reduce the heat and simmer for 15 minutes, or until the vegetables are tender. Cool slightly, then transfer to a blender or food processor and blend in batches until smooth, adding extra water if needed to reach the desired consistency. Do not overblend or the mixture may become gluey.

3 Season to taste with salt and black pepper. Ladle the soup into bowls, sprinkle with dried chilli and serve.

SWEET POTATO AND PEAR SOUP

INGREDIENTS

25 g (1 oz) butter
1 small white onion, finely chopped
750 g (1 lb 10 oz) orange sweet potato, peeled and cut into 2 cm (3/4 inch) dice
2 firm pears (500 g/1 lb 2 oz), peeled, cored and cut into 2 cm (3/4 inch) dice
750 ml (3 cups) vegetable or chicken stock
250 ml (1 cup) cream
mint leaves, to garnish

1 Melt the butter in a saucepan over medium heat, add the onion and cook for 2–3 minutes, or until softened but not brown. Add the sweet potato and pear, and cook, stirring, for 1–2 minutes. Add the stock to the pan, bring to the boil and cook for 20 minutes, or until the sweet potato and pear are soft.

2 Cool slightly, then place the mixture in a blender or food processor and blend in batches until smooth. Return to the pan, stir in the cream and gently reheat without boiling. Season with salt and ground black pepper. Garnish with the mint.

TOMATO AND BREAD SOUP

INGREDIENTS

750 g (1 lb 10 oz) vine-ripened tomatoes
1 loaf (450 g/1 lb) day-old crusty Italian bread
1 tablespoon olive oil
3 garlic cloves, crushed
1 tablespoon tomato paste (purée)
1.25 litres (5 cups) hot vegetable stock
4 tablespoons torn basil leaves
2–3 tablespoons extra virgin olive oil, plus extra, to serve

1 Score a cross in the base of each tomato. Place in a bowl of boiling water for 1 minute, then plunge into cold water and peel the skin away from the cross. Cut the tomatoes in half and scoop out the seeds with a teaspoon. Chop the tomato flesh.

2 Remove most of the crust from the bread and discard. Cut the bread into 3 cm (1¼ in) pieces.

3 Heat the oil in a large saucepan. Add the garlic, tomato and tomato paste, then reduce the heat and simmer, stirring occasionally, for 15 minutes until thickened. Add the stock and bring to the boil, stirring for 2 minutes. Reduce the heat to medium, add the bread pieces and cook, stirring, for 5 minutes, or until the bread softens and absorbs most of the liquid. Add more stock or water if necessary.

4 Stir in the torn basil leaves and extra virgin olive oil, and leave for 5 minutes so the flavours have time to develop. Drizzle with a little of the extra oil.

NOTE This soup is popular in Italy in the summer months when tomatoes are at their tastiest, and as a way of using up leftover bread. In Italy, the soup is called Pappa al pomodoro.

TOMATO AND CAPSICUM SOUP WITH POLENTA AND OLIVE STICKS

INGREDIENTS

2 tablespoons vegetable oil
2 tablespoons olive oil
2 red onions, finely chopped
2 garlic cloves, crushed
1 tablespoon ground cumin
¼ teaspoon ground cayenne pepper
2 teaspoons paprika
2 red capsicums (peppers), diced
90 g (⅓ cup) tomato paste (purée)
250 ml (1 cup) dry white wine
2 x 400 g (14 oz) cans chopped tomatoes
2 long red chillies, seeded and chopped
500 ml (2 cups) chicken or vegetable stock
3 tablespoons chopped flat-leaf (Italian) parsley
4 tablespoons chopped coriander (cilantro) leaves

Polenta and olive sticks

500 ml (2 cups) chicken or vegetable stock
185 g (1¼ cups) coarse polenta (cornmeal)
100 g (3½ oz) pitted Kalamata olives, chopped
125 ml (½ cup) olive oil, to deep-fry

1 Heat the oils in a large saucepan over medium heat and cook the onion and garlic for 2–3 minutes, or until soft.

2 Reduce the heat to low, add the spices and cook for 1–2 minutes. Add the capsicum and cook for 5 minutes. Stir in the tomato paste and wine, simmer for 2 minutes, or until reduced slightly. Add the tomato, chilli, stock and 500 ml (2 cups) water. Season. Simmer for 20 minutes. Purée the soup with the herbs.

3 To make the polenta and olive sticks, grease a 20 cm x 30 cm (8 inch x 12 inch) baking tray. Bring the stock and 500 ml (2 cups) water to the boil in a saucepan. Slowly add the polenta in a fine stream, whisking until smooth. Reduce the heat to low. Cook, stirring constantly, for 15–20 minutes, or until it starts to come away from the side. Stir in the olives, then spoon into the tray, smoothing the surface. Cover and chill for 30 minutes, or until firm. Cut into sticks.

4 Heat the oil in a large deep frying pan to 190°C (375°F), or until a cube of bread browns in 10 seconds. Cook the sticks in batches on each side for 1–2 minutes, or until crisp. Drain well, and serve with the soup.

VEGETABLE AND LENTIL SOUP WITH SPICED YOGHURT

INGREDIENTS

2 tablespoons olive oil
1 small leek, white part only, chopped
2 garlic cloves, crushed
2 teaspoons curry powder
1 teaspoon ground cumin
1 teaspoon garam masala
1 litre (4 cups) vegetable stock
1 bay leaf
185 g (1 cup) brown lentils
450 g (1 lb) butternut pumpkin (squash), peeled and cut into 1 cm (1/2 inch) cubes
2 zucchini (courgettes), cut in half lengthways and sliced
400 g (14 oz) tin chopped tomatoes
200 g (7 oz) broccoli, cut into small florets
1 small carrot, diced
80 g (1/2 cup) peas
1 tablespoon chopped mint

Spiced yoghurt

250 g (1 cup) thick plain yoghurt
1 tablespoon chopped coriander (cilantro) leaves
1 garlic clove, crushed
3 dashes Tabasco sauce

1 Heat the oil in a saucepan over medium heat. Add the leek and garlic and cook for 4–5 minutes, or until soft and lightly golden. Add the curry powder, cumin and garam masala and cook for 1 minute, or until fragrant.

2 Add the stock, bay leaf, lentils and pumpkin. Bring to the boil, then reduce the heat to low and simmer for 10–15 minutes, or until the lentils are tender. Season well.

3 Add the zucchini, tomatoes, broccoli, carrot and 500 ml (2 cups) water and simmer for 10 minutes, or until the vegetables are tender. Add the peas and simmer for 2–3 minutes.

4 To make the spiced yoghurt, place the yoghurt, coriander, garlic and Tabasco in a small bowl and stir until combined.

5 Dollop a spoonful of the yoghurt on each serving of soup and garnish with the chopped mint.

VEGETABLE AND PASTA SOUP

INGREDIENTS

2 teaspoons olive oil
1 onion, chopped
1 carrot, chopped
2 celery sticks, chopped
350 g (11 oz) sweet potato (kumera), chopped
400 g (13 oz) can corn kernels, drained
1 litre vegetable stock
1 cup (90 g/3 oz) pasta spirals

1. Heat the oil in a large pan and add the onion, carrot and celery. Cook the vegetables over low heat, stirring regularly, for 10 minutes, or until they are soft.

2. Add the sweet potato, corn kernels and stock. Bring to the boil and then reduce the heat and simmer for 20 minutes, or until the vegetables are tender.

3. Add the pasta to the pan and return to the boil. Reduce the heat and simmer for 10 minutes, or until the pasta is tender. Season the soup and serve immediately.

ZUCCHINI PESTO SOUP

INGREDIENTS

1 tablespoon olive oil
1 large onion, finely chopped
2 garlic cloves, crushed
750 ml (3 cups) vegetable or chicken stock
750 g (1 lb 10 oz) zucchini (courgettes), thinly sliced
60 ml (1/4 cup) cream
toasted ciabatta bread, to serve

Pesto
50 g (1 cup) basil
25 g (1/4 cup) finely grated Parmesan cheese
2 tablespoons pine nuts, toasted
2 tablespoons extra virgin olive oil

1 Heat the oil in a large heavy-based saucepan. Add the onion and garlic and cook over medium heat for 5 minutes, or until the onion is soft.

2 Bring the stock to the boil in a separate saucepan. Add the zucchini and hot stock to the onion mixture. Bring to the boil, then reduce the heat, cover and simmer for about 10 minutes, or until the zucchini is very soft.

3 To make the pesto, process the basil, Parmesan and pine nuts in a food processor for 20 seconds, or until finely chopped. Gradually add the olive oil and process until smooth. Spoon into a small bowl.

4 Transfer the zucchini mixture to a blender or food processor and blend in batches until smooth. Return the mixture to the pan, stir in the cream and 2 tablespoons of the pesto, and reheat over medium heat until hot. Season with salt and black pepper and serve with toasted ciabatta bread. Serve the remaining pesto in a bowl for diners to help themselves, or cover with olive oil and store in the refrigerator for up to 1 week.

ZUPPA DI FAGGIOLI

INGREDIENTS

2 x 400 g (14 oz) tins cannellini beans
1 tablespoon extra virgin olive oil
1 leek, finely chopped
2 garlic cloves, crushed
1 teaspoon thyme leaves
2 celery stalks, diced
1 carrot, diced
1 kg (2 lb 4 oz) silverbeet (Swiss chard), trimmed and roughly chopped
1 ripe tomato, diced
1 litre (4 cups) vegetable stock
2 small crusty rolls, each cut into 4 slices
2 teaspoons balsamic vinegar
35 g (1/3 cup) finely grated Parmesan cheese

1 Put one tin of beans and liquid in a blender or small food processor and blend until smooth. Drain the other tin, reserving the beans and discarding the liquid.

2 Heat the oil in a large heavy-based saucepan, add the leek, garlic and thyme and cook for 2–3 minutes, or until soft and aromatic. Add the celery, carrot, silverbeet and tomato and cook for a further 2–3 minutes, or until the silverbeet has wilted. Heat the stock in a separate saucepan.

3 Stir the puréed cannellini beans and stock into the vegetable mixture. Bring to the boil, then reduce the heat and simmer for 5–10 minutes, or until the vegetables are tender. Add the drained beans and stir until heated through. Season to taste with salt and cracked black pepper.

4 Arrange 2 slices of bread in the base of each soup bowl. Stir the balsamic vinegar into the soup and ladle over the bread. Serve topped with grated Parmesan.

NOTE This recipe is the authentic bean soup from Florence. If you like, spice it up by adding chopped chilli.

AVGOLEMONO WITH CHICKEN

INGREDIENTS

1 carrot, chopped
1 large leek, chopped
2 bay leaves
2 chicken breast fillets
2 litres (8 cups) chicken stock
75 g (1/3 cup) short-grain rice
3 eggs, separated
80 ml (1/3 cup) lemon juice
2 tablespoons chopped parsley
40 g (1 1/2 oz) butter, chopped

1 Place the carrot, leek, bay leaves, chicken fillets and stock in a large saucepan. Bring to the boil over high heat, then reduce the heat and simmer for 10–15 minutes, or until the chicken is cooked. Strain into a clean saucepan and reserve the chicken.

2 Add the rice to the liquid, bring to the boil, then reduce the heat and simmer for 15 minutes, or until tender. Cut the chicken into 1 cm (1/2 in) cubes.

3 Whisk the egg whites in a clean, dry bowl until firm peaks form. Beat in the yolks until light and creamy, whisk in the lemon juice, then 250 ml (1 cup) of the soup. Remove the soup from the heat and gradually whisk in the egg mixture. Add the chicken and stir over low heat for 2 minutes — do not boil or the egg will scramble. Serve at once with a sprinkle of parsley and dot of butter.

NOTE This soup will not stand well — make just before serving.

BEEF CONSOMME

INGREDIENTS

1 kg (2 lb) gravy beef, cut into small pieces
500 g (1 lb) beef bones including marrow, cut into small pieces (ask your butcher to do this)
1 leek, cut into small pieces
2 onions, quartered
2 carrots, chopped
2 sticks celery, chopped
6 black peppercorns
6 whole cloves
3 sprigs thyme
3 sprigs parsley
3 bay leaves
1 egg shell, crumbled
1 egg white, lightly beaten
2 tablespoons chopped parsley

1. Preheat the oven to moderate 180°C (350°F/Gas 4). Place the gravy beef and beef bones in a single layer in a baking dish. Bake for 45 minutes, or until lightly browned, turning once.

2. Put the meat, bones, vegetables, peppercorns, cloves, herbs, bay leaves and 1 teaspoon of salt in a large pan. Add 3 litres of water and slowly bring to the boil. Reduce the heat to low, cover and simmer for 4 hours. Set aside to cool slightly. Remove the larger pieces of meat and discard. Ladle the liquid through a muslin-lined sieve into a bowl. Discard the remaining meat and vegetables.

3. Cover the liquid and refrigerate for several hours, or overnight. Spoon off the fat from the surface. Return to a clean pan with the egg shell and the lightly beaten egg white.

4. Slowly heat the stock to simmering and simmer for 10 minutes. A frothy scum will form on the surface. Remove from the heat and leave for 10 minutes. Skim the surface and ladle the stock through a muslin-lined sieve. Reheat, season if needed, and serve with the chopped parsley.

BEEF PHO

INGREDIENTS

200 g (7 oz) rice noodle sticks
1.5 litres (6 cups) beef stock
1 star anise
4 cm (1 1/2 in) piece fresh ginger, sliced
2 pigs trotters (ask your butcher to cut them in half)
1/2 onion, studded with 2 cloves
2 stems lemon grass, pounded
2 garlic cloves, pounded
1/4 teaspoon white pepper
1 tablespoon fish sauce
400 g (14 oz) beef fillet, partially frozen, and thinly sliced
90 g (1 cup) bean sprouts
2 spring onions (scallions), thinly sliced on the diagonal
25 g (1/2 cup) fresh coriander (cilantro) leaves, chopped
25 g (1/2 cup) fresh Vietnamese mint, chopped
1 fresh red chilli, thinly sliced
fresh red chillies, extra, to serve
fresh Vietnamese mint, extra, to serve
fresh coriander (cilantro) leaves, extra, to serve
2 limes, cut into quarters
fish sauce, extra, to serve

1. Soak the noodles in boiling water for 15–20 minutes. Drain.

2. Bring the stock, star anise, ginger, trotters, onion, lemon grass, garlic and white pepper to the boil in a large saucepan. Reduce the heat and simmer for 30 minutes. Strain, return to the same pan and stir in the fish sauce.

3. Divide the noodles among bowls, then top with beef strips, sprouts, spring onion, coriander, mint and chilli. Ladle on the broth.

4. Place the extra chilli, mint, coriander, lime quarters and fish sauce in small bowls on a platter, serve with the soup and allow your guests to help themselves.

CHICKEN AND COUSCOUS SOUP

INGREDIENTS

1 tablespoon olive oil
1 onion, sliced
1/2 teaspoon ground cumin
1/2 teaspoon paprika
1 teaspoon grated fresh ginger
1 clove garlic, crushed
2 celery sticks, sliced
2 small carrots, sliced
2 zucchini, sliced
1.125 litres chicken stock
2 chicken breast fillets, sliced
pinch saffron threads, optional
1/2 cup (95 g/3 oz) instant couscous
2 tablespoons chopped fresh parsley

1. Heat the oil in a large heavy-based pan. Add the onion and cook over medium heat for 10 minutes, or until very soft, stirring occasionally. Add the cumin, paprika, ginger and garlic and cook, stirring, for 1 minute further.

2. Add the celery, carrot and zucchini and stir to coat with the spices. Stir in the stock. Bring to the boil, then reduce the heat and simmer, partially covered, for about 15 minutes, or until the vegetables are tender.

3. Add the chicken and saffron to the pan and cook for about 5 minutes, or until the chicken is just tender; do not overcook. Stir in the couscous and chopped parsley and serve.

CHICKEN AND GALANGAL SOUP

INGREDIENTS

5 x 2 cm (2 x 3/4 in) piece fresh galangal, peeled and cut into thin slices
500 ml (2 cups) coconut milk
250 ml (1 cup) chicken stock
4 fresh kaffir lime (makrut) leaves, torn
1 tablespoon finely chopped fresh coriander (cilantro) roots
500 g (1 lb 2 oz) chicken breast fillets, cut into thin strips
1–2 teaspoons finely chopped fresh red chillies
2 tablespoons fish sauce
1 1/2 tablespoons lime juice
3 teaspoons palm sugar or soft brown sugar
4 tablespoons fresh coriander (cilantro) leaves

1. Place the galangal in a saucepan with the coconut milk, stock, lime leaves and coriander roots. Bring to the boil, reduce the heat to low and simmer for 10 minutes, stirring occasionally.

2. Add the chicken and chilli to the pan and simmer for 8 minutes.

3. Stir in the fish sauce, lime juice and palm sugar and cook for 1 minute. Stir in the coriander leaves. Serve immediately garnished with extra coriander, if desired.

CHICKEN AND VEGETABLE SOUP

INGREDIENTS

1.5 kg ($2^{1}/_{2}$ lb) chicken
2 carrots, roughly chopped
2 sticks celery, roughly chopped
1 onion, quartered
4 parsley sprigs
2 bay leaves
4 black peppercorns
50 g ($1^{3}/_{4}$ oz) butter
2 tablespoons plain (all-purpose) flour
2 potatoes, chopped
250 g (8 oz) butternut pumpkin (squash), chopped into bite-sized pieces
2 carrots, extra, cut into matchsticks
1 leek, cut into matchsticks
3 sticks celery, extra, cut into matchsticks
100 g ($3^{1}/_{2}$ oz) green beans, cut into short lengths or baby green beans, halved
200 g ($6^{1}/_{2}$ oz) broccoli, cut into small florets
100 g ($3^{1}/_{2}$ oz) sugar snap peas, trimmed
50 g ($1^{3}/_{4}$ oz) English spinach leaves, shredded
$^{1}/_{2}$ cup (125 ml/4 fl oz) cream
$^{1}/_{4}$ cup (15 g/$^{1}/_{2}$ oz) chopped parsley

1 To make the chicken stock, place the chicken in a large pan with the carrot, celery, onion, parsley, bay leaves, 2 teaspoons of salt and the peppercorns. Add 3 litres of water. Bring to the boil, reduce the heat and simmer for 1 hour, skimming the surface as required. Allow to cool for at least 30 minutes. Strain and reserve the liquid.

2 Remove the chicken and allow to cool enough to handle. Discard the skin, then cut or pull the flesh from the bones and shred into small pieces. Set the chicken meat aside.

3 Heat the butter in a large pan over medium heat and, when foaming, add the flour. Cook, stirring, for 1 minute. Remove from the heat and gradually stir in the stock. Return to the heat and bring to the boil, stirring continuously. Add the potato, pumpkin and extra carrot and simmer for 7 minutes. Add the leek, extra celery and beans and simmer for a further 5 minutes. Finally, add the broccoli and sugar snap peas and cook for a further 3 minutes.

4 Just before serving, add the chicken meat, spinach, cream and chopped parsley. Reheat gently but do not allow the soup to boil. Keep stirring until the spinach has wilted. Season to taste with plenty of salt and freshly ground black pepper. Serve immediately.

CHICKEN, MUSHROOM AND MADEIRA SOUP

INGREDIENTS

10 g (1/4 oz) dried porcini mushrooms
25 g (1 oz) butter
1 leek (white part only), thinly sliced
250 g (9 oz) pancetta or bacon, chopped
200 g (7 oz) Swiss brown mushrooms, roughly chopped
300 g (10 1/2 oz) large field mushrooms, roughly chopped
2 tablespoons plain (all-purpose) flour
125 ml (1/2 cup) Madeira
1.25 litres (5 cups) chicken stock
1 tablespoon olive oil
2 chicken breast fillets (about 200 g/7 oz each)
80 g (1/3 cup) light sour cream
2 teaspoons chopped marjoram, plus whole leaves, to garnish

1. Soak the porcini in 250 ml (1 cup) boiling water for 20 minutes.

2. Melt the butter in a large saucepan over medium heat and cook the leek and pancetta for 5 minutes, or until the leek is softened. Add all the mushrooms and the porcini soaking liquid and cook for 10 minutes.

3. Stir in the flour and cook for 1 minute. Add the Madeira and cook, stirring, for 10 minutes. Stir in the stock, bring to the boil, then reduce the heat and simmer for 45 minutes. Cool slightly.

4. Heat the oil in a frying pan and cook the chicken fillets for 4–5 minutes each side, or until cooked through. Remove from the pan and thinly slice.

5. Blend the soup until smooth. Return to the cleaned saucepan, add the sour cream and chopped marjoram and stir over medium heat for about 1–2 minutes to warm through. Season. Top with the chicken and garnish with marjoram.

CHICKPEA, CHORIZO AND PORK RIB SOUP

INGREDIENTS

180 g (6 oz) dried chickpeas
300 g (10 oz) smoked bacon ribs
2 tablespoons olive oil
1 onion, finely chopped
1 clove garlic, crushed
2 tomatoes, peeled, seeded and finely chopped
1 potato, cubed
1 carrot, sliced
200 g (6½ oz) pumpkin, chopped
150 g (5 oz) chorizo or pepperoni sausage, sliced
¼ teaspoon dried oregano
6 cups (1.5 litres) chicken stock

1. Soak the chickpeas in cold water overnight. Drain.
2. Blanch bacon ribs in boiling water for 30 seconds, then plunge into iced water. Drain and slice into pieces.
3. Heat the oil in a large, heavy-based pan and cook the onion over medium heat for 3–4 minutes, stirring continuously. Add the garlic and tomato and cook for a further 5 minutes.
4. Add the chickpeas, ribs, potato, carrot, pumpkin, chorizo, dried oregano and stock. Bring to the boil, then reduce the heat and simmer, covered, for 30 minutes, or until the chickpeas are tender. Season to taste.

CREAMY CHICKEN AND CORN SOUP

INGREDIENTS

20 g ($^{3}/_{4}$ oz) butter
1 tablespoon olive oil
500 g (1 lb 2 oz) chicken thigh fillets, trimmed and thinly sliced
2 garlic cloves, chopped
1 leek, chopped
1 large celery stalk, chopped
1 bay leaf
$^{1}/_{2}$ teaspoon thyme
1 litre (4 cups) chicken stock
60 ml ($^{1}/_{4}$ cup) sherry
550 g (1 lb 4 oz) corn kernels (fresh, canned or frozen)
1 large floury potato (russet), cut into 1 cm ($^{1}/_{2}$ in) cubes
185 ml ($^{3}/_{4}$ cup) cream, plus extra, to drizzle
chives, to garnish

1 Melt the butter and oil in a large saucepan over high heat. Cook the chicken in batches for 3 minutes, or until lightly golden and just cooked through. Place in a bowl, cover and refrigerate until needed.

2 Reduce the heat to medium and stir in the garlic, leek, celery, bay leaf and thyme. Cook for 2 minutes, or until the leek softens — do not allow the garlic to burn. Add the stock, sherry and 500 ml (2 cups) water and stir, scraping up any sediment stuck to the bottom of the pan. Add the corn and potato and bring to the boil. Reduce the heat and simmer for 1 hour, skimming any scum off the surface. Cool slightly.

3 Remove the bay leaf and purée the soup. Return to the cleaned pan, add the cream and chicken and stir over medium–low heat for 2–3 minutes, or until heated through — do not boil. Season. Drizzle with extra cream and garnish with chives. If desired, serve with crusty bread.

DUCK, SHIITAKE MUSHROOMS AND RICE NOODLE BROTH

INGREDIENTS

3 dried shiitake mushrooms
1 Chinese roast duck (1.5 kg/3 lb 5 oz)
500 ml (2 cups) chicken stock
2 tablespoons light soy sauce
1 tablespoon Chinese rice wine
2 teaspoons sugar
400 g (14 oz) fresh flat rice noodles
2 tablespoons oil
3 spring onions (scallions), thinly sliced
1 teaspoon finely chopped ginger
400 g (14 oz) bok choy (pak choi), trimmed and leaves separated
1/4 teaspoon sesame oil

1 Place the shiitake mushrooms in a heatproof bowl, cover with 250 ml (1 cup) boiling water and soak for 20 minutes. Drain, reserving the liquid and squeezing the excess liquid from the mushrooms. Discard the woody stems and thinly slice the caps.

2 Remove the skin and flesh from the roast duck. Discard the fat and carcass. Finely slice the duck meat and the skin.

3 Place the chicken stock, soy sauce, rice wine, sugar and the reserved mushroom liquid in a saucepan over medium heat. Bring to a simmer and cook for 5 minutes. Meanwhile, place the rice noodles in a heatproof bowl, cover with boiling water and soak briefly. Gently separate the noodles with your hands and drain well. Divide evenly among large soup bowls.

4 Heat the oil in a wok over high heat. Add the spring onion, ginger and shiitake mushrooms and cook for several seconds. Transfer to the broth with the bok choy and duck meat and simmer for 1 minute, or until the duck has warmed through and the bok choy has wilted. Ladle the soup over the noodles and drizzle sesame oil on each serving. Serve immediately.

FIVE-SPICE DUCK AND SOMEN NOODLE SOUP

INGREDIENTS

4 duck breasts, skin on
1 teaspoon five-spice powder
1 teaspoon peanut oil
200 g (7 oz) dried somen noodles

Star anise broth
1 litre (4 cups) chicken stock
3 whole star anise
5 spring onions (scallions), chopped
15 g (1/4 cup) chopped fresh coriander (cilantro) leaves

1 Preheat the oven to moderately hot 200°C (400°F/Gas 6). Trim the duck breast of excess fat, then lightly sprinkle both sides with the five-spice powder.

2 Heat the oil in a large frying pan. Add the duck skin-side down and cook over medium heat for 2–3 minutes, or until brown and crisp. Turn and cook the other side for 3 minutes. Transfer to a baking tray and cook, skin-side up, for another 8–10 minutes, or until cooked to your liking.

3 Meanwhile, place the chicken stock and star anise in a small saucepan. Bring to the boil, then reduce the heat and simmer for 5 minutes. Add the spring onion and coriander and simmer for 5 minutes.

4 Cook the noodles in a saucepan of boiling water for 2 minutes, or until soft. Drain and divide among four bowls. Ladle the broth on the noodles and top each bowl with one sliced duck breast.

GRILLED ITALIAN SAUSAGE AND VEGETABLE SOUP

INGREDIENTS

500 g (1 lb 2 oz) Italian pork sausages
200 g (7 oz) piece speck (see note)
1 tablespoon olive oil
1 large onion, chopped
3 garlic cloves, crushed
1 celery stalk, cut in half and sliced
1 large carrot, cut into 1 cm (1/2 in) cubes
bouquet garni (1 parsley sprig, 1 oregano sprig, 2 bay leaves)
1 small red chilli, halved lengthways
400 g (14 oz) can chopped tomatoes
1.75 litres (7 cups) chicken stock
300 g (10 1/2 oz) Brussels sprouts, cut in half from top to base
300 g (10 1/2 oz) green beans, cut into 3 cm (1 1/4 inch) lengths
300 g (10 1/2 oz) shelled broad beans, fresh or frozen
2 tablespoons chopped flat-leaf (Italian) parsley

1 Grill (broil) the sausages under a hot grill (broiler) for 8–10 minutes, turning occasionally, or until brown. Remove and cut into 3 cm (1 1/4 in) lengths. Trim and reserve the fat from the speck, then dice the speck.

2 Heat the oil in a large saucepan over medium heat. Add the speck and reserved speck fat and cook for 2–3 minutes, or until golden. Add the onion, garlic, celery and carrot, reduce the heat to low and cook for 6–8 minutes, or until softened. Discard the remains of the speck fat.

3 Stir in the sausages, bouquet garni, chilli and chopped tomato and cook for 5 minutes. Add the stock, bring to the boil, then reduce the heat and simmer for 1 hour. Add the Brussels sprouts, green beans and broad beans and simmer for 30 minutes. Discard the bouquet garni, then stir in the parsley. Season to taste. Divide among four bowls and serve.

NOTE Speck is cured smoked ham or pork belly. It has a strong taste and is usually cut into small pieces and used as a flavour base.

HOT AND SOUR LIME SOUP WITH BEEF

INGREDIENTS

1 litre (4 cups) beef stock
2 stems lemon grass, white part only, halved
3 garlic cloves, halved
2.5 x 2.5 cm (1 x 1 in) piece ginger, sliced
90 g (1 bunch) coriander (cilantro), leaves and stalks separated, leaves chopped
4 spring onions (scallions), thinly sliced on the diagonal
2 strips of 1.5 x 4 cm (5/8 x 1 1/2 in) lime zest
2 star anise
3 small red chillies, seeded and finely chopped
500 g (1 lb 2 oz) fillet steak, trimmed
2 tablespoons fish sauce
1 tablespoon grated palm sugar or soft brown sugar
2 tablespoons lime juice
coriander (cilantro) leaves, extra, to garnish

1. Place the stock, lemon grass, garlic, ginger, coriander stalks, 2 spring onions, the lime zest, star anise, 1 teaspoon of the chopped chilli and 1 litre (4 cups) water in a saucepan. Bring to the boil and simmer, covered, for 25 minutes. Strain and return the liquid to the pan.

2. Heat a chargrill pan (griddle) until very hot. Brush lightly with olive oil and sear the steak on both sides until browned on the outside, but very rare in the centre.

3. Reheat the soup, adding the fish sauce and palm sugar. Season with salt and black pepper. Add the lime juice to taste (you may want more than 2 tablespoons) – you should achieve a hot and sour flavour.

4. Add the remaining spring onion and the chopped coriander leaves to the soup. Slice the beef across the grain into thin strips. Curl the strips into a decorative pattern, then place in the centre of four deep serving bowls. Pour the soup over the beef and garnish with the remaining chilli and a few extra coriander leaves.

THAI-STYLE CHICKEN AND COCONUT SOUP

INGREDIENTS

2 stems lemon grass, white part finely chopped, stem ends reserved and halved
6 cloves garlic, chopped
3 red Asian shallots, chopped
8 black peppercorns
1 teaspoon ready-made red curry paste
1 cup (250 ml/8 fl oz) coconut cream
400 ml (13$^1/_2$ fl oz) coconut milk
400 ml (13$^1/_2$ fl oz) chicken stock
2$^1/_2$ tablespoons thinly sliced fresh galangal
7 kaffir lime (makrut) leaves, shredded
400 g (14 oz) chicken breast fillets or thigh fillets, thinly sliced
2 tablespoons lime juice
2 tablespoons fish sauce
1 teaspoon grated palm sugar or soft brown sugar
3 tablespoons fresh coriander (cilantro) leaves
1 small fresh red chilli, thinly sliced

1 Process the chopped lemon grass, garlic, shallots, peppercorns and curry paste in a food processor to form a paste.

2 Heat a wok over low heat, add the coconut cream, increase the heat to high and bring to the boil. Add the paste and cook, stirring, for 5 minutes. Add the coconut milk and stock, return to the boil and add the sliced galangal, the kaffir lime leaves and reserved lemon grass stems. Reduce the heat and simmer for 5 minutes.

3 Add the chicken and simmer for 8 minutes, or until cooked. Stir in the lime juice, fish sauce, palm sugar, coriander leaves and chilli. Serve immediately.

JUNGLE SOUP

INGREDIENTS

2 teaspoons oil
1 medium onion, finely sliced
225 g (8 oz) butternut pumpkin (squash), peeled and diced
225 g (8 oz) fresh pineapple or mango, chopped
1 garlic clove, crushed
1 dried red chilli, finely chopped
2 teaspoons grated ginger
1 litre (4 cups) chicken stock
2 tablespoons lime juice
350 g (12 oz) chicken breast, skinned, cut diagonally into thin strips

1. Heat the oil in a large heavy-based pan and cook the onion for 5 minutes, or until golden. Add the pumpkin and cook for 5 minutes, or until just brown. Add the pineapple, garlic, chilli and ginger and toss together.

2. Add the stock and lime juice, bring to the boil and then reduce the heat to simmer for 20 minutes, or until the pumpkin is nearly tender.

3. Add the chicken and simmer for 5 minutes, or until the chicken is cooked. Serve immediately.

LEMON CHICKEN SOUP

INGREDIENTS

2 chicken breast fillets
1 lemon
1 litre chicken stock (see hint)
2 fresh lemon thyme sprigs, plus extra, to serve (see note)

1 Trim any excess fat from the chicken. Using a vegetable peeler, cut 2 strips of rind from the lemon and remove the pith. Place the stock, rind and lemon thyme in a shallow pan and slowly bring almost to the boil. Reduce to simmering point, add the chicken and cook, covered, for 7 minutes, or until the meat is tender.

2 Remove the chicken from the pan, transfer to a plate and cover with foil.

3 Strain the stock into a clean pan through a sieve lined with 2 layers of damp muslin. Finely shred the chicken and return to the soup. Reheat gently and season to taste with salt and freshly ground black pepper. Serve immediately, garnished with the extra sprigs of lemon thyme.

NOTE You can use ordinary thyme if lemon thyme is not available.

HINT If you don't have time to make your own stock, poultry shops or butchers sometimes sell their own. These may have more flavour and contain less salt than stock cubes.

LONG AND SHORT NOODLE SOUP

INGREDIENTS

300 g (10½ oz) minced (ground) pork
4 spring onions (scallions), sliced
3 garlic cloves, roughly chopped
2 teaspoons grated ginger
2 teaspoons cornflour (cornstarch)
125 ml (½ cup) light soy sauce
3 tablespoons Chinese rice wine
30 won ton wrappers
3 litres (12 cups) ready-made Chinese chicken broth, or home-made or ready-made chicken stock
200 g (7 oz) dried flat egg noodles
2 spring onions (scallions), extra, sliced on the diagonal

1 Put the minced pork, spring onion, garlic, grated ginger, cornflour, 1½ tablespoons of the soy sauce and 1 tablespoon of the rice wine in a food processor and process until well combined. Place 2 teaspoons of the mixture in the centre of a won ton wrapper and lightly brush the edges with water. Lift the sides up tightly and pinch around the filling to form a pouch. Repeat this process to make 30 won tons.

2 Place the chicken broth in a large saucepan and bring to a simmer over medium–high heat. Stir in the remaining soy sauce and rice wine.

3 Meanwhile, bring a large pan of water to the boil. Reduce the heat, add the won tons and simmer for 1 minute, or until they float to the surface and are cooked through, then remove with a slotted spoon. Return the water to the boil, add the egg noodles and cook for 3 minutes, or until tender. Drain and add to the chicken broth along with the cooked won tons. Simmer for 2 minutes, or until heated through.

4 Divide the broth, noodles and won tons among six large serving bowls, sprinkle with extra spring onion and drizzle each with a little sesame oil.

MOROCCAN LAMB, CHICKPEA AND CORIANDER SOUP

INGREDIENTS

165 g (3/4 cup) dried chickpeas
1 tablespoon olive oil
850 g (1 lb 14 oz) boned lamb leg, cut into 1 cm (1/2 in) cubes
1 onion, chopped
2 garlic cloves, crushed
1/2 teaspoon ground cinnamon
1/2 teaspoon ground turmeric
1/2 teaspoon ground ginger
4 tablespoons chopped coriander (cilantro) leaves
2 x 400 g (14 oz) cans chopped tomatoes
1 litre (4 cups) chicken stock
160 g (2/3 cup) dried red lentils, rinsed
coriander (cilantro) leaves, to garnish

1 Soak the chickpeas in cold water overnight. Drain and rinse well.

2 Heat the oil in a large saucepan over high heat and brown the lamb in batches for 2–3 minutes. Reduce the heat to medium, return the lamb to the pan with the onion and garlic and cook for 5 minutes. Add the spices, season and cook for 2 minutes. Add the coriander, tomato, stock and 500 ml (2 cups) water and bring to the boil over high heat.

3 Add the lentils and chickpeas and simmer, covered, over low heat for 1 1/2 hours. Uncover and cook for 30 minutes, or until the lamb is tender and the soup is thick. Season. Garnish with coriander.

MULLIGATAWNY SOUP

INGREDIENTS

500 g (1lb) chicken thigh fillets, excess fat removed
2 tablespoons plain (all-purpose) flour
1 tablespoon curry powder
1 teaspoon ground turmeric
30 g (1 oz butter)
1 onion, finely chopped
1 apple, peeled cored and finely chopped
4 cups (1 litre) chicken stock
6 whole cloves
⅓ cup (64 g/2¼ oz) basmati rice
1 tablespoon lemon juice
¼ cup (60 ml/2 fl oz) cream

1. Coat the chicken in the combined plain flour, curry powder and turmeric. Heat half the butter in a large pan and cook the chicken over medium heat for 3–4 minutes, or until lightly browned; turn frequently. Remove from the pan and drain on paper towels.

2. Add the remaining butter to the pan, then add the onion, apple and remaining flour mixture and cook for 3 minutes, or until soft. Return the chicken to the pan along with the stock and cloves. Bring to the boil, reduce the heat and simmer, covered, for 1 hour. Add the rice during the last 15 minutes and cook until it is tender.

3. Remove the chicken; allow to cool slightly and chop finely. Remove the cloves and skim any oil from the surface. Return the chicken to the pan. Reheat gently, stir in the lemon juice and cream, but do not allow the soup to boil. Season to taste with salt and freshly ground black pepper.

OXTAIL SOUP WITH STOUT AND VEGETABLES

INGREDIENTS

2 kg (4 lb 8 oz) oxtails, trimmed
2 tablespoons vegetable oil
2 onions, finely chopped
1 leek, finely chopped
2 carrots, diced
1 celery stalk, diced
2 garlic cloves, crushed
2 bay leaves
2 tablespoons tomato paste (purée)
1 thyme sprig
2 flat-leaf (Italian) parsley sprigs
3.5 litres (14 cups) chicken stock
375 ml (1 1/2 cups) stout
2 tomatoes, seeded and diced
100 g (3 1/2 oz) cauliflower florets
100 g (3 1/2 oz) green beans
100 g (3 1/2 oz) broccoli florets
100 g (3 1/2 oz) asparagus, cut into 3 cm (1 1/4 inch) lengths

1 Preheat the oven to 200°C (400°F/Gas 6). Place the oxtails in a baking dish and bake for 1 hour, turning occasionally, or until dark golden. Leave to cool.

2 Heat the oil in a large saucepan over medium heat and cook the onion, leek, carrot and celery for 3–4 minutes, or until soft. Stir in the garlic, bay leaves and tomato paste, then add the oxtails, thyme and parsley.

3 Add the stock and bring to the boil over high heat. Reduce the heat and simmer for 3 hours, or until the oxtails are tender and the meat falls off the bone. Skim off any scum that rises to the surface. Remove the oxtails and cool slightly.

4 Take the meat off the bones and discard any fat or sinew. Roughly chop and add to the soup with the stout, tomato and 500 ml (2 cups) water. Add the vegetables and simmer for 5 minutes, or until the vegetables are tender. Season.

PEA AND HAM SOUP

INGREDIENTS

1 tablespoon oil
2 onions, diced
2 carrots, diced
2 sticks celery, diced
1 parsnip, diced
$1\frac{1}{2}$ cups (330 g/$10\frac{1}{2}$ oz) green split peas
1 teaspoon black peppercorns
2 teaspoons dried thyme leaves
1 ham hock (850 g/1 lb 12 oz), cut into smaller pieces (ask your butcher to do this)

1. Heat the oil in a large pan and add the onion, carrot, celery and parsnip. Cook over low heat for 10 minutes, or until the vegetables have softened and the onion is translucent.

2. Add the split peas, peppercorns, thyme, the pieces of ham hock and 8 cups (2 litres) of water. Slowly bring to the boil, reduce the heat to low and simmer, covered, for $2\frac{1}{2}$ hours, or until most of the meat has fallen off the bones and the vegetables and split peas are very soft. Stir occasionally.

3. Remove the bones from the pan, pulling off any of the meat that hasn't fallen away. Chop any large pieces and return to the pan. Season well with salt and pepper, if necessary.

PORK AND BUTTERED CORN RAMEN SOUP

INGREDIENTS

200 g (7 oz) Chinese barbecued pork (char sui) fillet in one piece
2 small fresh corn cobs (550 g/1 lb 4 oz)
200 g (7 oz) dried ramen noodles
2 teaspoons peanut oil
1 teaspoon grated ginger
1.5 litres (6 cups) chicken stock
2 tablespoons mirin
2 spring onions (scallions), sliced on the diagonal
20 g (3/4 oz) unsalted butter
1 spring onion, extra, sliced on the diagonal
Cut the pork into thin slices and remove the corn kernels from the cob using a sharp knife.

1 Bring a large saucepan of water to the boil, add the ramen noodles and cook for 4 minutes, or until tender. Drain, then rinse in cold water.

2 Heat the oil in a large saucepan over high heat. Stir-fry the grated ginger for 1 minute. Add the chicken stock and mirin and bring to the boil. Reduce the heat and simmer for 8 minutes.

3 Add the pork slices to the liquid and cook for 5 minutes, then add the corn kernels and spring onion and cook for a further 4–5 minutes, or until the kernels are tender.

4 Separate the noodles by running them under hot water, then divide among four deep bowls. Ladle on the soup, then place 1 teaspoon butter on each serving. Garnish with the extra spring onion and serve at once.

NOTE This soup is traditionally served with the butter on top. However, for a healthier option, it is also quite delicious without the butter.

PORK CONGEE

INGREDIENTS

300 g (1 1/2 cups) long-grain rice, thoroughly rinsed
1/2 star anise
2 spring onions (scallions), white part only
4 x 4 cm (1 1/2 x 1 1/2 inch) piece ginger, cut into slices
3.5 litres (14 cups) chicken stock
1 tablespoon peanut oil
2 garlic cloves, crushed
1 teaspoon grated ginger, extra
400 g (14 oz) minced (ground) pork
ground white pepper
60 ml (1/4 cup) light soy sauce
sesame oil, to drizzle
6 fried dough sticks (see note)

1. Put the rice in a large saucepan with the star anise, spring onions, sliced ginger and chicken stock. Bring to the boil, then reduce the heat to low and simmer for 1 1/2 hours, stirring occasionally.

2. Heat the oil in a frying pan over high heat. Cook the garlic and grated ginger for 30 seconds. Add the mince and cook for 5 minutes, or until browned, breaking up any lumps with the back of a spoon.

3. Remove the star anise, spring onions and ginger from the soup and discard them. Add the mince mixture and simmer for 10 minutes. Season with white pepper and stir in the soy sauce. Serve with a drizzle of sesame oil and the dough sticks.

NOTE Fried dough sticks are available at Chinese bakeries and speciality shops and are best eaten soon after purchasing. If not, reheat in a 200°C (400°F/Gas 6) oven for 5 minutes, then serve.

RUSTIC HOT POT

INGREDIENTS

2 tablespoons olive oil
8 lamb shanks
2 onions, sliced
4 cloves garlic, finely chopped
3 bay leaves, torn in half
1–2 teaspoons hot paprika
2 teaspoons sweet paprika
1 tablespoon plain (all-purpose) flour
3 tablespoons tomato paste (purée)
6 cups (1.5 litres) vegetable stock
4 potatoes, chopped
4 carrots, sliced
3 sticks celery, thickly sliced
3 tomatoes, seeded and chopped

1. To make lamb stock, heat 1 tablespoon of the oil in a large, heavy-based pan over medium heat. Brown the shanks well in two batches and drain on paper towels.

2. Add remaining tablespoon of oil to pan and cook onion, garlic and bay leaves over low heat for 10 minutes, stirring regularly. Add paprikas and flour and cook, stirring, for 2 minutes. Gradually add combined tomato paste and stock. Bring to the boil, stirring, and return shanks to the pan. Reduce heat to low and simmer, covered, for 1 1/2 hours, stirring occasionally.

3. Remove bay leaves and discard. Remove shanks, allow to cool slightly and then cut the meat from the bone. Discard bones. Cut meat into pieces and refrigerate. Refrigerate stock for about 1 hour, or until fat forms on surface and can be spooned off.

4. Return the meat to the soup along with the potato, carrot and celery and bring to the boil. Reduce the heat and simmer for 15 minutes. Season and add the chopped tomato to serve.

SCOTCH BROTH

INGREDIENTS

1 kg (2 lb) lamb shanks, cut in half through the bone (ask your butcher to do this)
3 onions, chopped
3 turnips, chopped
2 carrots, chopped
1 tablespoon black peppercorns
$^1/_2$ cup (110 g/3$^1/_2$ oz) pearl barley
1 carrot, diced, extra
2 onions, finely chopped, extra
1 leek, chopped
1 stick celery, diced
2 turnips, diced, extra
chopped flat-leaf parsley

1 To make the stock, put the lamb shanks, onion, turnip, carrot, pepper-corns and 8 cups (2 litres) of water in a large pan. Bring to the boil, reduce the heat and simmer, covered, for 3 hours. Skim the surface as required.

2 Remove the shanks and any meat that has fallen off the bones and cool slightly. Remove the meat from the bones and finely chop, then cover and refrigerate. Strain the stock, discarding the vegetables. Cool the stock and refrigerate overnight, or until the fat has set on top and can be spooned off. Cover the barley with water and soak for 1 hour.

3 Put the stock in a large pan and gently reheat. Add the drained barley, extra carrot, onion, leek, celery and turnip. Bring to the boil, reduce the heat and simmer for 30 minutes, or until the barley and vegetables are just cooked. Return the meat to the pan and simmer for 5 minutes. Season well and serve with the parsley.

SPAGHETTI AND MEATBALL SOUP

INGREDIENTS

150 g (5½ oz) spaghetti, broken into 8 cm (3 in) lengths
1.5 litres (6 cups) beef stock
3 teaspoons tomato paste (purée)
400 g (14 oz) can chopped tomatoes
3 tablespoons basil leaves, torn
shaved Parmesan cheese, to garnish

Meatballs
1 tablespoon oil
1 onion, finely chopped
2 garlic cloves, crushed
500 g (1 lb 2 oz) lean minced (ground) beef
3 tablespoons finely chopped flat-leaf (Italian) parsley
3 tablespoons fresh breadcrumbs
2 tablespoons finely grated Parmesan cheese
1 egg, lightly beaten

1 Cook the spaghetti in a large saucepan of boiling water according to packet instructions until al dente. Drain. Put the stock and 500 ml (2 cups) water in a large saucepan and slowly bring to a simmer.

2 Meanwhile, to make the meatballs, heat the oil in a small frying pan over medium heat and cook the onion for 2–3 minutes, or until soft. Add the garlic and cook for 30 seconds. Allow to cool.

3 Combine the mince, parsley, breadcrumbs, Parmesan, egg, the onion mixture, and salt and pepper. Roll a heaped teaspoon of mixture into a ball, making 40 balls in total.

4 Stir the tomato paste and tomato into the beef stock and simmer for 2–3 minutes. Drop in the meatballs, return to a simmer and cook for 10 minutes, or until cooked through. Stir in the spaghetti and basil to warm through. Season, garnish with shaved Parmesan and serve.

SPICY CHICKEN BROTH WITH CORIANDER PASTA

INGREDIENTS

350 g (11 oz) chicken thighs or wings, skin removed
2 carrots, finely chopped
2 celery sticks, finely chopped
2 small leeks, finely chopped
3 egg whites
1.5 litres chicken stock
Tabasco sauce

Coriander Pasta
1/2 cup (60 g/2 oz) plain (all-purpose) flour
1 egg
1/2 teaspoon sesame oil
small bunch coriander (cilantro) leaves

1 Put the chicken, carrot, celery and leek in a large heavy-based pan. Push the chicken to one side and add the egg whites to the vegetables. Using a wire whisk, beat for 1 minute, or until frothy (take care not to use a pan that can be scratched by the whisk).

2 Warm the stock in another pan, then add gradually to the first pan, whisking constantly to froth the egg whites. Continue whisking while slowly bringing to the boil. Make a hole in the top of the froth with a spoon and leave to simmer, uncovered, for 30 minutes without stirring.

3 Line a large strainer with a damp tea towel or double thickness of muslin and strain the broth into a clean bowl. Discard the chicken pieces and vegetables. Season to taste with salt, ground black pepper and Tabasco sauce. Set aside.

4 To make the coriander pasta, sift the flour into a bowl and make a well in the centre. Whisk the egg and oil together and pour into the well. Mix together to make a soft pasta dough and knead on a lightly floured surface for 2 minutes, or until smooth.

5 Divide the pasta dough into four even portions. Roll one portion out very thinly and cover with a layer of evenly spaced coriander leaves. Roll out another portion of pasta and lay this on top of the leaves, then gently roll the layers together. Repeat with the remaining pasta and coriander.

6 Cut out squares of pasta around the coriander leaves. The pasta may then be left to sit and dry out if it is not needed immediately. Just before serving, heat the chicken broth gently in a saucepan. As the broth simmers, add the pasta and cook for 1 minute. Serve immediately.

SPICY LAMB SOUP

INGREDIENTS

2 large onions, roughly chopped
3 red chillies, seeded, chopped (or 2 teaspoons dried chilli)
3–4 garlic cloves
2 cm (3/4 inch) piece ginger, chopped
1 teaspoon ground black pepper
6 cm (2 1/2 inch) piece lemon grass, white only, chopped
1/2 teaspoon ground cardamom
2 teaspoons ground cumin
1/2 teaspoon ground cinnamon
1 teaspoon ground turmeric
2 tablespoons peanut oil
1.5 kg (3 lb 5 oz) lamb neck chops
2–3 tablespoons vindaloo paste
580 ml (2 1/3 cups) coconut cream
45 g (1/4 cup) soft brown sugar
2–3 tablespoons lime juice
4 kaffir lime (makrut) leaves

1. Put the onion, chilli, garlic, ginger, pepper, lemon grass and spices in a food processor. Process to a paste. Heat half the oil in a large pan and brown the chops in batches. Remove.

2. Add the remaining oil to the pan and cook the spice and vindaloo pastes for 2–3 minutes. Add the chops and 1.75 litres (7 cups) water, cover and bring to the boil. Reduce the heat; simmer, covered, for 1 hour. Remove the chops from the pan and stir in the coconut cream. Remove the meat from the bones, shred and return to the pan.

3. Add the sugar, lime juice and leaves. Simmer, uncovered, over low heat for 20–25 minutes, until slightly thickened. Garnish with coriander (cilantro).

TOM KHA GAI

INGREDIENTS

5 cm (2 inch) piece of fresh galangal or 5 slices of dried galangal
6 kaffir lime (makrut) leaves
1 stem lemon grass, white part only, quartered
2 cups (500 ml/16 fl oz) coconut milk
2 cups (500 ml/16 fl oz) chicken stock
3 chicken breast fillets, cut into thin strips
1–2 teaspoons finely chopped red chillies
$^1/_4$ cup (60 ml/2 fl oz) lime juice
2 tablespoons fish sauce
1 teaspoon soft brown sugar
$^1/_4$ cup (15 g/$^1/_2$ oz) coriander (cilantro) leaves

1 Peel the galangal and cut into thin slices. Mix the galangal, kaffir lime leaves and lemon grass with the coconut milk and stock in a medium pan. Bring to the boil, reduce the heat to low and simmer for 10 minutes, stirring occasionally.

2 Add the chicken strips and chilli and simmer for 8 minutes. Mix in the lime juice, fish sauce and sugar. Serve with the coriander leaves and garnish with coriander sprigs, if you want.

VIETNAMESE BEEF SOUP

INGREDIENTS

400 g (14 oz) rump steak, trimmed
1/2 onion
1 1/2 tablespoons fish sauce
1 star anise
1 cinnamon stick
pinch ground white pepper
1.5 litres (6 cups) beef stock
300 g (10 1/2 oz) fresh thin rice noodles
3 spring onions (scallions), thinly sliced
15 g (3/4 cup) Vietnamese mint leaves
90 g (1 cup) bean sprouts
1 small white onion, cut in half and thinly sliced
1 small red chilli, thinly sliced on the diagonal
lemon wedges, to serve

1 Wrap the rump steak in plastic wrap and freeze for 40 minutes.

2 Meanwhile, put the onion, fish sauce, star anise, cinnamon stick, pepper, stock and 500 ml (2 cups) water in a large saucepan. Bring to the boil, then reduce the heat, cover and simmer for 20 minutes. Discard the onion, star anise and cinnamon stick.

3 Cover the noodles with boiling water and gently separate the strands. Drain and refresh under cold water.

4 Remove the meat from the freezer and thinly slice it across the grain.

5 Divide the noodles and spring onion among four deep bowls. Top with the beef, mint, bean sprouts, onion and chilli. Ladle the hot broth over the top and serve with the lemon wedges.

WON TON SOUP

INGREDIENTS

2 dried Chinese mushrooms
15 raw prawns (shrimp)
100 g ($3^{1}/_{2}$ oz) minced (ground) pork
2 spring onions, chopped
1 teaspoon grated ginger
2 tablespoons canned water chestnuts, chopped
2 teaspoons chopped lemon grass, white part only
1 clove garlic, finely chopped
3 tablespoons soy sauce
225 g (7 oz) won ton wrappers
coriander (cilantro) leaves
6 cups (1.5 litres) beef stock
3 baby carrots, cut diagonally
3 spring onions, cut diagonally

1. Soak the mushrooms in hot water for 30 minutes. Peel and devein the prawns, then cut in half lengthways. Drain the mushrooms, remove the stems and chop the caps.

2. Mix the chopped mushroom with the pork, spring onion, ginger, water chestnut, lemon grass, garlic and 1 tablespoon of the soy sauce. Work with 1 won ton wrapper at a time, keeping the rest covered. Put 2–3 coriander leaves, half a prawn and a heaped teaspoon of the pork mixture in the centre of a wrapper. Brush the edges with water and lay another wrapper on top. Press to seal. Repeat with the remaining wrappers.

3. Bring the stock, remaining soy sauce, carrot and spring onion to the boil. Bring another large pan of water to the boil and cook the won tons in batches for 4–5 minutes; drain. Pour the hot soup over the won tons.

AVGOLEMONO (GREEK EGG AND LEMON SOUP)

INGREDIENTS

1.5 litres (6 cups) chicken stock
150 g (3/4 cup) long-grain rice
2 eggs, separated
125 ml (1/2 cup) lemon juice

1. Bring the stock to the boil in a large heavy-based pan. Add the rice and allow to simmer for 8–10 minutes until tender.

2. Beat the egg whites in a large dry mixing bowl until soft peaks form. Add the yolks and beat until they are combined.

3. Gradually pour in the lemon juice and then about 1–2 cups of the rice and stock soup, beating continuously. Gradually fold this into the pan of rice soup and serve immediately.

POTATO AND CHEESE SOUP

INGREDIENTS

30 g (1 oz) butter
4 rashers bacon, cut into strips
1 onion, finely chopped
1/2 teaspoon sweet paprika
1 kg (2 lb) potatoes, chopped
3 cups (750 ml/24 fl oz) chicken stock
1 cup (125 g/4 oz) grated Cheddar
chopped chives, to serve

1. Melt the butter in a large pan, add the bacon and cook until crisp. Remove the bacon from the pan with a slotted spoon, leaving as much fat as possible. Add the onion to the same pan and cook for 5 minutes, or until very soft and golden. Add the paprika and cook for a further 30 seconds.

2. Return the bacon to the pan and add the potato and stock. Bring to the boil, then reduce the heat and simmer for 30 minutes, or until the potato is very soft. Stir or mash lightly to break up the potato. Add the Cheddar and stir well, until it is melted through. Season with salt and pepper to taste and serve topped with a sprinkling of chopped chives.

STILTON AND APPLE SOUP

INGREDIENTS

40 g (1 1/2 oz) butter
2 tablespoons plain (all-purpose) flour
750 ml (3 cups) chicken stock
4 red apples
500 ml (2 cups) milk
250 g (9 oz) Stilton cheese
2 tablespoons chopped chives

1. Melt the butter in a large heavy-based pan. Sprinkle with the flour and stir over low heat for 2 minutes, or until lightly golden. Gradually add the stock, stirring until smooth.

2. Peel, core and slice the apples and add to the pan. Cook, covered, over medium heat for 20 minutes, or until tender. Cool, then purée in a processor in batches until smooth.

3. Return the soup to the pan, add the milk and reheat, stirring. Simmer gently and add the crumbled Stilton and chives. Stir until the soup is smooth and serve immediately.

SPICY PUMPKIN AND COCONUT SOUP

INGREDIENTS

1 small fresh red chilli, seeded and chopped
1 stem lemon grass, white part only, sliced
1 teaspoon ground coriander
1 tablespoon chopped fresh ginger
2 cups (500 ml) vegetable stock
2 tablespoons oil
1 onion, finely chopped
800 g pumpkin flesh, cubed
1 $^{1}/_{2}$ cups (375 ml) coconut milk
3 tablespoons chopped fresh coriander (cilantro) leaves
2 teaspoons shaved palm sugar or soft brown sugar
extra coriander (cilantro) leaves, to garnish

1. Place the chilli, lemon grass, ground coriander, ginger and 2 tablespoons vegetable stock in a food processor, and process until smooth.

2. Heat the oil in a large saucepan, add the onion and cook over medium heat for 5 minutes. Add the spice paste and cook, stirring, for 1 minute.

3. Add the pumpkin and remaining vegetable stock. Bring to the boil, then reduce the heat and simmer, covered, for 15–20 minutes, or until the pumpkin is tender. Cool slightly then process in a food processor or blender until smooth. Return to the cleaned pan, stir in the coconut milk, coriander and palm sugar, and simmer until hot. Garnish with the extra coriander leaves.

MISO SOUP WITH CHICKEN AND UDON NOODLES

INGREDIENTS

8 dried shiitake mushrooms
600 g chicken breast fillets, cut into 1.5 cm (1/2 inch) thick strips
1/4 cup (60 g/2 oz) white miso paste
2 teaspoons dashi granules
1 tablespoon wakame flakes or other seaweed (see note)
300 g (10 1/2 oz) baby bok choy, halved lengthways
400 g (14 oz) fresh udon noodles
150 g (5 1/3 oz) silken firm tofu, cut into 1 cm cubes
3 spring onions, sliced diagonally

1. Soak the mushrooms in 1 cup (250 ml) boiling water for 20 minutes. Drain, reserving the liquid; discard the stalks and thinly slice the caps.

2. Pour 2 litres water into a saucepan and bring to the boil, then reduce the heat and simmer. Add the chicken and cook for 2–3 minutes, or until almost cooked through.

3. Add the mushrooms and cook for 1 minute, then add the miso paste, dashi granules, wakame and reserved mushroom liquid. Stir to dissolve the dashi and miso paste. Do not boil.

4. Add the bok choy halves and simmer for 1 minute, or until beginning to wilt, then add the noodles and simmer for a further 2 minutes. Gently stir in the tofu and ladle the hot soup into large serving bowls. Garnish with the sliced spring onion.

Wakame is a curly-leafed, brown algae with a mild vegetable taste and a soft texture. It can be used in salads or can be boiled and served like a vegetable. Use a small amount as it swells by about ten times after being cooked.

CARAMELISED ONION AND PARSNIP SOUP

INGREDIENTS

30 g (1 oz) butter
3 large onions, halved and thinly sliced
2 tablespoons firmly packed soft brown sugar
1 cup (250 ml/8 fl oz) dry white wine
3 large parsnips, peeled, chopped
1.25 (42 fl oz) litres vegetable stock
1/4 cup (60 ml/2 fl oz) cream
fresh thyme leaves, to garnish

1 Melt the butter in a large saucepan. Add the onion and sugar, and cook over low heat for 10 minutes. Add the wine and parsnip, and simmer, covered, for 20 minutes, or until the onion and parsnip are golden and tender.

2 Pour in the stock, bring to the boil, then reduce the heat and simmer, covered, for 10 minutes. Cool slightly, then place in a blender or food processor and blend in batches until smooth. Season. Drizzle with a little cream and sprinkle fresh thyme leaves over the top. Serve with toasted crusty bread slices.

VEGETABLE RAMEN

INGREDIENTS

375 g (13¼ oz) fresh ramen noodles
1 tablespoon oil
1 tablespoon finely chopped fresh ginger
2 cloves garlic, crushed
150 g (5⅓ oz) oyster mushrooms, halved
1 small zucchini (courgette), sliced into thin rounds
1 leek, white and light green part, halved lengthways and thinly sliced
100 g (3½ oz) snow peas (mangetout), halved diagonally
100 g (3½ oz) fried tofu puffs, cut into matchsticks
5¼ cups (1.25 litres/42¼ fl oz) vegetable stock
1½ tablespoons white miso paste
2 tablespoons light soy sauce
1 tablespoon mirin
1 cup (90 g/3 oz) bean sprouts
1 teaspoon sesame oil
4 spring onions, thinly sliced
100 g (3½ oz) enoki mushrooms

1. Bring a large saucepan of lightly salted water to the boil. Add the noodles and cook, stirring to prevent sticking, for 4 minutes, or until just tender. Drain and rinse under cold running water.

2. Heat the oil in a large saucepan over medium heat, add the ginger, crushed garlic, oyster mushrooms, zucchini, leek, snow peas and tofu puffs, and stir-fry for 2 minutes. Add the stock and 300 ml water and bring to the boil, then reduce the heat and simmer. Stir in the miso, soy sauce and mirin until heated through. Do not boil. Stir in the bean sprouts and sesame oil.

3. Place the noodles in the bottom of six serving bowls, then pour in the soup. Garnish with the spring onion and enoki mushrooms.

BEEF AND BEET BORSCHT

INGREDIENTS

2 tablespoons olive oil
1 onion, chopped
2 cloves garlic, crushed
500 g ($17\frac{1}{2}$ oz) beef chuck steak, cut into 2 cm (1 inch) cubes
1 litre (34 fl oz) beef stock
2 small beetroot (250 g/9 oz)
200 g (7 oz) canned crushed tomatoes
1 carrot, diced
2 potatoes (280 g/10 oz), diced
$2\frac{1}{2}$ cups (190 g/$6\frac{3}{4}$ oz) finely shredded cabbage
2 teaspoons lemon juice
2 teaspoons sugar
2 tablespoons chopped fresh flat-leaf parsley
2 tablespoons chopped fresh dill
$\frac{1}{3}$ cup (90 g) sour cream

1 Preheat the oven to moderately hot 200°C (400°F/Gas 6). Heat the oil in a large saucepan, and cook the onion and garlic over medium heat for 3–5 minutes. Add the beef, stock and 1 litre water, and bring to the boil. Reduce the heat and simmer, covered, for 1 hour 15 minutes, or until the meat is tender. Remove the meat.

2 Trim the beetroot just above the end of the leaf stalks. Wrap in foil and bake for 30–40 minutes, or until tender. Unwrap and leave to cool.

3 Return the stock to the boil and add the tomato, carrot and potato, and season with salt. Cook over medium heat for 10 minutes. Add the cabbage and cook for 5 minutes. Peel and dice the beetroot. Return the meat to the pan and add the beetroot, lemon juice, sugar and $1\frac{1}{2}$ tablespoons each of parsley and dill. Cook for 2 minutes, or until heated through. Season to taste.

4 Remove from the heat and leave for 10 minutes. Serve with a dollop of sour cream and garnish with the remaining dill and parsley.

All our recipes are thoroughly tested in a specially developed test kitchen. Standard metric measuring cups and spoons are used in the development of our recipes. All cup and spoon measurements are level. We have used 60 g (2¼ oz/Grade 3) eggs in all recipes. Sizes of cans vary from manufacturer to manufacturer and between countries – use the can size closest to the one suggested in the recipe.

CONVERSION GUIDE

1 cup = 250 ml (9 fl oz)	1 Australian tablespoon = 20 ml (4 teaspoons)
1 teaspoon = 5 ml	1 UK/US tablespoon = 15 ml (3 teaspoons)

DRY MEASURES	LIQUID MEASURES	LINEAR MEASURES
30 g = 1 oz	30 ml = 1 fl oz	6 mm = ¼ inch
250 g = 9 oz	125 ml = 4 fl oz	1 cm = ½ inch
500 g = 1 lb 2 oz	250 ml = 9 fl oz	2.5 cm = 1 inch

CUP CONVERSIONS – DRY INGREDIENTS

1 cup almonds, slivered whole = 125 g (4½ oz)
1 cup cheese, lightly packed processed cheddar = 155 g (5½ oz)
1 cup wheat flour = 125 g (4½ oz)
1 cup wholemeal flour = 140 g (5 oz)
1 cup minced (ground) meat = 250 g (9 oz)
1 cup pasta shapes = 125 g (4½ oz)
1 cup raisins = 170 g (6 oz)
1 cup rice, short grain, raw = 200 g (7 oz)
1 cup sesame seeds = 160 g (6 oz)
1 cup split peas = 250 g (9 oz)

INTERNATIONAL GLOSSARY

capsicum	sweet bell pepper
chick pea	garbanzo bean
chilli	chile, chili pepper
cornflour	cornstarch
eggplant	aubergine
spring onion	scallion
zucchini	courgette
plain flour	all-purpose flour
prawns	shrimp
minced meat	ground meat

Where temperature ranges are indicated, the lower figure applies to gas ovens, the higher to electric ovens. This allows for the fact that the flame in gas ovens generates a drier heat, which effectively cooks food faster than the moister heat of an electric oven, even if the temperature setting is the same.

	°C	°F	GAS MARK
Very slow	120	250	½
Slow	150	300	2
Mod slow	160	325	3
Moderate	180	350	4
Mod hot	190(g)–210(e)	375–425	5
Hot	200(g)–240(e)	400–475	6
Very hot	230(g)–260(e)	450–525	8

INDEX

Published in 2006 by Bay Books,
an imprint of Murdoch Books Pty Limited.

ISBN 1-92120-850-3
978-1-92120-850-8

Printed by Sing Cheong Printing Company Ltd.
Printed in China.